For Robin Lane

ON THEIR OWN TERMS

Bringing Animal-Rights Philosophy Down to Earth

FOREWORD BY JAY TUTCHTON · COVER PHOTO BY JIM HANSEN

Other Books From Nectar Bat Press

Priscilla Feral and Lee Hall,
Dining With Friends: The Art of North American Vegan Cuisine
(2005).

Lee Hall,
Capers in the Churchyard: Animal Rights Advocacy in the Age of Terror
(2006).

Priscilla Feral,
The Best of Vegan Cooking
(2009).

Published in the United States of America by

Nectar Bat Press
777 Post Road, Suite 205
Darien, Connecticut 06820

Copyright © 2010 by Lee Hall
Friends of Animals
Internet: www.friendsofanimals.org
Phone: (203) 656-1522

Book Design: Mark Zuckerman

Published 2010

Printed in the United States of America on recycled paper

ISBN 0-9769159-3-5

Contents

Foreword

Lee Hall has written the book I wish I'd read when I was 20. Indeed, considering the false starts, detours, and sluggish pace of my own development as an advocate for animals "on their own terms," as Lee aptly puts it, this is the book I wish I'd read when I was 40—and the book I hope to re-read at 60 or 80, if I am so lucky as to enjoy four score years on Earth. It is not a book to leave on a shelf, but one to wear out, to scribble notes in, to take to the coffee shop and the campfire, to read, re-read, and ponder, to lend to our fellow travelers and discuss, because this book is part of a continuing conversation among friends about how we should live our lives.

I grew up in a house on what was then the edge of Denver, suburban-sprawl 1960s style. The place, no doubt the dream of some now departed realtor, was dubbed "Greenwood Village," though at the time it was neither "green," nor "wooded," or even a "village." It was a collection of new homes arranged in vaguely rectangular patterns on the tan, largely treeless prairie that previously ran unbroken to the mountains.

As many a small child does, I preferred to be outside. My mother, who strove to keep a neat house, often preferred it that way too. She tells me that among my first words the phrase "back outside," accompanied by stamping feet, was the most common. The prairie, or what was left of it beyond the embryonic yards and gardens of my neighbors, became my playground.

The prairie lends itself to children. It is short in stature, as they are, and its creatures are close at hand. I made small discoveries. Wolf spiders waited in the entrances to abandoned rodent burrows. Box turtles, horned lizards, and snakes wandered. Prairie dogs built towns of their own. Beetles and grasshoppers and ants went about their business among the bunch grass, and occasionally did battle with each other. Snails and crayfish lived in the creek and I hid in the shadows of the cattails with them. Pronghorn and coyotes, rabbits and foxes, left tracks for me to follow and wonder if prey escaped predator. I traveled and explored freely, like the creatures I observed—until, unlike them, I was called home for dinner.

Those prairies and most of the creatures who inhabited them are gone. My parents' house is gone as well, scrapped by new owners to make way for a bigger house. Today Greenwood Village is both green and wooded, courtesy of the extensive capture and diversion of mountain streams into the pipes of our civilization, and it is more than a village. It is a "bedroom community" of coddled lawns and privacy fences, office parks—with "excellent freeway and light rail access"—in a sea of such communities stretching in all directions for miles further than I ever wandered as a child.

In short, my story of Greenwood Village is that of any suburb in America that any of us remember as children. Our human "growth," our shallow concept of "progress" displaces things—important, special things that had lives of their own. That lesson spurred me, as it has many others who have watched the natural world vanish, down a lifelong path as an environmentalist. But that is not the immediate point of my recollection. What is important here is not what I remember but what I nearly forgot.

Like any child, in my play, I occasionally hurt myself. I would return home with a skinned knee or elbow, a bruise. My grandmother, who lived with us, would soothe my injuries with a kiss to the offended area "to make it all better" and a promise that a grandmother's kiss magically did so. I would stop crying. One such incident, from the dawn of my memories, when my world consisted of no more than the couple hundred yards from my parents' house that I could wander on four-year-old legs, stands out. The day the bird died.

The bird had flown straight into the glass of my little brother's bedroom window with a thud and dropped to the ground. Orange-shafted feathers glistened as I turned the body in my hands, but no life animated the wings. Though I couldn't then, I now identify the bird as a Northern flicker, *Colaptes auratus*. As a child all I knew was that this marvelous creature was hurt. I cradled the bird and ran to my grandmother insisting she "kiss it and make it better." My grandmother, the kindest light of my youth, told me there was nothing to be done. Her kisses wouldn't work on a bird. I pleaded. I didn't understand. Why wouldn't her magic kisses work for the bird? The bird had suffered an injury as I did. What worked for me should work for the bird. What was the difference? *We are all the same.* That is the memory I want to relate here—that as I child, like any child, I didn't draw distinctions between people and animals. We all deserved the magic of a grandmother's kiss. This, I nearly forgot along my journey.

But I didn't forget the destruction of my prairie playground. That was the omnipresent backdrop to my teens. Survey stakes would appear along invisible boundaries, earthmovers and construction crews would follow. In the hasty ways of youth, my friends and I fought back. We pulled the stakes out. We burned them. When we occasionally got creative, we rearranged them. We raided the construction sites and built barriers, with purloined lumber, in the new roads. We were children trying to say "no." But in our pain and frustration, we were only annoying. And we failed. One by one, the fields with the yucca and cactus, the prairie dog towns, the cattail marshes, disappeared and so did their residents.

At the time, I could have used the advice, found in Lee's earlier book *Capers in the Churchyard*, concerning the futility of vandalism and illegal action to promote peace with the natural world, but I wasn't ready yet. I was a disciple of Edward Abbey before I ever heard of *The Monkey Wrench Gang*.

Eventually, I found I different path. I went to law school. And I went with a single purpose in mind—to achieve the ends that had eluded me. To understand, and to change, the law—that set of societal rules that made fighting what I viewed as destruction a crime and the destroyers, "developers," and their works "progress." I got my first job, as an unpaid law clerk, with the former Sierra Club Legal Defense Fund, now Earthjustice. It was 1989, the year of the Exxon Valdez oil spill in Prince William Sound. They had agreed to let me help if I could find my way to Alaska. I called them from Los Angeles and arranged to meet at the airport in Juneau. I told them to look for a generic-looking white guy in a "leather flight jacket," a proud souvenir of my aborted career with the Navy that had helped put me through college. But what my new mentors heard over the garbled phone line was look for the guy in the "white leather jacket." We later joked that they worried that they had just agreed to work with a member of the Bee Gees.

Because I had no income while in Alaska and no place to live, I house-sat; one place I stayed was the home of one of the co-founders of EarthFirst! who was off in DC working to protect the Tongass National Forest from logging. I helped myself to his bookshelves. I met his friends. And I developed a philosophy of sorts that is relevant here. Like many a youth who grew up in the West, I was in love with the heroes of Western lore, the mountain men, the cowboys, the stories of Zane Grey, Louis L'Amour, Owen Wister's *The Virginian*. I also grew up a meat eater, a hunter and a fisherman. When I began to reflect on my meat-eating ways, I rationalized that if I was going to eat meat and take animal life, I should accept the personal responsibility of killing the animals I consumed myself. I should not purchase them in shrink-wrap on plastic trays from the store as though their lives never mattered and consisted of nothing more than "Grade A Beef." Not unlike philosopher Peter Singer, whose views Lee discusses, I believed that I reduced animal suffering by eating wild elk, deer, pronghorn, geese, ducks, and trout because, unlike their domestic counterparts, these wild animals were not subjected to manipulation, mistreatment, selective breeding, and confinement from birth to death. Rather, these wild creatures enjoyed natural, free, lives until their last day. I would eat only this "happy meat."

I was a "hook and bullet" environmentalist. A full adherent to the philosophy that by paying to hunt and fish I was providing money and economic incentives to those agencies that bought and preserved habitat— and thus thwarted those who would turn every wood and meadow into something else, displacing and killing the creatures who lived there. My own killing, I believed, was "sustainable use" of the wild. Or so the game and fish agencies told me. I never hunted for trophies or "sport" or anything

I didn't eat. And I hunted only creatures in places where those same game and fish agencies told me my prey was in excess of "management target" populations. I, and my hunting companions, tried to avoid the "unnecessary suffering" of the creatures we pursued. We strove for "clean kills" and passed on risky shots. We adhered to Teddy Roosevelt's notions of "fair chase." Though I was not so blind as not to notice, like Atticus Finch in *To Kill a Mockingbird*, that a rifle did offer some undeniably unfair advantages.

Yet I persisted. And, as my colleagues and I struggled to stop grazing by domestic cattle on public lands, grazing which destroyed wildlife habitat and spurred government programs to kill predators, I felt better about myself. I knew none of my money was going to support the livestock industry. My meat came from the natural world I was trying to preserve. But—though I didn't know it then—I was burning the village to save it.

It was the wisdom of my children that pulled me around and reminded me what I had forgotten and overlooked in my philosophy. Each in their own way; my two sons cried at the "game processing" butcher because the elk, hanging on hooks, gutted and with their hides removed, were "naked" and missing their heads. They remarked, "Dad, this is really sad," as they examined the beautiful tail feathers of a bunch of pheasants I was preparing to cook. And I was reminded of my own examination of the feathers of the flicker who had hit my brother's window, the body my grandmother's kisses could not restore to life. Still, I thought, they were just too young to understand.

It was my daughter who broke me. I had taken her to Rocky Mountain National Park to see the elk bugling in the fall. We spotted a herd from the jeep. She knew I hunted elk and tried to feed them to her by hiding them in spaghetti sauce and sausages. As I pulled her out of her car seat to get a better look at the herd, she said, simply and defiantly, "Daddy, if you are going to hurt the elks, I am not getting out of this car." I tried to explain that I wasn't going to hurt them today, that I really loved the elk, that I spent my days and nights and weekends filing all sorts of lawsuits to protect elk and the wildlands they needed to survive. She began to cry and asked, "Daddy, why? Why do you hate the elks?"

By then in my legal career, I had advised countless law students, struggling over what do with their lives and their powerful new degrees, to follow a guide I had used: "Try to explain your job to a child and see if they understand." It was a simple test to determine if you were being true to the ideals that had led you to law school. It was my own test. And I was failing it.

I stopped hunting. By my own standard, it followed that I should stop eating meat. But for a time, I made exceptions. I ate meat when friends cooked and I didn't want to give insult. Finally, when some friends dragged me to a famous barbeque shack in Kansas City, surrounded by a gluttonous orgy of meat eating, I became physically sick looking at the flesh of unknown type and origin on my plate. I stopped eating meat completely. Dairy products and eggs continued to be part of my diet—largely because I was an uncreative, lazy cook. I could have used the vegan cookbook, *Dining With Friends*, Lee co-authored with Priscilla Feral, but I hadn't met them yet.

I did know some vegans, friends I had represented in environmental lawsuits. They were delightful, caring, thoughtful, people. They invited me to their tables. I began to read books they recommended. We talked about ethics, health, the "carbon footprint" of meat-eating and the effects of animal agribusiness on the environment, the free-living wildlife that we loved and the endangered species that we fought to save with legal protection. Their vegan lifestyle made sense to me and I joined them.

In celebration at the new-found consistency in my life and with a sense of freedom that some fog had lifted, I walked out of my law office at the University of Denver, and gave my leather flight jacket, that source of embarrassing confusion in the Juneau airport years ago and my proud covering since, to the first homeless man I encountered. Yes, its leather perpetuated the use of animals to human ends, but he was cold, I was free, and perfection, which might never come, could wait.

My winding journey took its toll—and not only on free-living animals.

I would soon learn I had cancer. Cancer of a type associated with eating meat and consuming dairy products. Fortunately—or I wouldn't be writing this—I have thus far beaten the odds. My doctor says whatever I am doing with my vegan diet, I should, by all means, continue.

That is my own path to where I am now. A journey not particularly unique, but one that left me ready, indeed eager, to read the book you hold in your hands. I tell my story for a simple reason: because I came to be a vegan not from an animal-rights background, but from an environmental one. The great beauty of Lee's book is its blend of the values of environmentalism, reminiscent of Aldo Leopold's "land ethic," with a background springing from animal rights. We have arrived at the same place from different directions. Both the environment, the home of free-living wild animals, and the animals themselves deserve our respect and attention. The wild and its wildlife, living lives "on their own terms," are inseparable. There is no line between individual animals and their environment, just as there is no line between people and animals. Human rights are animal rights—indeed, a subset thereof.

Lee has penned a deeply studied guide; a thoughtful analysis of the philosophies that lead one to conclude a vegan life is the only theoretically consistent choice for an environmentalist or an animal-rights proponent. *We are all the same.* More important, Lee has written a practical guide for putting our shared theories and values into action. The vegan choice does more immediate good for animals and the environment than any other. And it does not require a lawsuit, of which I have filed so many. Through a simple, clean break with the philosophies of the past, a "subversion of the dominant paradigm" to paraphrase the old EarthFirst! bumper sticker, the vegan choice furthers the interests of advocates who arrive at this place either via environmentalism or in pursuit of animal rights.

Today, I live within a half-mile of the site where once stood my childhood home on the edge of the "undeveloped" prairie. When I again walk the paths of my youth, now paved, I walk among ghosts. Those of the creatures who lived here when I was young, and those of the creatures who lived here before I came along and whom I never knew because they were already gone: the bison, the prairie elk, wolves and grizzly bears. All of our "development," our "progress," has come at a steep price. My children inhabit a diminished natural world. There are remnants, islands of what was. These I fight to maintain. We all should. But I want to give my children what I had, more if possible. That is the dream of any parent.

To get there we must change. We can't keep score by the material measures of the past. We must begin to value Aldo Leopold's "land," our land, not only in terms of resources we might exact, but as a living community, of which we, and the animals with whom we share this world, are but interdependent parts. Becoming a vegan is to take simple, effective, direct and immediate action to save what we all love. And it will work. It has to. Let's continue this conversation among friends, and in the movement—our movement—that Lee so ably advances.

JAY TUTCHTON
CENTENNIAL, COLORADO
29 JANUARY 2010

Preface

This book is meant to supply a full spectrum of nutrients for animal-rights thinkers. It is suitable for everyone who has an interest in animal-rights theory, and designed to be especially relevant to those who've decided to advocate for animals' well-being, or are thinking about taking on this role. This book will have a particular relevance for readers who are right now interested in thinking about what a serious theory of animal rights means for the real world, and how to go about synthesizing that theory with activism. If you're such a person, you might be an animal-welfare proponent, an abolitionist, an environmentalist, or an eco-feminist. You might, at different times or even simultaneously, consider yourself all of these things.

Or perhaps you're not quite sure about the categories, but it matters to you that other animals are harmed by a lot of things humans do. You might be a chef, a dietician, a rescuer, a computer programmer, a woodworker, a book designer, a singer, a runner, an activist, or a person who talks with your friends and family, your students or teachers or clients. A rider on a train. And on your way, you have engaged in or welcomed the idea of advocating for animals.

It's an especially important time for you. The word's out that our little planet will be home to more than nine billion human beings by 2050, and that we'll need to vastly increase the world's food supply. This means the land and water allocated to the animals we domesticate is coming under some serious scrutiny. Life on this planet is facing rapid change. Today is the time for animal advocates to be up on the latest research, and ready to deliver the ethics.

Animal-rights thinkers are needed at the core of this urgent discussion, because without an ethic that permits us to see beyond dominance patterns, the changes we make will simply comprise reactions to emergencies. Some people are asking what and how to "cut back" in order to curb climate disruptions. But we need change at a much deeper level. The book you're about to read will make the case for undoing age-old thinking patterns surrounding the idea that other beings were put on Earth for us to control.

As New York City advocate Ellie Maldonado puts the point:

> In order to believe we are entitled to domesticate, exploit, and kill, we needed to believe the others are inferior to us, and that they can't think, feel, or experience emotions. Now we know better. No wonder this myth is losing believers, and that so many of us include other animals in our moral code.

Once we no longer subscribe to our idea of human entitlement, everything changes. Ask vegans for their own experiences, and you'll likely hear people who strongly feel that opting out of the human pattern of dominion has brought them a better quality of life and an abiding feeling of peace between themselves and other animals, a feeling that could not have been experienced any other way. In contrast, look at what we stand to lose, collectively and individually, if we don't overcome the habits connected with dominion over the planet's life—life which is currently in the throes of its sixth major extinction phase, this one moving in like a tornado because of the human activities propelling it. Because of our farming customs, deforestation, our exploitation of the land and seas, and our waste, extinctions are occurring at least a hundred times the normal background rate; that is at the most conservative end of the estimates. In January 2010, United Nations chief Ban Ki-moon went to Berlin for the launch of the International Year of Biodiversity to announce that human expansion is wiping out species at about *a thousand* times the natural rate of extinction, and that "business as usual is not an option."[1]

Of the animals known to scientists, at least one in four species of mammals—communities, they really are—face the risk of extinction.[2] Same goes for one in every three kinds of amphibians. About half of the world's known communities of reptiles and 52 percent of insects are in danger. All told, at least forty percent of the known species on the planet Earth are currently faced with an extinction risk. It's no good talking about rights for animals who will not be around to experience life at all.

There is one encouraging factor: We have a platform. The idea of animal rights has become kind of a big deal. Animal advocates are the stuff of talk-show conversations, even the main theme of a television sitcom. How can we translate this into support for a sustainable and fair future for conscious living beings on Earth? When we have a way to reach others, what are the most important things to say? How do we decide? How do we recognize animal-rights theory that's useful in activism, capable of supporting animals' interests in the real world? How do we apply it in our communities? And with all that's happened on this planet, is it realistic to insist that we can really make a difference to the big picture now? Where would we start?

Healing a culture begins with healing oneself; similarly, nurturing our movement begins with nurturing ourselves. Knowing who we are as individuals, and being clear about our personal goals, enables us to find like-minded people, put our support in the right places, and determine how to live and relish our days. It helps us nourish an organizational base for change—and that matters in our age, when animal use has become high-tech and regulated at the level of global economics.

No matter how we work, though, or even if we do not consciously advocate for anything at all, there's really no opting out of influencing society. Each person plays a political role every day. We can conform to the scheme of things, and that's one role. Alternatively, we can become conscious of the messages that run through our heads, adjust them, tune our thoughts to another wavelength, conceive other possibilities. We can then organize our lives, and perhaps whole communities, around a key idea. This takes stamina. Wherever we get together and dare to undo old hierarchies, we can anticipate vehement attacks that mischaracterize our efforts. The harshest attacks can come from other people who claim to be working for our goal. Expect resistance; it happens when one pushes for genuine moral progress. Yet we can be confident in our ability to transform our own being and our society. As children, before learning of classifications and hierarchies, we delighted in the variations of animals and enjoyed their presence. We, and everybody else, had to be *taught* that we're destined to control and consume them.

We can reverse this learning, and teach ourselves to live and move with respect. And it will grow from there. That's what organizing is about. Contrary to what some have said, we are not engaged in a social "war" and we are not going to prevail through targeting "the enemy." When the animal-rights message prevails, it won't look like an attack. It won't look like heroes trouncing villains, saints slaying dragons; no, it will look like invincible weeds, the roots of trees, rising up slowly from beneath the concrete.

Have you ever had a Henry Spira moment? Spira, known in the 1970s and 80s for campaigning to limit the use of animal tests and for promoting better handling of farm animals, recalled a moment of awakening: "I began to wonder why we cuddle some animals and put a fork in others."[3]

Most people wouldn't think of having an animal, or an animal product, as an act of domination. No hard feelings: It's just the way things are. Whether we stick a fork into an animal, ride, bet on, *or* expect to have animals we can cuddle, we tend not to examine why we've been doing any and all of these things. I hadn't thought of my leather jacket or my fried eggs or the animals I had known through this prism before another person took the time to tell me, unexpectedly, in the lobby of a music hall. With this help, it dawned on me that my life's catalogue of experiences was shaped by the dominion I'd exercised over others daily. Perhaps you too collected fireflies in a jar, asked for an animal as a holiday gift, pulled the most wondrous being out of the water by a hook, or witnessed a horse being broken? Except for the precise details and individuals who were present, my memories are yours.

Of the many early memories that rose into my mind, one was a childhood query I'd long forgotten: *Where do babies come from?* My mother was ready. Mothers get their babies from the zoo—the monkey exhibit, to be exact. Anticipating the objection that monkeys, unlike us, have tails, my mother had kept a copy of a photo essay about the tailless monkeys of Gibraltar. I was unconvinced, but the next time we went to the zoo I refused to approach the monkey exhibit. Spotting it from within one of the buildings, I was terrified to see these beings on display—almost as though we *could* pick them for ourselves if we wanted to.

While still in my twenties and learning to negotiate life as a vegan, I began working in the freight and baggage department of an airline company. My activism consisted of preparing completely vegetarian food and sharing it with others at work. My co-workers learned, day by day, about the idea of avoiding exploitation of animals for lunch, for work boots, for entertainment. In time, they were asking for the recipes and reciprocating, and there was a notable change in the air of our cavern under the airport. Our department became known as the most civil place to work.

But sometimes we saw monkeys transported in cages to labs, and puppies sitting in their messes in crates on their way to be sold. More than once, the sunrise would present us with a massive freight container full of tropical fish in ice blocks, thoughtlessly unloaded and abandoned to the night's cold. I would try to fix things for the animals, but was helpless to intervene in any substantial, lasting way. So I resolved to go to law school; there, I thought, was the key to changing the whole system. And eventually I did go to law school, and found out just how deeply the inferior status of other animals is etched into our social and legal relationships.

A couple of professors did agree, nevertheless, to support independent research into the idea that taking animals' interests seriously furthers the same impulse that confronts race bias, gender bias, and the plight of detainees, or the unfair situation of anyone who's intentionally dominated by others. I began to do research into, and write about, the concept of personhood. So far, the courtroom doors have been shut to non-human beings—except insofar as these beings are objects of some human's concern. But a narrow opening has appeared around that door frame. Today, a growing number of law teachers, philosophers and activists explain that we need not wait for a completely just human society before exploring issues concerning non-human beings—although human-rights issues are indeed well supported by animal-rights advocates. Nor need we wait for every conscious animal to be included before ensuring that the animals who can get respect do get it as soon as possible. Animal rights isn't about handing out privileges to any group. It's about simply letting them be.

Ecological realities play a key part in such a project. Dissolving the property paradigm that imprisons living beings must involve a revolutionary approach to environmental protection. For example, respecting non-human apes' own environmental needs on their terms (not because they attract tourists or are otherwise valued as our resources) will be immensely helpful, in turn, to other beings in the same territories—regions currently battered by war, deforestation, the spread of domestication and animal agribusiness, palm oil and biofuels, and climate disruptions. Sighing and writing off threatened animal communities to an inevitable doom or saying they'll only exist in "wildlife parks," as some philosophers do, is also an option—but the focus of this book will be another thing entirely.

Anyone can be pragmatic and tell us the habitat's practically gone and that life is everywhere being made into commodities. Wouldn't it be better to be surrounded by people who believe a world with room for animal rights is a world that's still possible? The vital key—no law school required—is our ability to refuse to be *consumers* of animal commodities. If legal personhood is the thin edge, then this general opting-out is the broad base for dissolving the for-sale status of other animals, and instead letting them thrive on their own terms in untamed spaces. It works like this. If we want to spare free-roaming horses from being rounded up and auctioned off, the answer cannot be limited to closing horse-slaughtering plants. Confronting slaughter makes sense, but as part of a broader perspective. In the United States, campaigners have allowed the public to become outraged over the idea that horses are the wrong animals to eat. Everybody knows, says the alerts, that "Americans don't eat our horses." Now, if Italians *do* think eating horse meat is proper, and U.S. residents continue to eat the flesh of pigs and cows (and export the popularity of burger or fried chicken restaurants worldwide), the argument becomes, on some level, one of cultural superiority. Only if the demand for the closure of horse slaughter operations comes as part of a whole vegetarian view is it consistent, respectful, and sensible.

Nor is the answer to impose birth control on free-roaming horses while cattle ranches expand. Nor is the answer found in auctioning the horses off, attempting to turn them into our children's pets or university mascots, or training them to police the borders. All of these ideas are being foisted on the horses, but the one respectful answer is to let free-roaming horses and burros do just that: roam free. That can happen if advocates successfully promote a vegan ethic: the permanent boycott of flesh and dairy products so animal agribusiness doesn't push these horses and burros off the land.[4] The environment should belong to these horses and to the other animals who live in it as free beings, and not to the ranchers who use animals as products.

Animal rights is first and last about objecting to the human war on other animals by conscientiously opting out of industries that displace, capture, breed, buy, sell, control and exploit conscious beings (beings, that is, who experience their lives). We can stop the exploitation only if we think big. An enormous segment of the human economy is based on taking advantage of conscious life, yet each one of us has the power to change this structure, and we all know and constantly encounter other people with this same potential. When they're ready, people do respond to reasoned optimism. The message of respect is not something we must (or can) force upon the world outside of ourselves. We're all implicated; we're all living and learning. If we accept opportunities for self-critique and growth, and enable a healthful balance of respectful critique and debate and co-operation in our movement, we can mature, and we can prevail.

And it might well be time for a reassessment of our whole movement. Animal law is becoming an important aspect of our social policy, with the model often involving pressure for courts to recognize, as animal law professors tend to put it, other animals' true value and special place in our homes. But law professor Catharine MacKinnon, in the 2004 essay "Of Mice and Men: A Feminist Fragment on Animal Rights," called for an entirely new way of understanding animal advocacy, observing that the primary model of animal rights to date "misses animals on their own terms."

The book you're holding is a response to that call. I cannot promise a faultless or complete answer. I can only invite you to take from these pages what best applies to the person you are, the humanity you stand for, and your deepest wish for all living beings. Take, adopt, adapt from this book that which resonates with your idea of the best animal-rights movement possible. A personal workshop for creative planning is included at the end of the book.

Thank you for meeting me in this work. Together, may we enjoy our progress in thinking about and engaging in activism. May we remember to appreciate the planet we're on right now. May we reflect on the strength and healing powers the animals know. Together, may we take time to learn from and actively collaborate with people in allied movements, to support our teachers and guides, and respect and sustain the publications that make social change possible. May we hang on to our optimism; it's our revolutionary spark. Diligently, with every word we speak, may we seek fairness for all who find themselves born to Earth.

Thank-You Notes

Thanks to you who take part in vigils, festivals, talks and conferences, and you who intervene on behalf of the deer, the moose and the wolves, the bees and bats, horses and burros—and the entire living communities in their midst. Thanks to you who desire and work to find the best in animal-rights theory, and cultivate a thoughtful and powerful movement. For you, and with your support, this book is written.

Thanks to the people whose work is mentioned here—including through a critical lens. Because you've developed and presented your contributions, this book has a base for its discussion. No writer or advocate works in a vacuum, and a book about finding the best potential in activism is, naturally, a work that owes much of its insight to experiences gained and ideas discussed with others. I hope and expect this work too will be developed, adapted, and improved by thinkers and thoughts yet to come.

Thanks to Marie Ansari and Serafina Youngdahl Lombardi for sharing many a conversation about the ideas in this book over a cup of green tea. I'm grateful also to Maryanne Appel, Harold Brown, Deanna Calderaio, Ryan Draving, Lisa Fillpot Walker, Chris Kelly, Curtis Hinkle, Cara Hunt, James LaVeck, Donald Leung, Jessica MacLachlan, Matthew McLaughlin, Ellie Maldonado, J. Muir, Benjamin Payne, Lee Ane Pompilio, Jason Pompilio, Dustin Rhodes, and Jenny Stein for their contributions to the creation of this book. Each has offered comments that made a substantive difference to a certain chapter—in a few cases, to the book as a whole.

The thoughts and questions explored here were presented for consideration and feedback in a variety of communities, courtesy of the employees, board members, donors and volunteers of Friends of Animals; Heather Steel (who offered the structure and the name for the website I

facilitate for Friends of Animals: *Veganmeans.com*); Peter White and the
Vegan Organic Network; *Dissident Voice.org*; Jenny Castle of Batten House
at Bryn Mawr College; the University of Victoria Law School; Michael
Harris and the Environmental Law Clinic of the University of Denver
Sturm College of Law; the North American Vegetarian Society; *The
Vegan* (quarterly magazine of The Vegan Society, based in Birmingham,
England); Catherine Burt; Rob Eccles; Roz Hendrickson; Óscar Horta;
Mark Zuckerman; Paula Casal; Alex Claridge; Catriona Gold; Robin
Lane; Joel Marks; Paul Saccone; Kris Weller; Fred Storck, Ray Deeney, and
the Unitarian Universalist Congregation of East Brunswick, New Jersey;
Claudette Vaughan; Jim Novak and Stacey Walder.

Jay Tutchton of WildEarth Guardians—an intrepid and highly
effective non-profit group based in Santa Fe, New Mexico of which I'm
glad to be a member—provided this book with its foreword. I am deeply
grateful to Jay for sharing both a personal narrative and an ecological
argument in support of hunting animals for food, and then the experience
of transcending this outlook. It seems the core of Jay's spirit, the little child
yearning to bring an injured bird back to life, came back to life itself at Jay's
young daughter's invitation. Jay writes, "Even for people who make as many
mistakes as I have there is always the potential to change."

Jay models that potential by carrying out some of the most promising
work in today's environmental law field. Representing a variety of clients,
Jay has challenged grazing, oil and gas extraction, logging, and assaults on
many communities of free-living animals, and has used energy laws to press
the federal government to address its own fuel habits. While heading up
Denver University's Environmental Law Clinic, Jay worked with Friends
of Animals to prevail over assertions made by the U.S. government and the
Safari Club, and thus successfully sealed up the legal loophole that enabled
trophy hunters to kill North African antelope at North American ranches.
Now, as General Counsel for WildEarth Guardians, Jay continues to work
with FoA in the interest of stopping the trade that displaces tropical birds
from their natural homes. If Jay's vision of the future prevails, Heaven will

be relieved of a great deal of rage.

And, before turning to Page One, a very special thanks to a valiant organizer and comrade, Priscilla Feral. For more than three decades, Priscilla has sought, struggled for, and represented the very best in animal rights.

Wherever humans think of other animal communities as threats, nuisances, or just not particularly useful, those communities are pushed off their lands and out of their waters. Priscilla is a virtuoso at unsettling these displays of dominance, and challenging others to do the same. Priscilla cares about the chickens and cows as well, and has shown us how to prepare attractive food and eat well in a non-exploitive way. The book Jay's foreword mentions, *Dining With Friends,* is a cookbook I had the pleasure of helping Priscilla produce. At one spot in the text, to explain the ethical problems with consuming dairy products, I had included a remark that milk comes from cows whose babies are taken away, so behind every mocha latte there's a veal calf. Our publishers were concerned about marketing the book and they asked us to remove that line; its tone, they pointed out, might not be good for sales. Rather than delete the calf, Priscilla preferred to start up a publishing house! And that's how Nectar Bat Press was formed, and how you're reading this book today.

Priscilla's day-to-day work has ensured the neutering of 2.5 million cats and dogs, and funded sterilizations of, and support for, feral cats. But imposing birth control on groups of independent animals, such as free-roaming horses, is human control over animals who are living naturally, and it's frequently accompanied by confinement—by government agencies, humane groups, or private owners. Priscilla has never tolerated this. Priscilla observes that addling or oiling the eggs of geese to keep them from hatching is disrespectful and a form of violence to geese, and that foisting contraception on free-living animals is an affront to a movement for animal rights. This is especially significant in an advocacy field in which even texts identified as abolitionist have urged the authorities to impose pharmaceutical control over communities of free-living animals, such as deer.

In short, if actions speak louder than words, then Priscilla articulated this book before I began to think about the ideas it contains. Priscilla has embraced the life of an activist, while writing animal-rights theory on activism's slate. Priscilla consistently places Friends of Animals' anti-fur interventions in their larger context, which is to insist that animals such as chinchillas, lynx, rabbits, mink and foxes could, but for this exploitive trade, live free on Earth; so to end the fur trade is, essentially, to extend animals their birthright of freedom. Animal rights presents a genuine and profound challenge to our culture, and Priscilla's activism conceives of the greatness of this challenge. It's not just about having sympathy for maltreated animals and outrage over what people do to them. It's even more than having our role as their masters abolished. It's about viewing them with respect and ensuring they can live in their own ways. Ultimately, it's not a work of anger and opposition, but a work of love.

PART ONE:

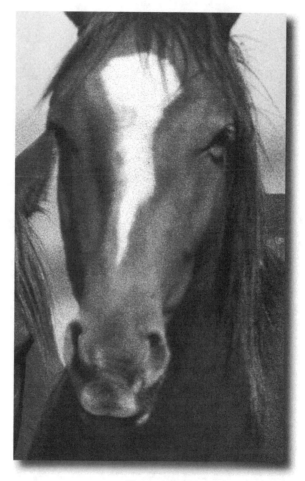

On Caring and
Being Fair

CHAPTER 1

Our Dialogue

C lear language is essential to a movement that seeks to be successfully explained and widely understood. Language describes, and should describe well. It also frames our understanding and helps to shape attitudes, and it should do that well, too. So let's carefully consider two problematic habits common to animal-advocacy dialogues. One is the idea that we must choose between a caring ethic and the language of animal rights. The other, closely related, is the convention of dividing advocacy into "animal welfare versus animal rights."

Distinct, yet complementary: rights and caring

What do we mean when we say animal rights?

Let's start by thinking about why we use the term "rights" at all. Our law treats everything and everyone on Earth as a person or as a piece of property. To our law, there's no meaningful category in between those two classifications—or beyond them. There's property here, persons there. Things, and owners.

Water and seeds and trees and beaches are all for sale. Conscious beings too are classified as property, available to be owned by persons. Persons may be those ubiquitous primates known as human beings, or, in certain circumstances, persons might be the businesses concocted by these same ubiquitous primates.

A piece of property is an appendage, whether of an individual or a community or an entire nation. It doesn't have rights; it never will. Only legal persons have rights—those socially created shields which oblige us to respect other people's interests.

People who are serious about animal rights want to change the social reality that labels conscious beings as property. More fundamentally, they want to end the custom of deliberately subordinating the needs of all other beings to human interests, and then systematically controlling these beings for human uses and conveniences.

The animal-rights idea is, at its core, uncomplicated. It takes no advanced education or special jargon to explain, and it's been around a long time. Henry Salt, author of *Animals' Rights Considered in Relation to Social Progress*, asserted that the human habit of raising other animals in order to consume them inflicts unnecessary harm on sentient beings.[1] "Fifty or a hundred years ago," Salt wrote in 1892, "there was perhaps some excuse for supposing that vegetarianism was a mere fad; there is absolutely no excuse at the present time."[2] Salt, as well as Anna Kingsford (who graduated from medical school in Paris in 1880, unique in doing so without having experimented on a single animal), influenced Mohandas K. Gandhi to publicly commit to a moral duty, as Gandhi put it, "not to live upon fellow-animals."

We are not the only ones born with interests, and so, as many have urged, we're not the only ones whose interests should be respected. Making that happen, however, is not so simple. The courts and other legal authorities we call upon to extend rights are the same institutions that have systematically, for the most part reflexively, defined the ubiquitous human apes as the only creatures on Earth whose interests really matter.

Courts have permitted their definition of personhood to evolve; but as rights theory is based on fairness—which, to judges, means treating similar cases in similar ways—animals such as gibbons, chimpanzees or orang-utans, who'll be perceived by legal authorities as most like current living persons, will probably get through the court's door first, and it will take longer to have the great many others acknowledged. The precedent-setting court will likely announce that it is only slightly relocating, rather than eroding, the border between persons with rights and all other beings. And such a novel case will have to survive a series of appeals before even the selected group's degrading status as property is changed for good.

Thus, while animal-rights theory would support efforts to secure legal rights for non-human beings where those rights might be within reach, most of its advocates, quite sensibly, are cultivating root-level changes in humanity's understanding, in order to bring about a culture that respects, and thus deliberately declines to violate, conscious beings.

In its ancient form, the concept of refraining from harm and cultivating respect appears in a rich variety of texts; it's inscribed on Jain temples of India with its Sanskrit name, *ahimsa*. Today it can also be found in the principles of vegan living. As a diet, veganism means the avoidance of dairy products, flesh, eggs, and honey. As a social movement, it entails the courage and sheer optimism to cultivate a society that renounces domination and systematic killing. By avoiding animal products, zoos, aquaria, animal racetracks and the like, vegans erode the power of the institutions that breed domestic animals into existence as commodities—institutions that, at the same time, use habitat needed by autonomous animals.

It's simple, and yet it's probably the biggest challenge humankind has ever faced, this journey to animal rights. It's the forthright claim that conscious beings should be allowed to live on their own terms, not the terms set down by those who seek to control and exploit. Each person who accepts this challenge treats other beings' interests with respect in an immediate way. And respect is the key to defining animal rights. Vegans put this ideal of non-exploitation into practice—right here and now.

Speaking of rights

Some feminist writers have urged us to avoid the language of rights, to steer clear of appealing to the legal authorities. Expecting officialdom to acknowledge or grant rights, they observe, is disempowering. The feeling is understandable. And yet we deal with the system of legal rights in some way daily; and daily, other animals feel the effects of their debasing legal status. So there's value in knowing what the law does, and confronting it if it's enabling unfairness. If the law is understood as comprising rules of conduct to which members of a given community agree to be bound, a statement saying "no, we do not all agree" sends a message that we reject an unfair standard, and that others should know and ask questions about the agreements established in their names.

For example, we can support efforts to dismantle the legal fiction that corporations are persons, requiring free speech rights or having due-process and equal-protection claims. Those are the key protections for prisoners, for communities that have endured hideous discrimination. Should they be the advantages of companies? Corporate personhood has done far less to hold businesses responsible for wrongdoing than to enable them to operate to the detriment of workers and non-human life. And how better to model tyranny than to extend the rights and privileges of personhood, say, to a cloning firm, while the law treats the animals its employees clone as a bundle of cells to be manipulated?

We could, and should, mount legal challenges to deforestation, to stop the expansion of grazing areas, to limit construction, and stop the pollution of wild places on land and in water. In various places throughout the world, this push to protect wild spaces is already resulting in new and expanded rules, such as the protection of Scottish coasts from water pollution. But not in the name of animal rights. This sentence from the BBC typifies the explanations that appear when these rules are established: "Environment Minister Michael Russell said the shellfish industry was worth £5m a year to the Scottish economy."

How can we bring animal rights into the dialogue, so that we can work at the causes of water pollution and deforestation as well as intervening legally to halt the direct damage? This will involve talking about the shellfish and other animals not as resources for our industries, but as actors on life's stage, just as we humans are. We can educate our communities about the ethical and ecological importance of a vegan culture, one that envisions a humanity beyond our current reliance on animal agribusiness.

And as for animal law, new legislation to stop aerial predator control is a good thing; evidently, the law already in place in the United States is no longer taken seriously. So let's push back. A bird protection group has noted that the U.S. law protecting migratory birds also must be taken seriously, and in August 2009 filed an action insisting that birds receive protection from pesticides used in their South and Central American wintering grounds, on coffee, oranges and bananas, and demanding a ban on the import of fruits and vegetables sprayed with chemicals such as diazinon, diquat and terbufos.[3] These advocates are finding their voices, and could become important allies in the animal-rights movement. Yet another example of a worthwhile legal challenge—and we'll get to more later—is a recent case on behalf of North African antelopes, who are endangered or near-extinct in their home regions. Until 2009, they could nevertheless be bred and killed for the fun and prestige of tourists willing to pay several thousand dollars to kill them at U.S. ranches. An animal-advocacy group and a law school clinic worked together to close that loophole in the Endangered Species Act.[4] Although this didn't give antelopes any rights, it did protect (or simply spare from being bred for such a violent and degrading purpose) a specific community of transplanted antelopes. It stopped a specific community of thrill-seekers from stalking them. It exposed the sham nature of the government's allowance for hunting ranches that claim to propagate endangered species while these same ranches pimp these misplaced animals to keyed-up trophy tourists. It brought advocates together to push back at the government's insidious strategy of splitting lists of shielded animals so that some animal communities might be bred, with the government's permission, into a completely controlled existence for human amusement or other uses. And it ended the hypocrisy involved in treating Africans as poachers for exploiting certain animals while treating wealthy Texas landowners as protected entrepreneurs for doing the same thing.

Wouldn't it be great if all the pushers-back got together for a conference and started a symposium on the importance of animal rights to the future of life on Earth? Wouldn't it be great if we said these patchwork pushbacks have been good so far, but let's join forces and do something that connects them all, by making the law understand animals cannot be our commodities, and we humans are not the only ones whose interests in territory counts?

The idea of pushing back—the resistance to those who would act against one's will, who would take unfair advantage—gets to the visceral core of what we seek when we speak of rights. Henry Salt expressed the trouble and the importance of discussing the abstract theory of natural rights—a phrase Salt deemed "confessedly vague and perilous"; nevertheless,

Salt added, there is "a solid truth underlying it—a truth which has always been clearly apprehended by the moral faculty, however difficult it may be to establish it on an unassailable logical basis." If people don't have rights, Salt wrote, "well, they have an unmistakable intimation of something very similar; a sense of justice which marks the boundary-line where acquiescence ceases and resistance begins; a demand for freedom to live their own life, subject to the necessity of respecting the equal freedom of other people."[5]

Still, some say we'd be largely better off avoiding legal confrontation and preferring an *ethic of care*. Often associated with the work of psychologist Carol Gilligan, the care ethic encourages the relationships we have with others to influence our approach to moral decisions.[6] Feminist writers have brought the care ethic to animal advocacy, and applied it to systematic relationships between humans and other animals.[7]

In their introduction to *Beyond Animal Rights: A Feminist Caring Ethic for the Treatment of Animals,* Josephine Donovan and Carol J. Adams describe rights theory as unsympathetic, arguing that it's meant for a "society of equal autonomous agents, who require little support from others, who need only that their space be protected from others' intrusions." Donovan and Adams then state: "Animals are not equal to humans; domestic animals, in particular, are dependent for survival on humans. We therefore have a situation of unequals," they write, "and need to develop an ethic that recognizes this fact."[8]

Yes, domesticated or dependent beings do need care, and, once they are here, they do benefit from that care. But by regarding the matter through the lens of dependency, Donovan and Adams have advanced a model which takes inequality—an effect of captivity or domestication—for granted.[9]

Our desire to care for other animals may become oppressive if we bring these individuals into being primarily so we can express that desire, as we do most notably with animals in our homes. Our urge to nurture can go into overdrive, creating the situations in which other animals continually need our help. Petkeeping, which has become a widespread social custom in the last 200 years (yes, we did without pet animals all those many centuries before), produces animals to suit us. Schnauzers and dachshunds didn't just spring out of nature; nor can they live in it. They depend on us, and there are millions in excess of the demand, each one an individual whose survival depends on the luck of being found by someone who's ready to rescue. When I and other advocates are working in the city, we see many cats; most are frightened by humans although they depend on waste bins or residents who might scatter food for them. An advocate can take and foster or keep a lucky cat here and there. Maybe.

Are we taking a hard look at how our good instinct to help and care has turned into a custom that forces other beings to look to us for care, and to be trapped inside this reliance? When we bring into existence other animals whose very being involves dependence upon us, a dependence they cannot outgrow, the unequal relationship is not mitigated by caring. Do we not need an ethic that questions the inequality?[10]

More than ever, we do. We need a social movement that inspires us to respect non-human animals, to want them to remain capable of living and moving freely in the habitats to which they've naturally adapted, rather than be alienated from those spaces. To leave birds in their forests rather than remove them and cage them as decorative or talkative pets; to let chimpanzees live in their natural territories rather than expect them to have babies in zoos and language labs; to let pronghorn antelope travel across the ground without our border walls fragmenting their communities; to respect turkeys' natural lives rather than consider their slaughtered bodies essential to our holiday buffets; to leave fish in their waters, swimming free; to let wolves be wolves and wildcats be wild.

A care ethic designed to fit human relationships is a poor fit for a movement striving to extend fairness and respect to animals who are not trying to be members of our social lives. Other animals arose on the planet as members of their own societies, and many of them were actors in intricately developed relationships well before we came along. In Earth's web of life, we comprise one of many communities. Why should any one group come along and expect all others to conform to its desires—and then justify this by applying the governing group's idea of care? Or, to put the point in slightly different terms, wouldn't a truly caring ethic include consciously transcending dominance and fostering respect? Authentic care involves taking others' interests seriously, and responding to others *on their terms.*

The first difficulty in the concept of animal rights, Donovan and Adams say, is that it requires an assumption of similarity between humans and animals.[11] But would a right for non-human beings to live on their own terms require us to assume other animals are just like ourselves? We'd just need to notice that we're not the only beings to experience life. In other words, respecting a right for other animals to live on their own terms requires no comparisons. It reflects a simple acknowledgment that other animals have interests.

So yes, let's say a theory of animal rights is needed. As important as caring is, it's as important to be fair. If we are to regard other animals as beings with individual dignity, our work must be about changing the habits and institutions that define and oppress them in groups—as well as regarding them as unique and caring about their individual well-being. When will we dare to stop putting other animals into dependent positions, and allow ourselves to instead be inspired by a deeper sense of our connection to those with whom we share this planet? Can we? If we are to have an animal-rights movement, we will. Fairness challenges us to intervene in the cycle of breeding dependent animals, and to stop sending domesticated cats, tropical birds, school-raised ducklings and other displaced animals into the world to fend for themselves in a biocommunity that's often ill-equipped to sustain or cope with them.

As "animal rights" means committing to an ethic that respects animals on their terms, we should carefully distinguish dependent animals from those who can live without human control. The theory of animal rights applies to the free-living communities, because freedom, along with life itself, is at the core of what rights are meant to defend. That doesn't mean we disregard purpose-bred animals; caring for domesticated animals is the ethical thing for animal-rights advocates to do. Domesticated animals are dependent on us, and thus do not have freedom, but they are living and they experience their lives and have an interest in continuing to live. Should there be social rules that oblige us to care for them? Of course, yes. Thus, an ethic of care *does* make sense for animals who, because they are in domesticated or captive situations, rely on our care, cannot live independently and shouldn't be sent off to do so, and simply cannot experience what we'd call animal rights.

Deserving rights?

One common objection to animal rights goes like this: "Identical rights for human and non-human beings will be impossible to achieve." In response, advocates say animal rights won't be the same as human rights.[12] Advocates aren't asking that other animals get to run for office, we add, and no, we're not trying to bring other animals into our social contracts or burden society with complex rules.

But wait a minute.

Truth be told, the prevailing idea of animal advocacy does focus on animals within human society. Although an essential premise of animal advocacy means protection for a being's interests shouldn't depend upon the capacity to perform duties, advocates do force animals into experiments or various positions of dependency, use their performance to show they deserve rights, or both. By doing so they offend precisely the right that makes sense, precisely the right other animals need: to be permitted to live on their terms, free of human interference and control.

Overwhelmingly, animal advocates talk about captive situations when discussing animals as candidates for moral or legal concern. I recently spoke with a film student who wants to do a documentary about a primate refuge. This student tells me advocacy is about elevating animals' position in society, and a good documentary should inspire viewers to try to have a relationship with other animals rather than use them. This is a common view of animal advocacy, but when animals have had a place in our society, their positions have never been on their terms. Many an animal lawyer asks that domestic animals, such as dogs, be elevated from the status of mere property. But neither is that what animal-rights theory proposes. Once we decide to respect their interests, other animals will not be deliberately bred to be dependent.

Many people, vegetarians and others, have embraced the growing movement to ensure all cats, dogs, rabbits, and other pet animals are neutered. That itself is a good trend; obviously, neutering stops the cycle of abandonment.[13] Neutering a domesticated cat is a positive action one can take to respect animal rights on several levels: When kittens aren't brought onto the scene, we have less occasions to (alas!) provide those animals pet food, or (alas, alas!) witness the death of a local chipmunk or sparrow. In many places, it might well mean the continued existence of wildcats. Yes, conservationists tell us that the greatest threat to the world's vanishing wildcats is interbreeding with abandoned domesticated cats.

It's to the undomesticated communities of wildcats, to wolves and free birds and rabbits, that the animal-rights ideal applies. Rights cannot be meaningfully extended to purpose-bred animals, beings perpetually at our mercy. Explaining this is not easy. We're used to smiling at a greeting card showing a puppy in a stocking, while a puppy wounded in a lab will draw outrage. But fundamentally, both animals are in the same position; both are bred for human purposes, and it's the luck of the draw that determines which one goes to the lab, or who owns and controls the one in the stocking.

In 2007, Harvard Law School held a "Future of Animal Law" conference. It was advertised as offering "cutting-edge legal strategies to stop the abuse of companion animals" and "educating prosecutors about how they can best seek maximum penalties for animal abusers." The conference's subtitle was "Remember When You Thought You Could Change the World? You Still Can." But locking up people for handling their animals improperly doesn't change the world. It reinforces the idea that cages and control are the answer to life's problems, while missing the real issue—that we think it acceptable to be the keepers of other animals—and suggests that everyone should just listen to experts to learn how to properly keep them. The United States has less than five percent of the world's population, yet has custody of twenty-five percent of the world's prisoners. Will sending more people to prison under maximum penalties help anyone to question the habit of keeping conscious life in cages?

We are not going to find every basement in which an animal is starving, and that wouldn't be a cutting-edge legal strategy in any case. I rescue animals who are bred as pets (actually, their discarded offspring), and I love these individuals. Because of my love for them as unique and special beings, I'm interested in finding out why they are in this position in the first place. So I ask animal lawyers: Rather than positioning ourselves as authorities on the proper use of animals bred as pets, couldn't lawyers and future lawyers be asking questions about how to help all animals, including humans, live as part of a sustainable planet's community? Rather than yet another conference based on concepts of management and control, how refreshing it would be to see an animal law conference question the custom of keeping other animals. This is not meant to discount work that stops violence against and abandonment of animals bred as pets. It's asking more: What about a conference on authentic rights issues, focusing on why animals are better left undomesticated, about the right to live on their terms and not ours? We'd start talking a lot more about habitat, and that would be very good. Connecting environmental law with this idea of transcending discrimination and dominance would signal vital progress.

All along, then, the best reading of animal-rights theory would guide us to make human care and intrusions less necessary and independence more possible. The basic idea is simple. Is there any point, readers might ask, in challenging human beings' desire to have and keep other living individuals? Most people we know probably associate having a pet with nearness and nurturing, and we've long associated a desire for nearness and nurturing with love between human beings. Yet animal rights is not an uncaring view. Striving for a society that seeks, as far as possible, to respect other animals' own ways of being on Earth is to care profoundly.

Now, then, why have most animal advocates yet to present plain-spoken challenges to human dominion over other animals? Perhaps it's because our field attracts many who so enjoy having, or interacting with, non-human animals; we were so often taught that having animals meant learning to appreciate life, to take responsibility, even to love. It is quite possible for well-meaning people to want to work with other animals, admire certain qualities of other animals and even learn from them without shedding our sense of superiority over them. I didn't give this a hard look until I was twenty-one. I believed I cared about animals as much as anyone alive. Even as a child, I knew I wanted to do something with animals, be surrounded by them. I'd imagine being a veterinarian like Dr. Doolittle, or tell people I'd grow up to have a farm with lots of dogs. In all likelihood, my early feelings for dogs and cats connect with my interest in sheltering animals today. I'm an adult now, and seeking to answer this question: How can I strive to learn and support what's really best for this world's other animals? For a free-living animal, the ultimate good, according to the best reading of the animal-rights principle, is to not be exploited. The ultimate good is the allowance to continue being free, interacting with other members of one's biocommunity in the way this animal evolved to do, propagating, flourishing.

A domesticated animal will never have that autonomy; the ultimate good in this case is the best care we know how to offer. An essential part of advocacy is sheltering dependent animals—these animals are the refugees of our customs of dominion, and a movement that fails to assist its refugees is reduced to a charade—but the point here is whether we are able to ask ourselves, and others, if bringing dependent animals into existence in the first place is a habit we could, and should, relinquish. Catharine MacKinnon has suggested that a significant problem facing activism for animals is our relationships with them.[14] The advent of animal-rights philosophy that asks such questions will defy many generations of our cultural patterns. I believe this is the central challenge for animal advocates today.

Taking animal welfare seriously

Animal welfare means, in ordinary conversation, the well-being of non-human animals. We'll use the term here in this ordinary, common sense, referring to a caring ethic for any animals who are unable to fend on their own and thus dependent on human care. It pertains, then, to efforts by a person or non-profit to ensure or improve the well-being of other animals who were raised in captivity and would be unlikely to cope well apart from human control, or to animals who were selectively bred—for example, as pets.

Genuine attention to well-being can honestly merit the term "welfare" or "care" and is distinct from concepts of proper maintenance of the commercially owned animal.

Decisions about individual or community welfare, usually understood as well-being, have a place in discussions of human rights. The word welfare fits the good work done at a refuge. We're right to look after humans in dependent circumstances, and we're right to ensure the welfare of all animals dependent on our care.

But the terms animal welfare and welfarist have been used in the past few decades to describe changes in the way animals are handled by businesses that use them. As we shall see, bioethics professor Peter Singer has talked of the "animal welfare movement" when discussing compromises between activists and companies that use animals, as though that's what welfare is all about. Welfare has become a dirty word. Watch how this is described by an animal sciences professor:

> At a 1991 animal protection symposium put on by the National Alliance for Animals, a call for the animal rights movement to distance itself from animal "welfare" was voiced by two prominent animal rights speakers: [Tom] Regan, of North Carolina State University, and Gary Francione of Rutgers University Law School. Though the style and substance of their oratory was markedly different, both Francione and Regan

characterized animal welfare as the "enemy" of animal rights; argued that the animal rights movement is being co-opted by proponents of animal welfare; and encouraged listeners to return to a belief in the fundamental principles of the animal rights doctrine, as articulated by Regan.

To Francione and Regan, the goals of animal "welfare" not only differ from animal "rights," they contradict them. In the words of Francione, "What you do when you merely ameliorate the conditions of enslavement is that you perpetuate the enslavement. And that is totally inimical to the goal of abolition." Regan stated that "people who work to improve the corrupt system of exploitation fail to understand this truth, a simple truth: to make injustice seem better is to prolong injustice…"[15]

To make injustice seem better might well prolong injustice, and we do need to be alert to that fine line that separates well-meaning attempts to improve the animals' lot from excitement over corporate promotions. But let's look at the word welfare. Is that concept, welfare, really what we'd want to distance ourselves from? Why would a group of animal advocates offer the public the idea that they would oppose something that means well-being? Surely the advocates would not mean to be understood as opposing animal well-being, and that is why it's a good idea to clean up the terminology. Today, people are called out for being welfarists when they agree with animal handlers to modify the way animals are shipped, stacked, stored, or slaughtered. Yes, those agreements with corporations are highly problematic—but do bargains with industries really concern animal welfare? Let's not call them that if we don't believe they advance the well-being of animals.

When theorists say we should distance ourselves from animal welfare, confusion arises. At its worst, this confusion manifests itself in the claim that animal-rights theory teaches disdain for the well-being of animals. That is, some people charge those who reject "welfare" as actually hoping for the worst conditions so that the status quo will change. (I doubt anyone really hopes animals will face the worst conditions, but the claim that the animal-rights proponent must eschew "welfare" assists in the making of the charge that we do.) After thinking for the last few years about the psychology and commercial effects of the linguistics here, I've decided to drop the word welfare from my vocabulary when discussing activists' negotiations with industries. We need to show clearly why husbandry (handling) is distinct from welfare (well-being).[16] Let's speak as clearly as we can.

Consider this real-world example to see why: After infiltrating some suppliers of a multinational fast-food chain, one animal charity, describing the chicken slaughter methods as "faulty and inefficient," devised, during the course of a long-sustained campaign, "animal welfare guidelines" for the chain's "animal welfare advisory panel" to adopt. The advocacy group said the standards, involving gassing chickens to death by a method called controlled atmosphere killing, "represent the most up-to-date studies and research into animal welfare."[17]

If birds and other animals could hold their advocates accountable, wouldn't this language and activism look different? Let us drop the term animal welfare where it doesn't apply. This international fast-food chain is a corporation that profits from the killing, frying, and vending of as many chickens as they can profitably handle. It cannot rightly claim to have an animal welfare advisory panel; and advocates who work with such a panel are pressing for handling adjustments and changes in killing methods—not the welfare (which, again, according to any common-sense definition, means well-being) of birds.

By the same token, let's say a critique of the animal charity should not include describing it as an animal-welfare or welfarist group. In Spanish, the term for welfarism is *bienestarismo*—which, translated exactly, would be well-beingism. Is that objective advanced at a restaurant that sells chicken parts, or the suppliers to the chain? It's animal husbandry that applies socially acceptable standards for humanity's systematic dominance over and use of other animals, the maintenance that enables animals to thrive insofar as they are useful to us. As Yi-Fu Tuan writes in *Dominance and Affection: The Making of Pets*, when one group dominates another, then puts that group to use, "[c]are is given them because tools must be kept in good order."[18]

Proper maintenance of the owned animal suits the owner either by enabling a good profit for a commodity, or by helping the animal produce longer and more efficiently. A U.S. park website explains that mules, used as "engines" of the Chesapeake and Ohio canal system, had a "longer work life than horses and could pull a canal boat for up to twenty years if they were taken care of" and quotes boat operator Lester Mose, Sr., as saying, "You had to take care of the mules. And the same way with the harness. You had to grease it and oil it."[19] Today, contact lenses are being developed for animals such as tigers, lions and giraffes with cataracts. One of the maker's clients is a sea lion with blurred vision at Sea World, a company whose profits rely on performing marine animals.[20]

Examine an industry manager's "welfare" claims carefully, and you'll find the real welfare being pursued is the shareholders'—that is, the well-being of the company's bottom line. The same problem arises with the U.S. Animal Welfare Act and its various international equivalents: The term deceives when the point is to set forth standards for keeping the living tools in good working order and the products in good shape.

In contrast, people who live with animals (not industries that exploit them) might care about their welfare. We might also care about the welfare of other people's animals, and if we see them in a sick or injured state, it's no misuse of our time to act. Let's put this, too, in real-life terms. Say you are living next to people who keep horses. You see an injured horse, so you go to the owner and point this out, in order that the horse may be treated. Even if we question the custom of trading, breeding, keeping and training horses, we nevertheless have empathy for an individual horse. We call for help. If we see a horse loose on the roadway, we don't turn away at that moment and write an article on animal rights; we call for the help this dependent animal needs—even though that means calling the horse's owner to return the horse to the paddock. After the horse is safe from the immediate danger, we can go and write an article on animal rights. If possible, we can share the thoughts it contains with the horse's owner. But animal-rights advocates don't shrink from promoting an animal's well-being, or welfare.

As long as domesticated and otherwise dependent animals exist and do need our help, a caretaking ethic—the ethic of genuine welfare—should co-exist with animal rights. Our theory is not a pass to ignore the welfare of animals who are already born into a domesticated life or otherwise dependent on us, even if we personally didn't put them in that position. Let's remember we're are all members of that class—the human class—that has long allowed ourselves the right to own all the others, and we each hold our share of the collective responsibility to care for the animals who therefore need looking after. It makes sense to reserve the word welfare to describe these genuine efforts of caregiving.

On a related note, let's consider the popular trend of objecting to factory farming—rather than simply objecting to all animal farming at once.

Most every environmental or animal advocate dislikes factory farming. We can agree on that starting point—vegans included. After all, those who energetically promote a cultural transformation to veganism are ensuring people do not consume the products of factory farming.

Yet to focus on the evils of factory farming is arguably to side-step reality, for even the small, family-run farm violates other beings' most basic personal interests. And such farms still use resources that could feed hungry humans; and with the waste they generate unnecessarily, they harm the ecology that sustains all living beings. There is no benign animal agribusiness. Not for the planet, ourselves, the animals we've domesticated or those we haven't. Thus the danger of campaigning pointedly against factory farms. When campaigns targeting high-volume farming channel their supporters' energies into projects designed to regulate the handling of animals, this could and almost surely will be read by some people as a message that there is a proper way for humanity to handle and use other animals.

In early 2009, Worldwatch Institute, a Washington, D.C. think tank long known for its reports on climate change, announced a partnership with the Stonyfield Dairy company. "Stonyfield does its best to ensure stringent animal welfare standards from its suppliers," the group's communications director told me, adding: "Stonyfield buys dairy from conscientious farmers and is constantly pushing those farmers to improve."[21] The partnership was no longer being advertised by the end of 2009; I'm one of the people who wrote to challenge it as inconsistent with Worldwatch's increasingly strong ecological critiques of animal agribusiness. But Stonyfield's animal-welfare claims were (and are) just as problematic. The notion that some dairy producers have animal welfare in mind, when their very purpose is to use animals up, is, well…hogwash.

Some animal-protection groups have perpetuated this same pattern. The World Society for the Protection of Animals, under the slogan "Make humane food choices," displays a picture of eggs, and tells readers where to buy "animal-friendly foods"—that is, how and where to buy animal products.[22] Chef and restaurateur Wolfgang Puck was bathed in accolades by the decision makers at two animal-protection societies (one, the wealthiest such non-profit in the world; the other, an internationally known and celebrity-supported farm animal sanctuary) for buying "sustainable seafood," for serving chicken and turkey flesh from farms that comply with "progressive animal welfare standards," and for indicating "interest" in processing plants that use a gas slaughter method.[23] Red flag! Animal advocacy should never be about making animal exploitation appear to work decently. More than a few of the farm animal sanctuary's employees and volunteers—people who do work for the welfare of rescued animals—felt queasy to see a person who loves to cook animals being praised for supposed attention to animals' welfare. I have listened to the views of people, just ordinary people, who've felt uncomfortable, even insulted, when hearing recommendations for certain kinds of meat and eggs from people claiming to be the animals' advocates.

With the above problematic campaigns in mind, and in an effort to make the idea of animal rights clear and not an insider's language—after all, unless those we reach understand our ideas, they're unlikely to pass them along to others—the word welfare will appear throughout this book in its ordinary, positive meaning, rather than as a code word for industrial concessions or corporate promotions. It would probably help the animal-advocacy movement a lot to reclaim the word welfare. It is not a word we ought to give up to industries.

Some young activists—confused, no wonder, by the derogatory use of the word welfare—avoid caregiving entirely, thinking it's not the work of animal-rights advocates. One day, I heard a young cat fosterer apologize to an animal-rights writer for failing to work full-time to advance the theory of animal rights. The young activist had read commentaries in which the word welfarist was used as a sort of warning that anyone falling into animal-welfare pursuits would become irrelevant to the development of animal rights. Indeed, some advocates deliberately refrain from rescuing and adopting homeless cats, dogs, rabbits and other animals. And this is one reason to challenge the use of the word welfare as a derogatory term. The too-common misunderstanding that rights advocates are not supposed to do welfare work can have some people shouldering a lot of the rescue work with others hanging back. Activists need to know that genuine animal-welfare work supports the movement and should be supported in return. The animal-rights proposal appreciates the efforts of one who traps domesticated cats in feral colonies, then returns them, neutered, to their areas and continues to feed and care for them and offer them as much shelter and comfort as possible.

So the rights-welfare debate—the idea that animal-rights goals could conflict with animal-welfare goals—usually presents a false dilemma, or at least confusing terminology. Animal-rights activists can, and usually do, promote the welfare of individual animals (those who must rely on our care) and promote a movement that respects free-living animals' autonomy.

Of course, some people are better suited, say, to speak and write about justice than they are to care for abandoned animals, and vice-versa.

Nevertheless, a rights advocate who offers shelter to (human or non-human) refugees applies a caring ethic to precisely those who need that, and is not, by doing so, working against rights. The rescuer, the fosterer, and the refuge facilitator can all be committed to ending human domination of other beings. Indeed, a person can oppose the degrading custom of owning conscious beings and still, in legal fact, own animals, in order to ensure the welfare of those who are forced to seek shelter. During times of enslavement, such protective ownership has been a fact of life.

Now, although rescue and caring are needed when we humans have caused an emergency in other animals' lives, or imposed dependency upon them, a respectful society will remember that animal communities don't need us to put ourselves in charge of them. Because an act of rescue means one party becomes dominant, rescue should, when possible and reasonable, be seen as a temporary intervention. One of my co-workers in the movement, Peter Wallerstein, works along the California coast, rescuing pelicans, seals and other animals who get caught in anglers' gear or fall ill with an algae-related poisoning that's becoming more frequent in a warming ocean. Peter has dedicated a lifetime to caring, yet believes rescues should be as temporary as possible. The aim of the Marine Animal Rescue project is to free animals from dangers humans have caused, and quickly return them to their normal lives. Occasionally, one of the stranded seal pups Peter reaches during the course of this work turns out to be suffering from a natural peril: A stingray's barb in a seal pup's face might, like a splinter, work itself out, but it can also can kill a pup, by boring up through the roof of the mouth and moving out through the eye or up into the head. Peter will remove a barb. Brief as it is, this is control over the animal, but only so the animal might flourish.

Some others—monkeys, birds and various animals kept in human settings and then discarded by their owners, for example, or orang-utans who are orphaned or left without habitat due to the effects of logging—need the ethic of care, and they need it for life. Rescue sites for monkeys and other non-domesticated animals should offer these refugees private space, and publicly challenge humanity's feeling of entitlement to use other animals or to take their habitat. And all rescue and rehabilitation projects—whether for domesticated animals or those who could have lived free—should make one thing crystal clear. It's high time for humanity to challenge the whole idea that all other animals' fates should hinge on our needs and our decisions. Unless refuges or farm sanctuaries are prepared to question domestication as well as captivity of non-human animals for human use, they can quickly take on the aura of a hobby farm or a petting zoo.

Promoting animal welfare and teaching animal rights:

An Example

Emberwood Lane Refuge is a sanctuary for domesticated animals rescued from abandonment. Many came from farms whose owners went out of business. Kelly Clark is the founder and is also a doctor of veterinary medicine.

Marty Pruitt is a guide there. This week, Marty meets the latest arrivals at the sanctuary: two donkeys. Marty tells the visitors, "All of the animals at our refuge experienced some type of maltreatment, even if that simply entailed being separated from their family at birth. Some have suffered years of torment and approached the end of their lives before a kind hand reached out to them. Here, each one is assured a place of safety and lifetime care, and as much freedom as we can provide the animals on 25 fenced acres of a natural setting, necessarily containing a variety of sheds to shelter them from the weather."

All of the animals at Emberwood Lane are purpose-bred—bred to be docile. Many obviously want and seek human contact. The pot-bellied pigs and a newer arrival, a pig who somehow escaped slaughter, are friendly and welcoming to the visitors. The rabbits and most of the ducks and other birds seem interested in doing their own thing. The goats appear to have all sorts of different opinions on the matter.

Kelly encourages all the resident animals to do as they wish (and explains this to visitors). The animals have plenty of space, trees, water containers, hutches and so forth, so individuals can decide whether they want to be out of view. The rabbits—who were bred to be pets, meat or fur, or as lab specimens—can dig, and have warrens underground. It's a cold day, but many are in the open air, active, and eating greenery.

The hens came from egg companies. When they lay their unfertilized eggs, these are fed back to the hens, to replenish their calcium.

One former veal calf had done what few in the world have ever done: grown up. What a massive individual, this ex-calf!

About the occasional tours of the refuge, Marty Pruitt says, "I invite visitors to share their own experiences, and always inject the message that these animals, much as I care for each one, shouldn't be here. This land was once brush and forest. Coyotes and bears, and wolves too, thrived here before farmers claimed the ground."

Once we decide to respect all animals' interests, Marty explains, other animals will not be deliberately bred to be dependent as these individuals were. By avoiding the products of animal farming, we could free up land for coyotes, and the bears and wolves as well, should they make their way back.

Working at a refuge is, of course, about animal welfare. The theory of animal rights applies to the free-living communities—those bears and coyotes and wolves. Marty and Kelly know that's important to say. Otherwise, their refuge fails to work for real change. Some visitors, of course, will dismiss their counsel. "Rabbits are much better off domesticated than living in the wild," says one guest. But others want to know more.

Marty presses on, giving practical tips on how each visitor could become vegan, using their current, individual circumstances as a starting point. "How can I cook without eggs? Aren't free-range eggs OK?"

Marty has well-tested recipes for eggless breakfasts and desserts on hand. "We don't need to take birds' eggs away from them to eat good meals," Marty answers. "And eggs are easier than you might think to replace."

On behalf of all refugees from human exploitation and indifference, Marty is working to ensure that visitors learn how they can help to prevent the tragedy that makes refuges such as Emberwood Lane a necessary component of the animal-rights movement.

Once this movement gets rolling, it will stop the whole machinery of animal agribusiness by showing that it need not be here at all. Meanwhile, some animals who are already born and escape the trap of commerce receive responsible care here. They're lucky. Roll-of-the-dice lucky, like the few turkeys who receive the privilege weirdly called the presidential pardon, the turkeys who, by luck of the lottery, get paraded in front of the television cameras every year during the Thanksgiving holiday while viewers cook these same birds' relatives. How, Marty asks, can we get these macabre jokes on other animals to end?

One day in October, Emberwood Sanctuary has a fundraiser. Many of the pieces of art and craft work for sale were made by young people in at-risk communities, who themselves are present, talking with supporters and taking turns volunteering at the grill where vegan pizza is being toasted. Marty gets a piece of pizza that's a bit overdone on the bottom, and praises its crispy texture and zesty taste.

The temperature is not too far above freezing, and it's drizzling. People huddle beneath the overhangs to enjoy their snacks, and interact with the animals who come to meet them. It's cold, but people have come, and most stay for several hours. A new barn is needed. It's a community's responsibility, and it's part of the bond that connects caring people, even if they haven't all got the same ideas about animal rights. Many will meet again; there will be time to talk and share.

Rescuers become a true force for change when they break ranks with the habitual breeding and selling of animals, and decline to help regulate such activities. No sanctuary should suggest that the animals rescued from that cycle have the best imaginable lives. In November, traditionally a month that features turkey-eating in the United States, an alert comes out from a sanctuary: "President Obama Urged to Send Pardoned Birds to 'Happiest Place on Earth' for Turkeys." Even as I write this chapter, I've received a fundraising message from a sanctuary self-described as "Paradise for Farmed Animals and the People Who Love Them." Such advertising numbs. As Marty points out, being vulnerable to human whim and mercy is hardly the best possible life. A refuge is no paradise; it depends on cleared land and systematic food production, and raises dilemmas about whether and how to control insects and rodents, not to mention the local carnivores who would perceive a confined animal as an easy meal.

On a small scale, these dilemmas come up for me. I've welcomed cats into my space, and so I buy commercial food, and sometimes medicines, wrapped in too much packaging, from corporations I want nothing to do with, at malls built on the land that once belonged to free animals. I clean up, and the waste, which might be toxic to water animals, has to go somewhere; it winds up carted on trucks in the heaps that make up the landfills. I offer the cats physical space: a bigger patch of Earth than I'd otherwise need. I don't consume animals, which helps contain my ecological footprint, and yet I'm walking with an entourage of animals on this increasingly fragile planet that's home to so many more communities than the human one.

We didn't ask to live together; they were in need, too near for me to turn away. I love each cat dearly, yet I'm not convinced it's fair to call them companions. At times it seems to me they are the trapped souls of wildcats. My ancestors were their ancestors' prey. Of that, I think maybe two of them have an ancient memory at about six in the morning, when they pounce on my ankles.

Rescuing animals and giving them safe homes may appeal to us. Perhaps, subconsciously, we regard their safety as assuring our own security in the world. We see ourselves as helping individual animals in distress, and that might be so; but overall, if it takes over as advocacy's mission, the view of advocates as rescuers may impede a serious movement for animals' autonomous lives. If so, there is value in struggling to find new ways of caring, so that the goal of advocacy isn't to make a Garden of Eden for other animals within our society, but rather to change society so we respect their own ways of being. As that respect grows, less charitable activity will be needed.

Vegan Society founder Donald Watson envisioned people all over the world cultivating acceptance of the ideal of non-exploitation, thereby abolishing vast industries and replacing them with peaceful methods of providing for ourselves. This ideal does not dismiss the welfare of human beings: The situation of human workers could be vastly improved in a culture that values organic growing, natural fertilizers, and peaceable, meaningful occupations.

In short, Watson believed in the power of ordinary people to work with each other and cultivate an extraordinary society: one that renounces dominion and systematic killing and thereby merits being called a civilization. Both simple and demanding, that idea is the core of animal-rights theory. The forthright claim that non-human animals should be allowed to live on their terms, not humanity's.

The responsible refuge: A checklist

Animal-rights activists do support animals' welfare, for it's unjust to neglect the well-being of animals whose vulnerability we created. Where we've caused dangers for other animals, we have an ethical duty to rescue. Where we've created dependency in other animals, we have a duty to care.

This is a task we should strive to share equally in the movement. For example, looking after feral cats should be supported by activists as a community effort. Regardless of gender, educational background, or title, we model this responsible action to everyone in our area. And if we steadfastly work with the animal-rights ideal in mind, fewer and fewer animals will be bred to live at the mercy of humanity, and less rescue and welfare work will be needed. At the same time, we'll cultivate respect for free-living animals' interest in having their habitats unmolested.

Refuges can adopt advocacy principles that encourage us to take animal welfare seriously, yet bring us closer to animal rights. As suggested guidelines, a sanctuary, shelter, or advocacy group:

- **Does not systematically kill animals.** Some charities regularly kill the animals they claim to help. Institutional killing retards social justice. It turns animal advocacy into animal control. **This is a non-negotiable commitment: A movement should support its refugees.**
- **Is prepared to create and support a refuge movement by strengthening viable or potentially viable no-kill shelters and sanctuaries, rather than resorting to convenience or giving up in despair.** The difficulty lies in balancing intake and individual animals' well-being; but the point is

to support a movement so that this societal responsibility can be shouldered. Animal-advocacy representatives in a position to personally offer refuge to animals, actively support the no-kill refuge movement, or both, should do so.

- **Is willing to state openly that rescue is a bandage; while it's often necessary and just, rescuing is neither the foundation nor the goal of the social movement known as animal-rights advocacy.** The point is to change the roots of the situation that puts animals in dependent positions.
- **Questions domestication of non-human animals for human use and enjoyment.** Rescue without this awareness turns cyclical and becomes part of the status quo.
- **Takes an unequivocal stand that rules out all stalking and killing of free-living animals, and opposes the confinement of animals in labs, agribusiness, zoos, aquaria, or for breeding to fight, work, race, or show.** Understanding systematic confinement as unfair, the sanctuary declines to become an apologist for supposedly benign, non-invasive or improved methods. Placing chimpanzees, gorillas, or bonobos in language studies, for example, is not acceptable. Except in genuine sheltering situations, all confinement is invasive and should be avoided as far as possible.
- **Turns down donations that hinge on compromises to the above positions.**

Advocacy means speaking with people in the language of justice. Our goals should never be hidden; our message must be clear and consistent for every audience. If animal sanctuaries need help, let's support them. But let's also cultivate the kind of thinking and discussions that will stop making these refuges necessary. Sanctuary workers, and people who report news about them, are best advised not to call the sanctuary's animals "retired" (one battery hen sanctuary, for example, describes its mission as "working with the farmers to retire these working girls into a wonderful, free-range life"). Not only is this language patronizing, but former industry animals were never willing employees in our society, and refuge isn't a payback for fair work. Nor should these animals be called by names that imply employment after being rescued (such as "ambassadors" for other animals of their kind or "educators" to the public); they owe us nothing, and it is our work to educate our society.

CHAPTER 2

Animal Rights,
As It's Commonly
Known

Confusion and debate abound over who speaks to the public for animal rights. In 2006, the British media identified Peter Singer as "the father of the animal-rights movement" when reporting that the bioethics professor had publicly called experimenting on a hundred monkeys justified if it would spare 40,000 humans from disease.[1]

Philosopher Tom Regan immediately wrote to correct some misunderstandings: Peter Singer, said Regan, is not an advocate of rights and doesn't speak for animal-rights advocates. Regan explained that Singer holds the views of a utilitarian, believing that overall consequences of a given action determine moral right and wrong. Regan disagrees. "The basic moral rights of the individual," wrote Regan, citing the rights to life and bodily integrity, "should never be violated in the name of reaping benefits for others."[2]

Regan's words matter. Regan, after all, is the western philosopher most identified with the development of a modern-day case for animal rights,[3] distinct from the anti-cruelty model of traditional humane societies. But then, Singer does preside over a group called Animal Rights International— which, in turn, exerts considerable influence over activists, at least in the United States. *The New Yorker* has said Singer's beliefs "gave birth to the animal-rights movement"; and Singer's 1975 book *Animal Liberation* has been called "a canonical text of the animal rights movement."[4] One might understandably wonder if the definition of animal rights, like that of beauty, is in the eye of the beholder.

Let's continue, then, into a brief and general discussion of the two prevalent views currently associated with what's commonly called animal rights. To say "currently associated" is important because, as political philosopher Rod Preece has written, "Contrary to the impression one receives in so much of the literature, a recognition (and even sometimes the language) of animal rights is no new phenomenon but is a part of general human consciousness"—even though "[m]any influential animal rights advocates wish to be seen as a vanguard rather than a historical continuity."[5]

With that caveat in mind, let's examine the views of Peter Singer and the people who have applied them to animal advocacy, and then take a brief look at Regan's abolitionist perspective.

Following that, we can proceed to anticipate the path animal-rights theory can travel if it is genuinely consistent with the goal of ensuring fairness. This path isn't for the faint of heart. Animal rights, as old as the idea's roots are, calls for a revolution in human thought.

Major lifestyle adjustments will, in any case, be forced on us by harsh changes, already underway, in the weather and ecology. But without an ethic that permits us to see beyond dominance patterns, the change will simply comprise reactions to emergencies. We need change at a much deeper level. Humanity needs a radical change of heart.

Singer's reduction-of-suffering model: Is it animal rights?

A guarantee of a pain-free life doesn't work on Earth. No one has ever had the right not to suffer. Pain is a survival mechanism that signals us to avoid injury, or to carefully protect an injured area. It enables conscious beings to live and look after themselves on our planet. If we consider the interest in life worth defending, we must acknowledge that pain has a role in (not against) that theory, for *pain promotes our ability to survive and thrive.*

In 2006, researchers identified six children from three Pakistani families with mutations that inactivated one particular gene. None of the children had ever felt pain. Each one had bruises and cuts. One, who was known for hand-stabbing and walking on hot coals, died after jumping off a roof.[6]

Although suffering is, of course, an undesirable sensation, animal advocacy at its best will accept risk and unplanned suffering as a part of being alive, self-conscious, and aware of life experiences. Ending animal suffering, in contrast, would mean ending conscious life as we know it. Yet it appears to be the entire premise for Peter Singer's view. Singer has described *Animal Liberation* as "what seemed to me then—and still seems to me basically, really, now—an incredibly simple and yet very logical argument based on values that most people accept that suffering is a bad thing..."[7] Today, numerous advocacy groups, with missions focusing on most every current human use of other animals, heed Singer's call to lobby for adjustments in industrial methods of handling animals in order to lessen their pain.

Animals can't be understood as containers of pain. Moreover, the well-known campaigns for handling changes misunderstand even physical pain. While acute pain serves as a protective response when tissue is damaged, chronic pain is the lingering distress known to people who have had on-the-job injuries that fail to heal properly, or arthritis, or the neuropathic pain of amputees or people suffering a serious disease. It's not unreasonable to assume that commercially used animals experience acute as well as chronic pain. Only some factors will be noted in advocacy or advertising campaigns. And some assessments might be outright wrong as well as insufficiently contextualized. When the now-fashionable and purportedly less-miserable "uncrated" veal calves are taken from the dairy cows who gave birth to them and put on slotted or solid floor space in groups, the frustrated young beings commonly mount or suck each other, or fight. To deal with aggression and still get them fed, the site managers will restrain them.[8] Animal-science professor Joy Mench has reported that out-of-cage hens are more likely to fall victim to cannibalism or to illnesses associated with increased exposure to their manure, and that most laying hens suffer from osteoporosis, so hens are more likely to break bones when moving through the barn or on the range; yet activists typically disregard these facts as they campaign to change the storage methods of live hens.[9]

Changing the way we confine hens has become an unwavering call of several of the world's animal-protection societies—both the Humane Society of the United States and the Vancouver Humane Society have praised companies that buy from suppliers who use alternatives to the standard cage as "putting the chicken before the egg"—and it has long been an aim of Singer's. Chickens are seen as both numerous and badly abused, confined in high-volume (also known as "battery") cage storage by modern agribusiness. "One of the first things we campaigned about in the 1970s when I got interested in this," Singer has said, "was the battery cage for hens. People laughed at you and said you'll never get rid of that, people don't care about hens anyway, how can you prove they're suffering, all of that sort of stuff, and now the whole of Europe is getting rid of the battery cage."[10]

But if the whole of Europe is doing it, doesn't that mean it's evolved into yet another form of mass production? The answer is yes. Continental Europe's egg market is still a high-volume affair. A multi-tiered storage system packs many birds inside buildings.[11] In Germany, where barren battery cages were outlawed in 2009, a replacement system called "colony cages" offers only minimal improvements; an egg business owner who proposed trying this system in California said the enclosures would have 50 square feet of indoor space for 60 birds—still not even a foot per bird—whereas common battery cages cram eight hens into a four-foot space.[12] Wherever they become popular, the "cage-free" and "free-range" offerings are typically mass-produced commodities involving no pastures at all. These situations can be better than standard cages, but not much better. The hens who get less than a foot of space each don't know it could've been worse, and they all meet the same dreary end. Nevertheless, Peter Singer has pressed Princeton University to follow other schools and switch to the more expensive "cage-free" eggs, calling this trend "among the most successful efforts of the American animal-welfare movement."[13]

The press has called Singer "an internationally recognized expert on ethical treatment of animals, even those raised for meat."[14] And this description gets to the heart of the problem with Singer's philosophical model. When asked if universities could serve an ethical hamburger, Singer replied, "It's not a black-and-white answer," and added, "But a hamburger can be much more ethical. I would be satisfied if we move it in the right direction."[15] Singer's suggestion that we can ethically raise any conscious beings in order to consume their flesh replicates the wrong that animal-rights advocacy sets out to confront.

That confronting came in 1944, when, in the spirit of profound respect for conscious life on the planet, Donald Watson and a small group of like-minded "non-dairy vegetarians" founded The Vegan Society. Watson knew and declared that no animal farm would ever be idyllic. "I suppose I was one of millions of children with a very similar, orthodox background," recalled Watson at the age of 92. "One of my earliest recollections in life was being taken for holidays to the little farm where my father had been born," Watson continued. "And my first impression of those holidays was one of heaven...."

Watson explains why:

> I was surrounded by interesting animals. There was the big Shire horse, who pulled the plough. There was a horse of lighter build, that pulled the trap, which in those days was the equivalent of the modern motor car, which took my granny into local markets to sell her butter and eggs. There were the cows, there were the pigs; there were no sheep on the farm—they lived in a field hundreds of yards away. There were hens, there was a cockerel; there were two cats, the farm dog, Rover...The cows "gave" milk, the hens "gave" eggs, the cockerel was a useful "alarm clock"—I didn't realize at that time that he had another function too! The sheep, I knew, "gave" wool...I couldn't for the life of me see what the pigs "gave"; and they seemed—there were usually two—such friendly creatures, always glad to see me, and grateful for almost anything that was thrown to them in the sty.

One day, something strange was going on when Donald came downstairs for breakfast. Donald's grandmother was busy boiling one pan of water after another on the fire. "What was all this about?" the child wondered, watching two farmhands walking past the kitchen window, carrying a trestle, with handles on each end, to the sty. Then the business of killing one of the pigs began.

> And I still have vivid recollections of the whole process
> from start to finish—including all the screams of course, which
> were only feet away from where this pig's companion still lived.
> And then, when the pig had finally expired, the women came
> out, one after another, with buckets of this scalding water, and
> the body of the pig was scraped; all the hairs were taken away.

Donald was shocked that "Uncle George, of whom I thought very
highly, was part of the crew," and that day decided that "farms, and uncles,
had to be re-assessed."

> And it followed that this idyllic scene was nothing more
> than Death Row. A Death Row where every creature's days
> were numbered by the point at which it was no longer of service
> to human beings.

And this, said Watson, is the story on which our present civilization
is built. Quite early in life, this straightforward thinker concluded that a
report on human progress would have been summed up in "the comment
beloved of schoolteachers: *Could do better.*" It would be from that seed that,
in 1944, The Vegan Society was planted into the human consciousness.[16]

By the latter half of the 1970s, Peter Singer had arrived on the
scene, insisting that purpose-breeding and killing—both quintessential
acts of domination—could be acceptable to the advocacy platform. Singer
understood non-human animals as interested in avoiding suffering, but not
in their futures; so killing them, Singer decided, is morally acceptable if they
can be killed after having experienced lives that Singer deems reasonably
pleasant.

Donald Watson saw the injustice in capturing, keeping and breeding
other animals for our own ends even if their lives, up until their last moments,

were idyllic. In the vegan paradigm, therefore, and in contrast to Singer's, breeding animals into a domesticated existence does not benefit them.[17] The vegan movement established a bright-line position: Animals' interests will never be respectfully met as long as we go on using them. Indeed, as early as 1892 the general idea that Singer proposed was rebuffed as a "gross absurdity" by Henry Salt, who observed:

> The common argument, adopted by many apologists of flesh-eating, as of fox-hunting, that the pain inflicted by the death of the animals is more than compensated by the pleasure enjoyed by them in their lifetime, since otherwise they would not have been brought into existence at all, is ingenious rather than convincing, indeed being none other than the old familiar fallacy already commented on—the arbitrary trick of constituting ourselves the spokesmen and the interpreters of our victims.[18]

Singer's utilitarian view drew interest and criticism to the plight of commercialized animals, but it did not arise to help us challenge our dominion over other conscious beings; it prescribed, instead, a way to exert it. Negating what the vegan principle seeks to preserve—other animals' freedom and autonomy—Singer's influence over the past few decades has accepted the existence of, and directed the spotlight to, the animals we can protect, such as captive turkeys, pigs, cattle, and chickens, whose prolonged ordeals we can at least shorten, or whose air we can at least freshen. And even this limited prescription is flexible, with Singer asking people to do little beyond what's convenient. "If it's a big burden on us, that's surely different," Singer says, but "we ought to be prepared to pay more for eggs so that the chicken can enjoy its life, and not be frustrated and deprived and miserable."[19]

Wrapping animal products in labels meant to assure people that the beings from whom these items came were handled relatively carefully, and weren't deprived, could thus reduce misgivings about consuming them.

Stating that paying more for eggs is not a big burden, Singer implies that removing eggs from our diet *is*. That implication is even stronger when Singer reassures people that "the entire European Union is already saying you can't keep hens as confined as American hens" and concludes, "So you can do it, and it doesn't mean that people can no longer afford to eat eggs."[20]

It's not surprising, then, that Singer elides the ethical difference between the conscientious objector to animal agribusiness—the vegan— and those continuing to support animal-based businesses. "If you can be vegetarian or vegan," Singer states, "that's ideal."[21] As dairy products are in many foods, says Singer, "avoiding them entirely can make life difficult... Personal purity isn't really the issue. Not supporting animal abuse—and persuading others not to support it—is."[22] Singer allows for eating anything at a fine restaurant, if the visits are infrequent: "A little self-indulgence, if you can keep it under firm control, doesn't make you a moral monster, and it certainly doesn't mean that you might as well abandon your principles entirely."[23] Similarly, Singer finds it "appropriate to praise the conscientious omnivores" for how much they do.[24]

Whether or not one agrees that such praising is appropriate, we can see a vast gulf between this and Donald Watson's view, which, as far as possible, rules out the subordination of conscious beings. Focusing on factory production, a relatively new form of rearing animals and processing their bodies, Singer recently stated:

> I sort of in a way hoped that people would just read the book *[Animal Liberation]* and say, "Yes, this is right, I've got to do something about it, I've gotta stop abusing them, I've gotta pass this book on to my friend, and then my friend will say the same thing and so the movement will rapidly spread. And these industries will collapse, factory farming will collapse, because people will stop demanding its products."[25]

This hasn't happened, so Singer says we have to think about "what else can we do to stop the immense amount of suffering that happens to factory farmed animals in particular. I focus on that because…that's where the greatest amount of animal suffering is. That's where the numbers are so overwhelmingly much larger than any other form of human abuse of animals."[26]

Most people who hear Singer would likely agree: much suffering happens in high-volume animal production. So much, that trying to address its various components (cage dimensions, the searing of beaks, transport conditions, slaughter methods, and so forth and so on) everywhere it's happening, even as the industries become ever bigger and more complex, anticipating the demand of perhaps nine billion people by 2050, would mean perpetually chasing after the outer edges of the worst scenarios. Singer insists that animal agribusiness needs to be cut back. For humane reasons and also considering the "environmental costs of intensive animal production" Singer says "we need to cut down drastically on the animal products we consume."[27]

But does that mean a vegan world? That's one solution, but not necessarily the only one. If it is the infliction of suffering that we are concerned about, rather than killing, then I can imagine a world in which people mostly eat plant foods, but occasionally treat themselves to the luxury of free-range eggs, or possibly even meat from animals who live good lives under conditions natural for their species, and then are humanely killed on the farm.[28]

But in today's world, that scene involves an industry catering to the wealthy few—encouraging the problematic association of wealth with animal products. Enabling animals to graze freely is simply out of the financial reach of many farmers; in Europe, for example, acreage is extremely expensive, and actual grazing could only be managed at the call of the well-heeled. Land would be used up as far as industry could take it—farmers can tell us that letting calves amble and graze in a field will quickly make the ground bare—putting free-living animals' essential needs behind people's desire (for it's not a need) to eat animals. And while some maintain that at least "humane farming" promotions make people contemplate the cruel treatment of animals, those people willing to think seriously about such things are presumably the same people who would opt out of animal agribusiness if they received a straightforward explanation of why business built on domination can never be uncruel.

By framing animal advocacy as a challenge to assembly-line practices, by calling the situation of purpose-bred animals "natural," and by thinking of animal products as our treats, Singer has stalled the holistic activism that a serious segment of the vegetarian movement had been promoting for well over a century: withdrawing our support for animal agribusiness.

John Davis, historian for the International Vegetarian Union, writes of the first vegetarian society and its defined mission: "In the early 1850s the magazine representing the Society had quite clearly defined it as: 'Vegetarian: one who lives on the products of the vegetable kingdom.'" By the early 1900s, Davis reports, the Vegetarian Society's *Vegetarian Messenger* expressly supported a diet free of eggs and dairy, listing both ethical and health objections to the use of these foods. It is from this background that the early vegans emerged. Free-range farming is no step in the right direction in the vegan paradigm; in fact, it was a free-range farm that Donald Watson found unacceptable. Watson also said, "We can see quite plainly that our present civilization is built on the exploitation of animals, just as past civilizations were built on the exploitation of slaves..."[29] Defining veganism for the record in 1951, Leslie Cross (as vice president of The Vegan Society) wrote that veganism "possesses historical continuity" with the anti-slavery movement, and further explained:

> [V]eganism is not so much welfare as liberation, for the creatures and for the mind and heart of man; not so much an effort to make the present relationship bearable, as an

uncompromising recognition that because it is in the main one of master and slave, it has to be abolished before something better and finer can be built.[30]

And so a movement had emerged, explicitly connecting vegetarianism with a liberation call, based on the conviction that *humanity has no right* to exploit other creatures for our own ends; and this new movement set out to discontinue the use of other animals for human food, work, hunting, vivisection and all other deliberately exploitive purposes. The vegan's diet would thus be derived entirely from "fruits, nuts, vegetables, grains and other wholesome, non-animal products" and exclude "flesh, fish, fowl, eggs, honey and animal milk and its derivatives."[31] More than a diet, it is a principle in itself, for the early vegans took the war-resister's principle of conscientious objection and expanded it to encompass all conscious life. The modern animal-rights movement had begun. But then...

Singer's model goes to market

When Whole Foods Market unveiled a concept called the Animal Compassion Foundation, and announced that new rules would be devised for the handling of animals bred, raised, and killed for the upscale grocer's butcher aisle—apparently reframing the act of shopping for animal flesh as a charitable act—Friends of Animals objected.[32] On the 19th of January 2005, Whole Foods' CEO John Mackey replied: "I agree with you that it is not ideal or perfect. I agree with you that it would be better if human beings would stop killing, eating, enslaving, and exploiting animals and I'm personally committed to that very philosophy."

The following day, Priscilla Feral of Friends of Animals wrote back:

> You agree that "it would be better if human beings would stop killing, eating, enslaving, and exploiting animals" and yet you, John, with your Animal Compassionate Standards, are investing millions so that those human beings can think in

precisely the opposite terms. You are sugar-coating, and thus promoting, what you personally acknowledge as enslavement.

Five days later, the grocery chain's website showcased a letter from Peter Singer on Animal Rights International letterhead, co-signed by seventeen

Animal Rights International

John Mackey
Chief Executive Officer
Whole Foods Market
500 Bowie Street
Austin, TX 78703

January 24, 2005

Dear John,

The undersigned animal welfare, animal protection and animal rights organizations would like to express their appreciation and support for the pioneering initiative being taken by Whole Foods Market in setting Farm Animal Compassionate Standards. We hope and expect that these standards will improve the lives of millions of animals.

Animal Rights International (ARI)
Animal Welfare Institute (AWI)
Animal Place
Animal Protection Institute (API)
Association of Vets for Animal Rights (AVAR)
Bay Area Vegetarians
Christian Vegetarian Association
Compassion Over Killing (COK)
Doris Day Animal League
East Bay Animal Advocates
Farm Sanctuary
Humane Society of the United States (HSUS)
People for the Ethical Treatment of Animals (PeTA)
Mercy for Animals
Northwest In Defense of Animals
Vegan Outreach
Viva!USA

Sincerely,

Peter Singer

President, Animal Rights International

ANIMAL RIGHTS INT'L (ARI) PO Box 532 Woodbury, CT 06798 · Tel: 203.263.8532 · Fax: 203.263.8533
Email: info@ari-online.org · Website www.ari-online.org · Contributions to ARI are tax-deductible.

Founder: Henry Spira President: Professor Peter Singer Administrative Officer: Sarah Whitman
Campaigns Advisor: Mark Graham Legal Advisor: Elinor Molbegott, J.D.

"animal welfare, animal protection, and animal rights organizations" to express their "appreciation and support for the pioneering initiative being taken by Whole Foods Market in setting Farm Animal Compassionate Standards."

The day after that, this international grocery chain rolled out a fundraising day around this concept, advertised by posters with animal silhouettes—with the backing of seventeen animal-protection charities.[33]

What next?

In our age, when farm animals are being cloned, some people are looking to biotech researchers (who test their endless parade of ideas by injecting a noxious, painful chemical into animals' paws, shocking them, or burning them) to produce industrial animals without sensitivity to pain. One proponent of genetic engineering for this purpose is Adam Shriver, a philosopher at Washington University in St. Louis, who says, "I'm offering a solution where you could still eat meat but avoid animal suffering."[34] What does Peter Singer think of animals being reduced to such a state?

Although animals' pain is not the only factor in Singer's assessment of animal factories, it's a central one, and in the interest of achieving a reduction in overall suffering, Singer sees the genetic engineering idea as a plus. When an interviewer asked for an opinion on the possibility of producing chickens without brains, Singer, apparently in earnest, answered, "It would be an ethical improvement on the present system, because it would eliminate the suffering that these birds are feeling. That's the huge plus to me."[35] In Singer's reduction-of-suffering model of advocacy, human decisions to develop certain traits in other animals can easily be accepted as good for the animals themselves; again we see this view accepting domestication, even to the point of laboratory-based gene manipulation. The view that more intensive handling, not less, is best for animals is emerging in the promotional rhetoric of the biotechnology industry itself, which, for example, insists that breeding clones will improve the overall health and disease resistance of animal populations, and that cloning should reduce animal suffering over time.[36]

Perhaps most unnerving of all is Singer's ability to suggest engineering birds out of their minds and in the next breath compare the movement for improving our treatment of other animals to anti-slavery movements, anti-Nazi activism, and feminism.[37] (Singer tells the interviewer: "We have expanded the circle beyond our own race and we reject as wrongful the idea that something like race or religion or gender can be a basis for claiming another being's interests count less than our own." Singer further says that "nonhuman animals are conscious beings" and we ignore their suffering "just as the Nazis ignored the suffering of the Jews, or the slave traders ignored the suffering of the Africans.") Lobotomy—partial destruction of the brain—was tested to reduce aggression in chimpanzees at Yale in the 1930s. Subsequently, political rebels and unruly women (including John F. Kennedy's younger sibling, Rosemary), and individuals of various other kinds whom society has decided don't deserve or need respect, were subjected to lobotomies.[38] Psychiatrist Walter J. Freeman, who once headed the American Medical Association's certification board for neurology and psychiatry, would perform numerous ice-pick lobotomies in the 1940s, assembly-line style. The operation was a success if, in the words of Freeman and Dr. James Watts, the patient was "adjusting at the level of a domestic invalid or household pet."[39] Tractable individuals, deliberately deprived of their minds or their feelings, and thus their will to resist control, aren't any nearer to liberation; on the contrary, they're even more dependent on others, and easier to manage in institutional settings.

Here it might be argued that the chickens' intellectual and emotional lives would be far from those of the lobotomy patients. But we need not compare and contrast. The point here is that challenging institutional suffering shouldn't mean conjuring up new procedures by still more institutions. We need not institutionalize people for being strong-willed; nor need we institutionalize other animals and deprive them of their autonomy.

Singer's focus on maximizing satisfaction and reducing suffering leads animal advocacy down other paths of absurdity as well. Singer has declared that "sex with animals does not always involve cruelty" and that, between a homeowner and a dog, for example, "occasionally mutually satisfying activities may develop."[40] Dogs are deliberately rendered less independent during selective breeding, then trained to conform to individual human environments, and to be anxious to please their owners. One can hardly imagine a more vulnerable position.[41]

Singer's reduction-of-suffering model is antithetical to rights theory. It does not ask us to stop exploiting or killing other animals, but instead advances the notion that we can make these things bearable, or at least less uncomfortable, for the individuals being controlled.[42] It is prepared to justify all manner of exploiting animal bodies, individually and systematically, simply by obtaining assurances that such actions don't exceed some vague level of physical pain. It offers much leeway for human indulgences, and appears to take for granted that *Homo sapiens* have and will keep certain prerogatives. It has reduced animals *to* suffering by influencing activists to regard the animal body as a repository of measurable pain.

"Oddly, by arguing that disabled children should sometimes be killed, Singer seems, if anything, to be worrying too much about their pain," wrote Michael Specter in 1999 for *The New Yorker*. "He is so devoted to the prevention of suffering—in a hen, a cow, or a human infant—that he dismisses the possibility that there might be more than that to many people's lives."[43]

It's a dim philosophy indeed that fails to value the lives and interests of conscious individuals as infinitely more remarkable and complex than the sum of their suffering. Singer's philosophy seems eerily dismissive of what it's ill-equipped to compute, including animals who aren't valued for fulfilling human preferences—those who might live free of our manipulations. When asked about a "scenario where animals are no longer bred for human use" and "allowed to roam free," Singer has answered:

> Tragically, we've destroyed so much habitat that for some species, this is not a great option. Chimpanzees, bonobos, gorillas and orang-utans, for example, have few safe havens now. So—in the real world, anyway, rather than in some utopia—it

might still be best for some species to live under human control and protection.[44]

True, few safe havens remain for many animals. But this does not mean it is best for some groups of animals to live under human control and protection. At this point, humanity has already changed so much habitat and manipulated the lives of other animals so thoroughly, part of letting other animals live on their terms must include strong environmental law—law that stops seeing the environment as a background to human affairs, law that takes the interests of all living inhabitants seriously. That will entail a direct challenge to several human institutions, most notably the business of purpose-breeding animals. A leading reason for the planet's lack of safe havens is the sheer vastness of our use of the globe's surface for domesticated animals. With them, the environmental footprint of nearly seven billion of us is multiplied several times over. And yet Singer also suggests that an ethical person would accept the human custom of breeding animals, including for the agribusiness sector. Singer, with Jim Mason, in *The Way We Eat*, writes:

> Raising lambs in the Welsh hills, for example, is a traditional form of husbandry that has existed for many centuries and makes use of land that could not otherwise provide food for humans. If the lives of the sheep are, on the whole, good ones, and they would not exist at all if the lambs were not killed and eaten, it can be argued that doing so has benefits, on the whole, for both human and animals.[45]

Similarly, discussing what is, in reality, manipulating the reproductive systems of pigs and having them bear more pigs so their flesh can be consumed by others, Singer accepts that "as long as the pig has a good life and a quick death, it is a good thing (or at least not a bad thing) for the pig that he or she exists."[46] Pigs can appear, in our eyes, to have a good life in captivity because breeders have purposefully selected the docile animals and eliminated the inconvenient autonomy of free-living pigs. Humans have decimated those earlier, autonomous pigs and cleared the land they once roamed and covered it with factories, industrial yards, and roads. So here again is the argument for dominion: they're happy because we tamed them, because we took away from their communities all that made them free.

In a multitude of ways, Singer's position reverses the vegan call to organize for conscientious objection to the human war on others. Singer's position accepts the system of animal agribusiness as benign if we agree (at least when convenient) to carry out its exploits with a promise to lessen the standard level of pain. All in all, what I've outlined here—which is by no means an attempt to sum up all of Singer's prolific work, but which, I believe, does give a fair, if stark, idea of how Singer's model affects everyday animal advocacy—compels us to agree with Regan's assertion that Peter Singer is not an advocate of animal rights as the term "rights" is generally understood. Singer's suffering-reduction plan could lead us to a place where the world's animals exist under the dominion of a single species, not unhappy with their lot—even if ridding them of their distress means taking out their brains.

Because Singer declines to consider an end to our dominion, control, and commodification of other conscious animals as ethically necessary, Singer's theory of equal consideration disappoints. For animal rights isn't properly understood as a way to create satisfying interactions between humans and other animals or to reduce suffering. Instead, it's about challenging and transcending human supremacy.

CHAPTER 3

Abolition:
Is It Animal Rights?

L et's turn to the second popular conception of "animal rights." To distinguish it from Singer's view, we'll call it abolitionism. Abolitionists talk of meaningful safeguards for non-human animals as requiring the end of daily, institutional animal use; or they speak of the imperative to completely remove non-human animals from the category of human-owned property. For those committed to developing a respect-based movement, the abolitionist theory, we shall see, fares better than Singer's.

Tom Regan, who, in 1983, published *The Case for Animal Rights*, explains the book's central thesis as asserting that all beings who are conscious of their lives, human and non-human, "share the fundamental right to be treated with respect."[1] All such beings, Regan asserts, have an "inherent value" which is independent of the way they might be useful to others.[2] Regan's concept of "inherent value" is not economic. It's what we talk about when we say we value our life, our freedom, our body, our dignity, our privacy. *The Case for Animal Rights* tells us avoiding injustice would require us to believe that all who have inherent value have it equally: "Possession of moral rights does not come in degrees. All who possess them possess them equally, whether they are, say, white or black, male or female, Americans or Iranians."[3] Along with humans, Regan asserts, other animals who are psychological beings, or "subjects-of-a life," share the "basic moral right to respectful treatment."[4] Regan states: "My value as an individual is independent of my usefulness to you. Yours is not dependent on your usefulness to me. For either of us to treat the other in ways that fail to show respect for the other's independent value is to act immorally, to violate the individual's rights."[5]

Applying the rights perspective beyond humanity, Regan asserts:

> In the case of the use of animals in science, the rights view is categorically abolitionist. Lab animals are not our tasters; we are not their kings…It is not just refinement or reduction that is called for, not just larger, cleaner cages, not just more generous

use of anaesthetic or the elimination of multiple surgery, not just tidying up the system. It is complete replacement. The best we can do when it comes to using animals in science is—not to use them. That is where our duty lies, according to the rights view.

Addressing animal agribusiness, Regan takes the same position:

> The fundamental moral wrong here is not that animals are kept in stressful close confinement or in isolation, or that their pain and suffering, their needs and preferences are ignored or discounted. All these *are* wrong, of course, but they are not the fundamental wrong. They are symptoms and effects of the deeper, systematic wrong that allows these animals to be viewed and treated as lacking independent value, as resources for us—as, indeed, a renewable resource.

Highlight that; there we have Regan pointing out that addressing the symptoms and effects of use will generally result in superficial changes. Over and over, the outcome is the same. Humans will still think it's acceptable to treat animals as our resources, so animals will repeatedly be placed in positions where close confinement, isolation, or pain can be imposed. In other words, says Regan: "You don't change unjust institutions by tidying them up."[6] We know managers don't like to lose profits, and they can't endure losses for long if they are to survive in the corporate world. Achieving some sort of concession over the standards of confinement might well result in the company cutting corners in, say, the transportation contract in order to make up any financial losses from the change. Or the company might vaunt the new, improved confinement standard in its promotional material and succeed in selling more animal products, or in selling them at a higher price. Today, the Whole Foods Market chain sells packets of sausages with labels showing pigs rooting around. It claims to "give shoppers peace of mind" when buying the bodies that once belonged to individuals like those pictured on the labels. The chain is reportedly working with state and federal authorities to establish a fleet of "state of the art" Italian-built mobile slaughterhouses, starting in Massachusetts, Connecticut, and New York, to expand their customers' access to meat from chickens raised according to the Whole Foods Market "access to pasture" standard—which, one writer has said, may involve the presence of a door to the outside that's rarely used, but will effectively preclude the raising of birds *on* pasture.[7] This is because space in the northeastern United States is at a premium, and supplying a buyer the size of Whole Foods will inevitably mean keeping birds indoors, where they can be more densely packed.

When we think of close confinement or isolation, pigs and other domesticated animals come to mind. But of course free-living animals are used as mass commodities too, and campaigns addressing symptoms and methods arise here as well. At seacoasts such as the edge of Newfoundland, young seals are killed in the hundreds of thousands annually, mainly for their skin and fur. And every year, there are protests. Lately, in Spain, there has been a spate of nude demonstrations, in which activists streak their bodies with red dye, the exposed skin presumably connected to the horror of seals not only clubbed and shot, but also in some cases skinned alive in the haste and chaos.[8] When television reporters come, activists and spectators alike are seen on video clips saying it's terrible that the seals are skinned alive. An international group with headquarters in Massachusetts has taken legal action to force seal kill crewmembers to poke seals' eyes to ensure they are dead before skinning them. The activists are involved in an important issue, and giving much of their lives to it. For this reason, and not to dismiss their commitment, we might call for more thought: Could the focus on the risk of animals being skinned alive fixate people on a symptom of the kill, rather than understanding the killing itself as the central wrong?

It *is* wrong, intensely wrong, that seals are skinned alive—just as it would be if human prisoners of war were skinned alive, which would unquestionably be called an atrocity. Yet attempting to mandate an end to the live skinning but not the kill itself would be regulating the kill, and this is not the work of the vegan activist. As long as there is slaughter (as long as human warring on other animals is considered acceptable and normal), there will also be atrocities. So the unremitting, unequivocal pressure must be against the Canadian government's decision to hold this annual kill. The animal-rights movement, Tom Regan writes, "seeks to end human tyranny over other animals, not make our tyranny more 'humane.'"[9] Even if the seals were quickly killed by expert sharpshooters, after a long life, and if, apparently, this did not hurt even for a moment—and no matter how much satisfaction it gives anyone to wear a seal's skin—the kill would still be wrong. Until humans acknowledge this, all kinds of atrocious things will happen to the non-human beings of the world, often behind closed doors, with activists only able to campaign against some of the most obvious and grotesque.

Tom Regan has also addressed the sexual use of other animals by humans—specifically, Peter Singer's position that such activity could be carried out humanely. Regan writes that "consistent with his utilitarian philosophy, when satisfaction is optimized, Singer can find no wrong."[10] No serious advocate of animal rights agrees, says Regan. "An animal cannot give informed consent." For this reason, "engaging in sexual activities with animals must be coercive, must display a lack of respect, thus must be wrong." Insofar as Regan rejects allowances for some to be valued by how they satisfy others' preferences, we could comfortably say that it merits being called a theory of animal rights.

On at least one occasion, Regan's theory goes astray, and although it's an exception and not the rule in Regan's case for animal rights, we'll briefly look at it here mainly for its relevance to some questions Regan did *not* address, but which will be important as we move on.

Animal-advocacy theorists have, from time to time, used a hypothetical emergency to consider whether discrimination on the basis of species is ever acceptable. Picture a lifeboat that's not strong enough to carry everyone in a group of humans and dogs to safety. Who should be pushed out to drown? In Regan's version of the lifeboat crisis, four humans and a dog need the boat. It's the dog who should be pushed out, Regan answers, explaining that invoking "an equal right to be treated with respect" won't tell us how to handle the daunting task of deciding what to do when, no matter what, someone will be harmed.[11] Regan does see the humans and the dog as having equal moral significance, because all of them experience their lives, so all have a moral worth that draws equal consideration for basic rights. Yet Regan distinguishes the *value of the lives lived* by various subjects from the value of the subjects who live them. To show equal respect for the equal rights of the two kinds of beings, Regan explains, one must count their equal harms equally, not their unequal harms equally. Regan states that the value of a life "increases as the number and variety of possible sources of satisfaction increases"; and to Regan, the human's life typically offers much more in terms of possible sources of satisfaction than does a dog's. So we could rank the harm represented by death, Regan states, as "a function of the number and variety of opportunities for satisfaction it forecloses" to the living individual.[12] Spot must die, as "no reasonable person would deny" that the death of any of the four humans would be a greater harm than the dog's death would be.[13] Thus, Regan prescribes the sacrifice of any number of dogs in order to save the humans.[14]

It doesn't seem surprising that a person who has only experienced life as a human believes a human life would offer more possible sources of satisfaction than any other kind of life. But this is a questionable justification for taking advantage of another. Henry Salt might have answered that here Regan is being ingenious rather than convincing, bringing back that familiar fallacy: constituting ourselves the spokespeople and the interpreters of our victims.

When Regan says it's the human who can "bring impartial reasons to bear" on moral decision-making, by invoking such concepts as the Golden Rule or the principle of utility,[15] we might pause for a moment. There's likely much more to many other animals' experiences of life, and how they decide to act in given situations, than we can know. Early in 2008, a dolphin guided two stranded whales safely away from a New Zealand beach.[16] A conservation officer reported that a parent and baby whale seemed confused by a sandbar just off Mahia Beach and unable to find their way back to open water. "Over the next hour and a half I pushed them back out to sea two or three times and they were very reluctant to move offshore," Malcolm Smith recounted. Normally, whales in this situation die, but then a dolphin arrived. Smith reported, "The whales made contact with the dolphin and she basically escorted them about 200 metres parallel with the beach to the edge of the sandbar. Then she did a right-angle turn through quite a narrow channel and escorted them out to sea and we haven't seen those whales since."

We can see other animals' fear, hear their pain, observe their excitement; but we can't know everything they sense and how intense, how complex, how excruciating or exhilarating their experiences might be. Dogs' sense of smell is some ten times stronger than a human's. With an estimated 200 million receptors in their noses, compared to five million in a human nose, dogs can distinguish aromas much more acutely than we can.[17] A sense of smell is not only based on the structure of a dog's nose; it relies on having a brain that can make sense of all that's being sniffed. And discussing the social interactions of wolves, the free-living ancestors of dogs, the late scholar and teacher Robert C. Solomon contended, "A wolf who is generous can expect generosity in return. A wolf who violates another's ownership zone can expect to be punished, perhaps ferociously, by others."[18]

The ownership zones Solomon mentioned, we might predict, would involve a peculiar set of issues when wolves encounter human encroachment in the wildlands they inhabit. Describing an experience in the 1890s, wolf-hunter Ernest Thompson Seton wrote, in the book *Wild Animals I Have Known,* of a wolf whose band targeted farm animals. From time to time, according to the ranchers of the region, the band would kill simply for the satisfaction of it, leaving sheep bodies uneaten. Of course, some humans act in much the same way; some see hunting as sport—claiming either a cultural interest apart from the food, or simply a thrill—and perhaps this band of wolves did act for the thrill of it. But likely not. It's normal for wolves to regard sheep as prey; wolves hunt free-roaming sheep in their northern habitats, and sometimes more animals are killed than eaten as pups are taught to hunt.

A number of other reasons could further explain this seemingly capricious activity. The grizzly bears of British Columbia don't eat all of the fishes they catch, but this seems to fit the ecological plan of their native territory. Each autumn, the bears drag multitudes of spawning salmon out of Glendale Cove. At first, the hungry bears eat the fish whole. But as the season progresses, they may simply scoop out the roe (eggs) and toss the body away. Overall, grizzly bears leave up to half their salmon catch on the forest floor, feeding mink and weasels, coyotes and foxes, mice, shrews, and squirrels, as well as crows, ravens, jays, seagulls, dippers, hawks and eagles, and nourishing cedar, hemlock, spruce and berry trees, and all the rainforest's greenery, with vital minerals.

Wolves appear to have a similar impact. Corpses of wolf-hunted moose create hotspots of forest fertility on Isle Royale, Lake Superior, by enriching the soil with nitrogen, phosphorous, and potassium, causing intense growth in microbes and fungal fatty acids, and providing extra nutrients for plants—including large-leaf asters, a key food for moose.[19] The foraging moose then add more nutrients in the form of their bodily wastes. Significantly, when researchers demonstrate how this cycle works, they point out that it hasn't been well understood or reflected in policy; yet anyone who must deal with government officials will likely agree that they approach many—probably most—decisions as though they know better than nature. In the Arctic tundra, musk ox carcass sites continue to affect vegetation dramatically a decade after the animals are killed.

The band of wolves that lived on in Seton's memory would avoid rangers and traps and guns and dog packs. (Yes, strangely, we've made the descendants of wolves our guards and their enemies.) The band had the wits to avoid eating any animal killed and left by a rancher, and thus carefully avoided numerous servings of strychnine, arsenic, cyanide, and prussic acid set out over the years. Eventually, the band's elusive leader, whom the ranchers called Lobo, became the object of the highest recorded wolf-bounty of the era. Lobo would deliberately use stones to spring traps, or pick up poisoned morsels of cow's flesh disguised with stewed cheese and move them a distance—the latter act, as Seton understood it, an expression of utter contempt for the would-be trapper. But after numerous failures to trap Lobo, Seton finally succeeded in luring the elusive individual's mate—"She was the handsomest wolf I had ever seen," wrote Seton—and used her blood to drive Lobo into a trap more emotional than physical:

> All that day I heard him wailing as he roamed in his quest and when he came to the spot where we had killed her, his heartbroken wailing was piteous to hear. It was sadder than I could possibly have believed. Even the stolid cowboys noticed it, and said they had "never heard a wolf carry on like that before." He seemed to know exactly what had taken place, for her blood had stained the place of her death. Poor old hero, he had never ceased to search for his darling, and when he found the trail her body had made he followed it recklessly, and so fell into the snare prepared for him. There he lay in the iron grasp of all four traps, perfectly helpless, and all around him were numerous tracks showing how the cattle had gathered about him to insult the fallen despot, without daring to approach within his reach.[20]

For two days and two nights Seton left the wolf losing blood and without any way to eat or drink, struggling to exhaustion. When Seton finally approached, Lobo rose up, roaring, fur bristling, making an effort to attack, but the determined hunter had chained the traps to heavy logs and buried the logs well underground. And yet, Seton recalled: "How his huge ivory tusks did grind on those cruel chains, and when I ventured to touch him with my rifle-barrel he left grooves on it which are there to this day."

The wolf also managed to tear a lasso into two pieces midair. Eventually Seton—after another trip to the ranch, and reinforced by ranch hand, a horse, and more rope—splinted and tied the wolf's jaws and feet; and the conquerors took their victim away. Lobo would die in a pasture sometime during the third night in a collar and chains.

> I set meat and water beside him, but he paid no heed. He lay calmly on his breast, and gazed with those steadfast yellow eyes away past me down through the gateway of the canyon, over the open plains—his plains—nor moved a muscle when I touched him. When the sun went down he was still gazing fixedly across the prairie. I expected he would call up his band when night came, and prepared for them, but he had called once in his extremity, and none had come; he would never call again.

Seton reportedly stopped stalking animals from that point on.[21]

Regan has accepted that "sympathy, self-sacrifice, loyalty, and courage" might be found in non-human beings, and people have described the richness of the lives and the relationships of non-human animals wherever their world of experience and ours have met. To the extent such traits are found, Regan considers the lives of other animals as equal in value to human lives. Nevertheless, insists Regan, relevant differences remain, for humans can "pursue aesthetic, scientific, and sacramental interests that other animals lack."[22]

This assertion is reminiscent of the view Jane Goodall expressed in the field chronicle *In the Shadow of Man.* Goodall wrote, "It should not be surprising that a chimpanzee can recognize himself in a mirror. But what if a chimpanzee wept tears when he heard Bach thundering from a cathedral organ?"[23] The shadow to which Goodall's title refers represents a vertical hierarchy of being, with the chimpanzees beneath us. "Just as he is overshadowed by us," Goodall wrote, "so the chimpanzee overshadows all other animals."[24] So the chimpanzees, special as they are deemed to be, then become a foil: a proof for our still *more* special status.

If, that is, we happen to be considered normal. As Regan puts it, "Five survivors find themselves in a lifeboat. Four are normal adult human beings."

"...Someone must go or all will perish. Who should it be?..."

Whoever dies will lose everything, but Regan believes the "everything" each of the humans would lose amounts to more than everything lost to the dog. What about the non-normal human beings? Evidently, their "everything" too would be less. To believe that *all* humans, being human, have something of value to lose that no other animals possess would, says Regan, amount to species bias—or, to borrow Richard Ryder's term, speciesism. But is Regan then judging the value of these beings' lives on the basis of another *ism*—ablism? Regan has refined the hypothetical to include an "irreversibly comatose human" and states that the rights view would mean sacrificing that person, but goes further, by leaving the door open for the sacrifice of mentally disabled people. Regan states:

> [W]e do have, on the rights view, the basis utilitarians lack for protesting against, for example, those who would use animals in terminal research, but not humans, when the death caused these animals marks a greater loss, and thus a greater harm, than it would in the case of some humans who might be used in their place. For the magnitude of the harm that death is, is a function of the number and variety of opportunities for satisfaction it forecloses, and there is no credible basis on which to claim that the death of a normal, adult animal is not a greater loss, and thus a greater harm, than the death of a less aware, retarded human, one who possesses fewer desires, less competence to act intentionally, and is less responsive to others and to the environment generally.[25]

Being conscious, experiencing life, supplies most every individual with a tenacious will to continue doing so. If we respect all lives, based simply on those who live them experiencing a role in life, we need not decide whose life has more nuances or potential for satisfaction. We need not do something so hurtful as to measure the value of a purportedly abnormal person's life against someone's definition of normal. We need not decide which species have which interests and thus get which rights, or the degree to which pain and emotional responses in each may be anticipated, or where to draw the line around who gets meaningful rights.

Regan assures readers that lifeboat-type crises are rare, and the rights view doesn't entitle some to dismiss the interests of others on an everyday basis. Regan writes, "Nothing relating to the justice of social practices or institutions follows from anything I have said. Only in extreme cases would differences in the value of different lives matter."[26]

Compare the assertion of Gary L. Francione, who has also written of decisions between saving humans or other beings in extreme cases. Francione writes: "If we are going to make good on our claim to take animal interests seriously, then we have no choice but to accord animals one right: the right not to be treated as our property." Francione adds: "Moreover, recognition of this right would not preclude our choosing humans over animals in situations of genuine conflict."[27] In *Introduction to Animal Rights*, Francione says most of us share the view that we should choose humans over animals in situations of true conflict—a conclusion Francione claims stems from conventional wisdom—and that the animal-rights position can accommodate this view.[28]

Perhaps there's an argument that it can. We might say animals of every kind save each other, and that members of humanity act similarly; that saving our own kind is just something biology and evolution dictates— not evidence of biased evaluations.[29] And yet, if we are going to work out a theory of animal rights, we would need to develop a concept that interrogates human supremacy even as it takes into account our impulses and our biological natures. And we know it's in the extreme case or the genuine conflict, quite often, that rights matter most. And once lives are differently valued, oppressive results are unlikely to wait for rare emergencies. After all, if less aesthetic, scientific, and sacramental interests means expendability in an exceptional case, the way is open for the claim that overriding another being's interests on an ordinary day could be ethical—to lay the groundwork for success in the exceptional case, to provide a cure for a more sophisticated individual in a life-or-death situation. That's how vivisection has often been justified, whether performed on vulnerable humans or on other beings. Insofar as it's decided that some lack certain abilities, and thus are expendable, the Other is dominated, enslaved, used up, or pushed aside. Daily.

Regan distinguishes the way the dog got into the boat from the way test subjects were forced into a lab:

> More fundamentally, animals who are in laboratories already have had their rights violated, already have been treated with a lack of respect. How otherwise could they be there? When it comes to the survivors on the lifeboat, by contrast, the scenario functions as a prevention case only if we assume that no one's rights have been violated.[30]

And should we assume no one in the boat has had their rights violated? One of Regan's challengers said the dog's rights were violated when humans made a decision to bring the dog out to sea.[31] Regan decides that the decision to take the dog on the voyage wasn't coercive, or at least not in a way that rises to a violation of rights.

Both Regan and Regan's challenger miss the key point. The essential question about "violation" is a far deeper one: Is a community's integrity not violated by being selectively bred, genetically domineered, and put "in the same boat" with humans constantly? What "rights" can a dog or any domesticated animal really have? Every day, they're bought and sold. Bred for us to handle, they come into the world with the status of articles to be exchanged. Fish are easily flushed away or dumped into a pond when the owner finds them inconvenient. Today, it's not uncommon to see horses turned out and starved, the hapless victims of the economic woes of their owners.[32] Some cats get left outside when the owner moves, or even when they approach sexual maturity at just a few weeks or months of age. Then, the minute one is disowned and outside, the same cat humans just "loved" becomes transformed into an object of hatred. Those of us who run offices for animal-advocacy groups regularly receive phone calls from people who want to abandon ("donate," some say) their cats, rabbits, and dogs.

In 2008, *CNN* reported on the five-figure cost of keeping a dog for life, and said some people are "opting to give up their pets" because "[o]wners either have to move to dog-unfriendly accommodation or can no longer afford to care for the animal after losing their job."[33] Throughout China, there are one-dog-per-family rules; when the city of Guanzhou adopted this rule, the already-owned dogs were not shielded from government roundups. We see similar policies in North American cities where dogs considered especially aggressive have been banned, but it's not just a breeding ban to prevent biting dogs from being born; it actually forces the owners of dogs of a certain breed who already exist (whether the dogs have bitten anyone or not) to turn these animals over to the authorities.

Dogs from breeds in which aggression is disproportionately common, or dogs who turn out to be assertive or unpredictable, are often regarded with a wary eye or even outright anger, and are at particular risk of being rejected or killed. A pet practically has to have a cheerful personality and a strong attachment to humans—maybe an ESFP personality on the Myers-Briggs test—to survive. *This Extraverted Sensing Feeling Perceiving being is fun-loving, lives in the moment, and adores people, generally treating everyone as a friend.* I'm only half-joking, of course. It's risky to be a rebellious cat or dog, or even one who's too nervous to sense and act on the expectations of an owner.

Yi-Fu Tuan writes, "A pet is a personal belonging, an animal with charm that one can take delight in, play with, or set aside, as one wishes." A sign of just how little regard we have for relationships between the animals themselves appears right when they are born: Cats and dogs and other animals are routinely separated from their birth families at their owners' discretion. We might put a clock in a blanket so the tick-tock rhythms will soothe a puppy, but the ticking clock is no real substitute for a mother's heart. Puppies are praised, punished, or left to wait alone in places for long periods at the owner's whim, often to be rejected because of an allergy, a move, or a new baby; and they enjoy the pleasures of living only as long as the luck of the draw places them with benign human beings, and just for so long as those humans are in the position to continue caring for them. To put a dog's vulnerability starkly into perspective, imagine coming across a wolf in a boat with a group of humans. The humans would be unlikely to last long while deciding who will be sacrificed; in any case, just imagine them trying to throw that wolf out!

So Regan's insistence that no one is in the boat due to disrespectful treatment makes sense only if we're talking of an *immediately obvious* lack of respect. Abolitionist animal-rights theory has largely neglected the immensely important point that wolves (like apes, deer, and all free-living animals), as long as they and their habitats exist, could genuinely benefit from legal rights; dogs could not. Some animal lawyers and bloggers believe that achieving "rights" for domesticated dogs makes sense, and they're focusing on further ingraining petkeeping in society, for example, by using softer phrases about the custom: substituting "guardian" for owner and "animal companions" for animals who have been purpose-bred to depend on us. This has been accepted as a form of public advocacy: Rhode Island rewrote its statutes concerning pets, replacing the word "owner" with "guardian." A few cities, including West Hollywood, California, have done the same. Activists have promoted such legislation, claiming it might help owners recover substantial damages for human carelessness, including veterinary malpractice.[34] Humans are the owners of animals bred as pets. That is a fact. If we decline to face it straightforwardly, we miss the core point of the abolitionist mission. Because improving health maintenance of animals bred as pets does not make us any less their owners, the use of the word "guardian" instead of "owner" is euphemistic. (Abolitionist books and pamphlets have frequently and prominently included endearing dog and cat illustrations in a way that unwittingly contributes to the confusion.)

Regan's lifeboat prescription has been challenged by several writers, yet to my knowledge none has straightforwardly stated that dogs ought to have been permitted to flourish as wolves.[35] Bookmark this concern. We'll revisit it throughout this book. For now, here's one more important point. Given global climate patterns, situations resembling the lifeboat scene might not be rare at all.[36] From glacial regions to low-lying coastlands, we see ominous signs that such emergencies will be part of the world's daily life, as physical reality changes more quickly than could have been predicted when many animal-rights texts were written. One only need recall the images of hurricane Katrina to observe scenes uncannily similar to Regan's hypothetical emergency. And climate change will bring ever more extreme weather conditions as this century unfolds. At the same time, we're all being affected by changes in the economic climate. As I write, refuges are doing all they can with strained resources to help the animals who arrive at shelters because people have lost their jobs and believe they can no longer afford to keep their pets. Refuges have to decide whether to take in more animals or keep paying support staff; sometimes, there isn't money for both. Deciding between helping humans and helping dependent animals is surely not rare.

Lifeboat scenarios also affect many free-living animals as well, of course. In India, environmentalists have questioned a Tribal Rights Bill—meant to redress discrimination --that would allocate land to several million indigenous forest-dwellers at a fatal cost to the region's last few hundred tigers. The BBC wildlife commentator and natural historian Valmik Thapar has said, "Wherever you have humans and tigers living in the same area, they just do not coexist." Now, is that an acceptable scenario because the tigers would have had less possible sources of satisfaction than the members of indigenous tribes? Or does ethical decision-making on our planet require a thought process more complex than that? There are several layers of injustice in the India forest dilemma to be carefully outlined and grappled with if social and ecological wisdom is to prevail. Ranking interests involved in the emergency is likely to worsen the problem; that habit makes up a key part of the emergency's cause.

Regan's and Francione's grant of an advantage for human beings deals with hypothetical dogs, but it carries over to their view of conflicts between humans and free-living animals. When those animals' interests most matter, they are trumped by the convention that we should prefer our own species: As we shall see, both Regan and Francione will allow for imposing contraception on free-living animals when there is a perceived conflict over space between humans and them. Were the conflict between human groups, one forcing contraceptives on the other would raise alarm bells over human rights and reproductive autonomy.

About the lifeboat question, Regan has written, "Personally, I think the attention showered upon my treatment of such cases is vastly disproportionate to their importance within my general theory."[37] But a general theory can't just fit a particular writer; it must fit our changing planet, just as human pressure has overcome our physical surroundings and affects everyone else in our midst. As one who appreciates Regan's general theory, I believe the lifeboat section does have serious, albeit unintended, illogical aspects and unfair ramifications; and there's a reason it's drawn so much attention. I also think it is an exception, a loophole within that theory and one that should be rethought by abolitionists and, *with respect for the theory as a whole*, withdrawn.

Before we move on from Regan's lifeboat, it's worth taking note of a classic, real-life extreme case. In Regina vs. Dudley and Stevens (1884), an English judge considered the acts of two sailors who survived in a boat by eating the body of a younger survivor. The youth, Parker, had swallowed seawater and seemed fatally ill when killed by the two older seafarers. In a case that drew wide sympathy for the convicts, the court showed some leniency to the pair of surviving sailors, but nevertheless decided Dudley and Stevens had taken the youth's life—and that was murder. The pair's argument that this was an extreme case, and that killing young Parker was necessary to save them, didn't change that. Had someone vounteered to go overboard, or had all castaways drawn straws (as was done in an earlier case of the same kind), the verdict would likely have been different. Because Parker already appeared to be near death, casting lots might well have resulted in the death of more people than one; but that, the court suggested, was what morality compelled.

Of course, in our society, a criminal court and public opinion would have little patience with any animal-rights advocates who let one of their human friends risk death before a dog, or who picked or assigned straws, drew them randomly, threw one of their party overboard, and kept the dog safe. The mores of our culture would compel the survivors to sacrifice the dog or live as outcasts. Animals are not considered persons; so when push comes to shove they go overboard.

A bind? It's a boat I wouldn't want to be in. Let's admit that one group making assessments about which group's members lives most merit sustenance doesn't answer the question from an animal-rights perspective. In the panic of emergency, any of us might save ourselves over Bach. Moreover, practical reasons might prompt the decision for having the dog go overboard; were it a case of only one individual remaining on the boat, a dog might lack the ability to survive (or the patience to stay) on the boat alone. Perhaps, combining the abilities of ourselves and the other animal(s) with us, we'd come up with a better answer; for example, if each took a turn swimming by the side of the boat, all might reach help faster and make it to shore alive. It may be that the best response is to try to suggest more such alternatives to simply throwing someone over—especially because these emergency scenarios will be happening in real life more and more frequently.

In summary, the decision to sacrifice the dog for being a dog is indeed a hole in the fabric in the standard theory of animal rights to date. And whatever answer we may give, the lifeboat dilemma, at least as it's generally been discussed, doesn't pose the real question for the future of animal-rights theory. The final violent blast to Lobo lasted three days and three nights. The process of taking the autonomy out of wolves so we could have schnauzers took centuries.[38] Is the second series of actions less violent than the first? As we clear more space for our houses, roads, yards and paddocks, as we bring domestic animals onto the planet in ever greater numbers, what has happened to the free-living animal communities? Where are the wolves and other animals who once walked over the land on their terms? Have we trapped their wild hearts, trophy-like, into living beings whose purpose is to amuse, guard, or adore us?

Abolitionist animal-rights theory, refined

Gary L. Francione both expanded and distilled Regan's abolitionism. Whereas Regan had focused on mammals as having clear psychological identities that call for the extension of rights, Francione insisted that any animal possessed of sentience would have an equally strong claim for such protections. In Francione's view, "the only characteristic that is required for personhood is sentience, or the ability to feel pain. If a non-human can feel pain, then we have a moral obligation not to treat that non-human as property, or exclusively as a means to our ends. If a sentient being has other interests, then we ought to accord equal consideration to those interests as well, but the basic right not to be treated as the resource of others should not be connected to any characteristic other than sentience."[39]

It should be noted, however, that Regan's *Case for Animal Rights* acknowledged:

> It may be that the snail and animals even less like us are conscious, despite our disinclination to say or think so. If they are, the theoretical grounds for thinking that they are must come from the same source that underpins the attribution of consciousness to mammalian animals...*Where one draws the line* regarding the presence of consciousness in no easy matter, but our honest uncertainty about this should not paralyze our judgment in all cases.[40]

Francione's position, as asserted nearly two decades later, doesn't seem far from that:

Are insects sentient? Are they conscious beings with minds that experience pain and pleasure? I do not know. But the fact that I do not know exactly where to draw the line, or perhaps find drawing the line difficult, does not relieve me of the obligation to draw the line somewhere or allow me to use animals as I please. Although I may not know whether insects are sentient, I do know that cows, pigs, chickens, chimpanzees, horses, deer, dogs, cats, and mice are sentient. Indeed, it is now widely accepted that fish are sentient. So the fact that I do not know on what side of the line to place insects does not relieve me of my moral obligation to the animals whom I do know are sentient.[41]

In 2008, Francione stated: "Sentience is necessary to have interests at all." (Not necessarily so, if sentience is defined as the awareness of pain; plain consciousness, or the ability to regain consciousness, is arguably a better word for identifying the locus of interests. Remember the Pakistani children who couldn't feel pain, but who clearly had interests?) Whether insects and mollusks are sentient and thus have interests, Francione continues, is unclear.[42]

Where to "draw the line" around communities of beings requiring ethical consideration, is, of course, a perennial question. It was answered most firmly in the vegan platform, formally established in 1944, which rejected the use of *all* animal products, and all forms of exploitation of, and cruelty to, the animal sphere. It urged us to disconnect from our reliance on flesh, fish, fowl, eggs, honey, animal milk and its derivatives, and has encouraged the use of alternatives for all commodities derived wholly or in part from animals. Just as much as veganism is about stopping exploitation, it's also about preserving the freedom of those who live on their terms. Donald Watson carefully gardened with a fork, not a spade, to avoid harming earthworms.[43]

But our main point here is that Francione fine-tuned the abolitionist proposal in this way: "I argue that all sentient beings should have one right:

the right not to be treated as our property—the right not to be valued exclusively as means to human ends."[44] This picked up a spoon that had been poised to stir the legal pot since 1789, when utilitarian Jeremy Bentham wrote, "Other animals, which, on account of their interests having been neglected by the insensibility of the ancient jurists, stand degraded into the class of things."[45]

Francione asserts that death is a harm to a sentient being: "The death of a healthy animal (or human) is a deprivation because it represents an ultimate and irreversible closure to the satisfaction of further preferences. This is the case whether the death is painful or not."[46] Singer, on the other hand, does not see death—at least not a quick death—as a harmful loss. Unlike Singer, Francione does not believe that bringing an animal into life as property is a benefit. Francione has urged that the right not to be property would involve "abolishing and not merely regulating animal exploitation because our uses of animals for food, experiments, product testing, entertainment, and clothing all assume that animals are nothing but property. If we accepted that animals have the right not to be treated as our property, we would stop—completely—bringing domestic animals into existence."[47]

Francione's call for this moral imperative highlights a key aspect of the vegan position. Here is how Vegan Society founder Donald Watson put the point at a 1947 conference:

> The present relationship between man and animal was deplorable. Man has appointed himself lord and master over everything that breathed, and he had filled the world with millions of creatures for no other purpose than to exploit them for personal gain and kill them when it no longer served his purpose to keep them alive.[48]

Note that Watson is talking about the fundamental issue *underlying* property status: our self-appointment as "lord and master"; that is, dominion. Campaigning to release non-human beings from property status is a critical component to ending the "deplorable" relationship, to ending our master role, our enslavement of non-human animals. No matter how benign the slaveholder, or how protected a slave may appear to be in some cases, no matter that a slave might even be loved, the rule against enslavement is a key moral commitment. Thus, Francione's pinpointing of the need to end the animals-as-property model is aligned with the vegan platform. We must, however, consider a few further points. For *human* beings, the end of enslavement means individuals are released to begin anew the struggle to reach their full potential within human society. Other animals are in a markedly different position. Today, animals are selectively bred to be the choices on menus and the objects of racing and betting, showing and petting. The abolition of those customs would indeed mean the discontinuation of purpose-breeding. And as for non-domesticated animals, their freedom would not involve gaining admittance to human society, but staying out of it.

It's in their habitats and social networks, not within human society, that the respect taught by animal-rights theory will apply. It's in their world, not ours, that animal rights will have meaning. It's essential that they have their habitats, and the freedom to pursue the interactions and experiences that comprise their lives. And that's why, just as an individual life involves more than experiencing or avoiding suffering, it involves more than not being property. We could, after all, have a world in which animals weren't property and, with continued habitat depletion (in addition to hunting, and the increasing use of contraception on free-living animals or egg-addling and other birth control measures), see non-human communities collapse. To put it into the language of human rights, it would be as though we've spared groups of people from slavery only to subject them to genocide. Wholesale extinctions of non-human communities are already occurring.

If we think other animals could harm us, or even if they just look at us sideways, we eliminate them. A cougar, already being tracked through a radio collar, walked through a national forest campground near the

Grand Tetons, stopping about 25 yards from a camper before moving on. The cougar was tracked down and killed. For looking. A biologist who objected was barely more tolerant, suggesting that authorities could have instead trained the cat to avoid the campground by electric shocks or rubber bullets.[49]

Logic tells us that such interactions are increasingly inevitable. After all, humans are turning up everywhere. If our control over others is the default mode, they will be wiped off the continent; it's only a matter of at what rate. In the rare event that a mountain lion is spotted in California, residents will say these big cats are beautiful, but "they don't belong here" and the answer is to "take them out."[50] Why? This raises the issue an environmentally aware society needs to face openly: We are afraid, and we have been self-preserving for a long time. *How we deal with fear makes the difference.*

The deepest and most comprehensive question for our social movement is why and how modern human society has developed through patterns of domination; and the greatest challenge we face is imagining humanity without the master role. Is it our fear of free animals' power (over our children, our dogs, our cows, the back yard at night, the woods our government claims for the people, our own bodies) that keeps us from imagining another identity for ourselves?

Although decommodifying conscious life (that is, abolishing their legal property status) is important, these questions about domination, and what we'd be if we redefine humanity, take us deeper still. While abolition addresses what other animals will not be, and this is indeed important, what's essential is what and who they are, and how we come to grips with that. This all depends on what and who *we* strive to become. Are we willing to relinquish our authority, our control?

So animal rights is not just an idea of what they will stop being; it affirmatively expects other animals to express their lives as they will, to flourish on their terms. Although other animals will not be brought into our societies for their best interests to prevail, other animals' well-being has something in common with ours: it's a positive concept. Consider the definition of health offered by the World Health Organization's Basic Documents. In 1948, the WHO said health is a positive concept: "physical, mental, and social well-being, not merely the absence of disease and infirmity."

Similarly, animal-rights theory, inseparable from veganism, is an idea that's fresh, whole, positive and life-affirming. Animal-rights theory does not just need to be refined. It needs to be reconceived—as part of the vegan paradigm.

CHAPTER 4

The Vegan Paradigm

I n this chapter, we'll look at rights for animals in an environmental context, recalling that the environment is simply the animals' home. This sets the stage for real respect for non-human animals. When we consider other beings' autonomy as the focus of animal rights, animal-rights advocacy is not so much about generating pity for animals, or about looking for ways to show how cruel we are to them, as it is about the triumph of their natural freedom and power.

Abolitionist animal-rights theory, reconceived

As noted in the previous chapter, "abolition" is part of animal-rights theory, because other animals should be able to experience their lives without being human property. So far, so good. But we could stop bringing other animals into being for our purposes and still ignore the loss of communities who already *do* live free in their habitat. In other words: There are animals, outside our windows right this moment, who are living as they would live if our society accepted the animal-rights ideal. These animals have usually been offered only fleeting attention in the popular animal-rights literature. One scholar has said, for example, "If we stopped treating animals as resources, the only remaining human-animal conflicts would involve animals in the wild." But these animals need to be accounted for directly and affirmatively in an animal-rights position, and not left until some later time. Many human actions presently affect free-living animals' individual dignity and the integrity of their communities and habitat: the classification of free-living animals as game; the fragmentation of the spaces in which they live by road-building and construction; transportation, pollution and greenhouse gas emissions; our habit of moving various animals between regions; our own expanding population; our expanding use of water and land space to hold our purpose-bred animals; and mass eradication plans, including the use of fertility control against animals throughout the world. Everywhere we look, the homes of free-living animals are being paved over, polluted by industrial waste, sold and built upon. The waterfront city of Baltimore has covered the water's edge with shopping malls and, ironically, the National Aquarium.

The ecology of every bay and every forest matters to animal rights. And animal-rights thinking matters right back to the green movement, as environmentalists who express respect for the autonomy of free-living animals are the strongest kind. They present the most serious challenge ever brought to those who deforest the land, commodify life, and pollute the earth, water, and atmosphere. A robust animal-rights position will require us to control our own numbers. It will mean that we value plants, the health of oceans, air and land, as well as the interests of animals. For just as our environment matters to us, it matters to all animals it supports. So, when asked whether the ecology matters to the animal-rights ethic, let us say yes. It matters critically. Nectar bats cannot pursue life on their terms without drinking from the flowers of the agave plants they pollinate; pronghorn antelope cannot pursue their interests in traversing the land we call the United States and Mexico with border walls in their way.

Today, the future of conscious life, and of all life as we know it, is at stake. Had respect for animals' autonomous lives played the part it merits in the environmentalists' platform all along, we—all life on the globe, that is—wouldn't be facing climate catastrophe today.

Some scientists think we've passed the point of stopping severe disruptions caused by excess greenhouse gas in our atmosphere. We're going to spend massive resources trying to adapt to the changes already set in motion. Could we have reached such a point had we taken animal rights seriously? Consider the rainforests of the Amazon—or rather the quarter of them that remain, choking on the flow of warming gas. So many animal communities have been hurt by the commercial grazing that steals their land. Had we respected the lives and futures of pink dolphins, marmosets, jaguars and tamarins, could we have torn the trees down to make way for an industry that creates hamburgers? Surely we could never have devoted the great plains of North America to single-crop feed growing operations, full of herbicides and pesticides, interspersed with cattle feedlots, had we taken seriously the interests of river otters, whooping cranes, burrowing owls, long-billed curlews, wolves, black-footed ferrets, coyotes and kit foxes. Insisting that free-living animals' interests be respected would keep natural areas intact, force humanity to confront its dependence on animal agribusiness, and address the root causes of our climate crisis.

So, now that we're in this fine mess, what do we do about it?

Our grandparents' habit of connecting animal products with affluence can't be ours. The psychology of making this change needs special attention. There is surely a social psychology that says eating animals makes us stronger, more prestigious, better or safer somehow. As an indicator, take a look at a 2008 study in the *Journal of Consumer Research* in which people who prized traits such as authority and wealth rated "beef" rolls tastier than "vegetarian" rolls—regardless of what was actually in the wrap.[1]

The shift to organic, vegan growing methods is going to be a big change for affluent people—and struggling people too. But it will encourage fairer distribution among us. We now know the exploitation of otherness is intertwined, as several Asian and South American countries devote vast lands and resources to produce soybeans to feed the cattle they exploit, cattle whose bodies they in turn ship off to be eaten by those who pay for the imports. Who wants this to keep happening? We can stop this harmful chain, but not by waiting for governments to present technological fixes. It's not up to scientists and the big corporations to lead the way out of current problems. We the people need to find our way, to combine ethical values with practical measures to secure healthful and abundant food.

If we all come together, we might just make it through this time of melting ice caps. We can do it by learning our lesson about dominion, so that the human primates will stop defining ourselves as a group apart and above. We can instead become truly respectful and fair members of the entire community of conscious life on Earth. We'll enjoy Bach or a breath of fresh air and we'll know other animals are enjoying their songs, their air, and those they love, with a love perhaps stronger than their fear of death.

What we'll add to the abolitionist proposal, then, is the acknowledgement of all other conscious animals' interest in living on their own terms. When those individuals and communities receive our respect, decisions about proper treatment and handling of them will no longer be the point. If we truly respect them, we can envision them living in their own ways; and as we impart this vision to others, we become contributors to a movement. And although the most well-known advocacy model to date has involved a pattern of compromise between human groups over the details of systematic animal use, we can, today, put a stronger animal-rights theory into action.

Incremental steps?

We can find the most refreshing kind of animal advocacy when we recall its vegan principles. In recent years, anti-cruelty fundraising campaigns and abolitionist theorists alike have focused much attention on the conditions of animals in commerce. When the abolitionist argument treads inside institutional systems of use, we lose the idea's authentic spirit. The idea of disallowing battery cages for hens might *seem* a step on the way to the lifting of property status (as the activist claims the rule increases costs, and inconveniences the business owners); it might *seem* aligned with abolitionist theory (as the activist claims to be abolishing the use of cages); but the idea that such a move would hasten emancipation is highly questionable.

Throughout the 1996 book *Rain without Thunder*, Gary L. Francione noted good reasons for the animal advocate to steer clear of designing laws and regulations under which the industrial use of animals would be carried out.[2] Yet Francione did deem it *possible* that a narrowly tailored campaign for such a provision could proceed without offending abolitionist principles.[3]

Francione considers the egg factory, which typically crowds several chickens in each laying cage (also called *battery cage*), and posits: "Assume that a prohibition abolishes the battery cage *entirely* and replaces it with a rearing system that accommodates *all* of the hen's interests in freedom of movement and thereby fully recognizes the interest of the hen in bodily integrity." Francione declares that "this sort of substitution differs considerably from that in which two hens are merely removed from the cage: although we have not yet abolished the institutionalized exploitation, the substitution eliminates the exploitation involved in the confinement system through a *full* recognition of the interest of the hens in their freedom of movement."[4] Although Francione calls this "a *possible* exception" to the rule that any adjustment in the birds' living arrangements will substitute one form of exploitation for another,[5] even this tentative claim problematically suggests that genuine freedom could be furthered through acts within the industry itself.

Another writer, Joan Dunayer, has since objected that urging restricted business practices will fail to reinforce the point of abolitionist theory wherever the recommendation would—as *Rain without Thunder* did, at times—leave the animals inside the exploitive enterprise. No husbandry change that leaves birds inside the bird-selling business, or any animal within the system of use, is helpfully dubbed a ban, Dunayer argues. All such changes amount to standards, not prohibitions.[6] Dunayer's is an important point to consider if we are to see abolitionism in its most consistent and powerful form. Indeed, we need to ask whether Francione's starting premises are inconsistent (or at least unclear); a reasonable reader might well get the idea that a purpose-bred animal could have meaningful rights when Francione cautions against activism involving the egg industry that trades away a "basic right of the hens" and "falls short of recognition of the basic right, or the complete protection of some interest that the animal has, for example, in bodily movement."[7]

Many students and activists are now confused by the growing pains in animal-rights theory: Shall we stop considering changes at animal farms? Is there really no point in seeking handling adjustments as increments on the way to the end of animal use? Most people will agree that a pattern has emerged: When activists campaign for changed conditions, they tell their supporters it's important to give more space or improved handling rules to industry chickens or calves now; regulation always comes first and something called animal rights is to occur in the distant future. And so it goes. Capable activists are pulled into full-time attempts to gain community support for changes in the way cows or chickens are stored, transported, and put to death. How is an animal-rights future being achieved through this?

Some say at least it gets people to pay attention to animals. But there are ways of doing that without becoming involved in the husbandry regulations that take for granted humanity's use of animals.

Not *all* laws and rules should be ignored, though. We can distinguish between codifying husbandry methods such as slaughter or modes of confinement on one hand and, in contrast, the potential of rules that could, with creative attention, ease human pressure on free-living animals, such as bars against tropical bird shipments to northern regions, an end to sonar testing that affects marine animals, a designation of waters as boat-free sanctuaries, off-limits to anglers; a resolution against road-building on public land; designation of parks and buffer areas surrounding them as gun- and trap-free zones—with an eye, of course, to winning complete respect for the animals treated as targets: decisions to end aerial gunning, stalking, hunting and trapping of animals.

This is not to suggest that the Airborne Hunting Act or any similar law to date has established animal rights, but rather to say that if one were to strive to make the law work on behalf of non-human animals, environmental law presents a far more promising area of legal work than the sphere of husbandry regulation. What I am noting and asserting, in contrast to Francione, is that the animals who are trapped at large differ in a key way from those living in institutions such as agribusiness, as the trapped animals could, if only they'd be left in peace, have what we'd call meaningful rights. Rather than suggesting modes of institutional control, or trying to define other animals' pain or comfort from our viewpoint, sound environmental rules may potentially provide animals the support to live autonomously. I stress again that this has yet to happen in a way that makes non-human animals' interests the locus of legal concern; and as none are now persons under the law, working with the law to provide respect for autonomous animals will be an intensive undertaking.

I see it, quite simply, as an outright mistake that Francione or any writer would look to the industrial site as the locus of the legal work to stop human uses of other animals. The focus of an animal-rights advocate, when asked how we can deal with the matter of animal farms, is best placed on straightforwardly and decisively encouraging people to eat peaceable meals.

A more complex discussion will involve legal challenges where they can actually advance animal rights: in habitat. If animal rights means respecting animals' interest in living on their own terms, we should intervene to stop assaults on free-living animals. Can legal interventions meaningfully focus on a particular form of exploitation such as leg-hold traps (as Francione has asserted they "easily" can if the campaign doesn't promote another type of trap)?[8] Or must we insist on complete bans, on eliminating whole practices at once? What is a whole practice? Bans on every kind of leg trap and body-crushing trap would, to be meaningful, be sought together, and the bans would need to anticipate new technology that substitutes for either; in effect, the plan would need to rule out traps generally, including snares. (Cage traps for the purpose of assisting animals would not be banned.) This effort to discontinue the use of land-based hazards would need to be part of an overall platform that seeks to end the war on undomesticated animals, and that affirmatively seeks to let them thrive.

Laws devised to control ordinary people are limited; people need to *want* to act in a certain way, not be coerced, if we are to transcend oppressions rather than chase people down for them. Cockfighting is a felony in Texas, for example, but that hasn't stopped the practice. The optimal approach is outreach, not clampdowns. Stopping a state-sponsored assault on animals, however, can be fully effective and worthwhile. If, because of advocacy, the state stops handing out permits for hunting animals, that's a situation in which a harmful example by the government stops, a particular system closes down, and a group of animals is free from this systematic, state-condoned attack. Legal work challenging official actions and plans, then, to close out systems of violence, is arguably far more valuable, positive, and fair than instituting laws that track down and punish certain people.

At times, it might be unclear whether ending a given practice is, say, tailored to a specific community of animals in a way that makes it unacceptably narrow. And it's true that ending one form of assault (such as trapping) might leave open others (such as stalking with weapons). Specific cases are unique, and need careful thinking, with an eye to defending animals' autonomy and outreach to the public—not just the easiest "victory" obtainable. As a general rule, when any community of animals is, as a result of advocacy, empowered to experience autonomous life in habitat, the "incremental" move is probably a worthwhile step on the path to a society that accepts animal-rights ideals. (Again, note we are situating this legal intervention to provide respect for *autonomous* animals—that is, free-living beings.) At the same time, cultivating a vegan worldview is needed, because it will answer the question of demand for *all* kinds of fur etc., and challenge the notion that other animals, any and all, should live on humanity's terms and for our purposes.

For the most part, instead of following that trajectory, *Rain without Thunder* provides guidelines for deciding whether or not particular regulations in industrial settings could be consistent with rights theory."[9] As we've seen, the rule against battery cages is discussed in light of its potential to allow freedom of movement for hens within commercial settings:

> For example, if egg batteries are abolished but hens, still regarded as property, are kept under circumstances that would be appropriate were their property status abolished entirely (i.e., they have freedom of movement and are otherwise kept as they would be were they no longer regarded as property), then, although the hens will continue to be exploited as property, the prohibition of battery cages recognizes an interest that the animal would have were the animal no longer regarded as property, and the prohibition may be said to prohibit a constitutive activity of exploitation.[10]

Is it plausible that "although the hens will continue to be exploited as property"—confined by a business whose point is to market the products of their bodies—the "prohibition of battery cages recognizes an interest that the animal would have were the animal no longer regarded as property"? Is it plausible to suggest that an owned hen would have freedom of movement parallel to that of an unowned hen if the birds will always be available to be caught and handed over for rendering? Is that plausible, if they are born and exist within human commerce, from which they never have the freedom to walk away?

Early on in *Rain without Thunder,* Francione states that rights theory completely rejects the institutionalized exploitation of animals.[11] Yet in the book's final chapter, Francione posits: "If animal exploiters accommodate animal interests and eliminate the battery cage in favor of some other form of hen enclosure that continues their status as property and does not fully respect their interest in, for example, body integrity, that does not necessarily undermine the incremental eradication of property status" because the new form of containment is "forcing the property owner to recognize, albeit in a limited way, that the animals have inherent value that must be respected whether or not the property owner thinks that such respect is cost-justified in light of the status of the animal as property."[12] But what inherent value can be considered only temporarily, yet deemed respected? Claims of respecting the animal's "inherent value" are treacherous illusions where animals are born and remain in a commercial system. *Rain without Thunder* urges: "The position that is consistent with rights theory, it seems, is that the veal crate should be prohibited or that the battery cage ought to be prohibited."[13] A rights advocate, Francione writes, should endorse an alternative storing system only "when that alternative *fully respects some relevant animal interest.* In such a case, the alternative removes some form of exploitation and grants a protoright, which requires treatment of the animals that, at least with respect to the relevant interest, would be required were the animal no longer regarded as property at all."[14] (The term "protoright" appears in earlier writings by Tom Regan, meaning a precursor to full rights.) But how is no longer being regarded as property at all possible, for a purpose-bred calf? Removing a calf from an individual stall and devising some other form of confinement might result in a less harsh type of handling, yet it doesn't make the calf anything but a purpose-bred calf; that doesn't change by degrees. If we subscribe to the concept of rights, we know animal rights will belong or pertain to those whose interests are protected by them. They cannot belong to those whose lives are fundamentally controlled by another party. As a purpose-bred calf will *always* be under the control of another party, there can be no rights, proto- or otherwise, for such a being.

Francione revisited the veal calf issue in 2007, writing: "A prohibition on the production of any veal is to be preferred to promoting non-crated veal."[15] But promoting "non-crated veal" isn't an action to be less preferred; it should not be untaken at all. And a legal ban on veal production is an odd concept. The calves who are deemed excess to the dairy industry—offspring of the lactating cows from whom milk is taken—are turned into veal cutlets. Thus, it's actually vegan education, which explains the ethic of renouncing dairy products, that will end the production of these baby cows in the first place. So we're back to the only effective way to address animal agribusiness: The focus of an animal-rights advocate, when asked how we can deal with the matter of animal farms, is best placed on straightforwardly and decisively encouraging people to eat peaceable meals.

Francione's conflation of what we can get for a calf and the idea of animal rights shows the importance of starting out by distinguishing selectively bred animals from communities of animals who could actually be freed from property status and experience autonomy.

Rights for purpose-bred animals would be, according to a sound theory of animal rights, a contradiction in terms. Charting a sensible advocacy path to animal rights would mean a movement to defend non-human animals' and communities' ability to live autonomously—that is, on their terms and not on the terms of a domineering (human) class. Cows, alas, will never experience independence from human keepers. They are domesticated beings whose ancestors no longer live. As commercial cows became widespread, their free-living ancestors, the aurochs, went extinct in the seventeenth century, when a poacher shot the last one. In the 1920s, two German zoo directors attempted to breed the aurochs back into existence from modern cattle, resulting in "recreated aurochs," also called Heck cattle (after zoo directors Lutz Heck and Heinz Heck)—animals shorter and less heavy than the powerful, free animals they were bred to replicate. Because today's commercial cattle cannot be emancipated from human dominion, saying that ruling out the transport of injured cattle, ending the use of individual veal stalls or crates, or targeting horn removal could be steps on the route to animal rights is to send a confused message. *Rain without Thunder* considers eliminating veal crates or painful dehorning as possible steps in the direction of animal rights; but cattle rights is a contradiction in terms.[16]

Francione also accepts "a complete prohibition" on the selling of crippled cattle.[17] The above critique applies again here. And in real-world terms, keeping all animals walking until they are slaughtered won't be carried out on account of any distinct factor of respect; it will invariably stop the public avoiding—essentially rebelling against—flesh products. In August 2008, the food safety wing of the U.S. agriculture department proposed an amendment to the federal meat inspection law to forbid slaughter of "non-ambulatory" cattle, instead ensuring that they be "condemned and properly disposed of."[18] The reasons offered by the government were regulatory clarity, consumer confidence in the food supply, and humane handling.

Francione states: "It does not help the overall cause for animal advocates to secure prohibitory legislation by telling people that they will feel better about eating meat if they do not have to contemplate the agony of disabled animals."[19] But the government has done so, by mentioning humane handling as one of the three reasons for the rule change, and it's likely that the advocates who have pushed for this move also feel better for the change, and of course no sensitive person would want cattle to be dragged to slaughter, but it's unclear if this restriction would move humanity closer to the ideal of non-exploitation or even the end of flesh production than a campaign unrelated to the grotesque circumstances of animals who are crippled on the way to slaughter.

The real-life language of the announcement addressing this rule change was the most eerie antithesis of rights:

> Under the proposed rule, cattle that become non-ambulatory disabled from an acute injury after ante-mortem inspection will no longer be eligible to proceed to slaughter as "US Suspects." Instead, FSIS [Food Safety and Inspection Service] inspectors will tag these cattle as "US Condemned" and prohibit them from proceeding to slaughter.

None of this means we should go out and oppose adjustments to industrial conditions or feel disdain for the people who work for them in the hope of getting some measure of relief for animals in bleak places. But we know keeping and using other animals disrespects the dignity of conscious life; the acceptance of the keeping and use is what continually creates the bleak places, so the acceptance itself needs our attention. Once again: The focus of an animal-rights advocate, when asked how we can deal with the matter of animal farms, is best placed on straightforwardly and decisively encouraging people to eat peaceable meals.

Francione maintains that "rights theory objects to the use of the animal exclusively as a means to an end" and that certain changes within industry can treat animals "as more than means to human ends."[20] But why should we accept treating them even partially as means to ends? They are not human workers; they cannot consent to *any* form of use.

Cass R. Sunstein has asked, when reviewing Francione's work, why other animals ought to be off-limits to use. "In many domains," Sunstein points out, "human beings seem to be 'used,' and the relevant practices are not objectionable for that reason."[21] Sunstein offers examples: plumbers, cleaners, lawyers, and other professionals being treated as means, not as ends. Francione responds:

> We cannot enslave the incompetent plumber in a forced-

labor camp; we cannot use her as a nonconsenting subject in a biomedical experiment or as an unwilling organ donor. Even if we do not value the plumber as a plumber, she still has residual value that prevents us from valuing her fundamental interests at zero. In the book that Sunstein was reviewing in the context of making these comments, I use the plumber example and distinguish between treating the plumber as a means to an end and treating her exclusively as a means to an end.[22]

Neither scholar's argument should satisfy us. Other animals are not our plumbers or lawyers or cleaners. They needn't—and, on the rights view, shouldn't—be used by us *at all*. Chickens won't do well to retain "residual value" in order that their fundamental interests be valued at more than zero. The point of animal rights is not treating other animals as more than *mere* means to our ends. It's not about refusing to treat them *exclusively* as means to our ends. Can we accept that they are here for ends of their own? If so, the issue isn't about how we treat them; it's about leaving them free from such interactions.

It seems we must decide whether humans could simply let other animals be, and organize now around that future. Otherwise, we might be talking sincerely about animals' interests, but we fall short of respecting their dignity. Once they are domesticated or captive, once they are in our sphere, they've lost autonomy, and everything else boils down to the details of handling. I wonder if we can really improve upon the vegan message, which asks us straightforwardly to reject products and enterprises that wage war on other animals, and replace them with animal-free offerings. For surely there is no better, more straightforward advocacy for animals used in industries than to opt out of using them—by becoming vegan. Let people know that they can do this, and that's just what we must do to address the situations of industry-owned animals. Then we can really talk about animal rights: the ability of undomesticated animals to live on their terms.

Francione writes: "What is essential in seeking any incremental change is that rights advocates recognize that their efforts must be accompanied by a continuing and unrelenting political demand for the complete eradication of the property status of animals."[23] But advocacy that seeks to impose rules on an industry in order to establish the idea that the industry mustn't exist is like trying to head east and west at once. The political demand for the complete eradication of the property status of animals means pointing out the bright line between (a) animals in institutions of use and (b) animals who are apart from them, and making a realistic assessment of what can and should be done on behalf of each of these groups.

Agribusiness necessarily perpetuates the property status of the animals it owns—their minds and every cell in their bodies—and cannot be expected to sabotage itself any more than it can be expected to respond positively to sabotage. If it is a lawful business, government cannot be expected to sabotage it either. It's important to be clear, crystal-clear, about this: Animal rights is not dedicated to changing rules and conditions inside profit-making industries. When we get down to it, the question being decided here is whether we are going to identify other animals as ours for the taking or not. In short, no matter how cautiously we select our campaigns, when we focus attention on changing handling and killing methods for domesticated animals, we focus on animals who can't be released from our dominion—who wouldn't be born apart from our desire to use them as producers and products. The right not to be property, for one who is purpose-bred, would mean not being bred into existence at all. Francione has in fact concluded that "the right of nonhumans not to be treated as property" requires us to "stop producing domestic nonhumans for human use."[24]

How crucial it is to relay the message that animals, free animals, should exist, live, experience, thrive! How important it is for us to say not just what animals won't be, but who they *will* be. Animal rights will be found, and should be sought, in the oceans and rivers; in the air, on the tundra, and in the forests. Animal rights will *not* be found in the shop, lab, factory or farm. To those institutions, the clearly appropriate, rights-based approach is simple conscientious objection.

Let's take a closer look at what domestication has done, and why our approach to domesticated animals cannot be conflated with pursuing animal rights. Many animals have been so thoroughly purpose-bred for agribusiness over centuries that they couldn't live on the tundra or in the forest. They can't carry out basic activities of daily life. If modern commercial turkeys and chickens (the ones bred for their flesh) are held longer than usual before slaughter, they continue to grow, become too heavy for their own legs, and soon become unable to get food. Harold Brown (a former cattle farmer, now an environmental and animal-rescue advocate) remembers how the chickens rescued from hurricane Katrina grew rapidly and died a very short time later from heart attacks or becoming so heavy that their legs could not support them:

> Some of the broiler chickens tipped the scale at 20 pounds! Even though the turkeys fared better, they were still incapacitated to some degree. And occasionally a few of them would break their legs or dislocate their hips. They have been selectively bred to have their breasts grow so fast that if they survive past slaughter age, they inevitably have problems.

Laying hens aren't going to enjoy anything tantamount to freedom as long as they are bred for commerce, even before the ultimate indignity and horror of slaughter. Most laying hens suffer from osteoporosis, for example, and the idea of comfortably cage-free hens vanishes when we learn they're more likely than caged hens to break bones while moving through a shed or across the ground.[25] That's a fact we won't find on the box of "cage-free" eggs, but we should: *Cage-free hens are more likely than caged hens to break bones while moving through the barn or on the range.*

And even if discontinuing conventional caging could, in the most narrowly tailored circumstances, lead us in the direction of eroding the property status of animals, Francione's thought experiment fails to notice the crucial reality that using spacious areas for commercial egg operations will remove those areas from indigenous animals at the start; and were predators to come back, the property owners will kill them. How, then, can allocating space to agribusiness be aligned with, or even neutral to, animal-rights theory? Moreover, if one introduces domesticated birds into a natural landscape in an attempt to provide freedom of movement, the introduction could destabilize an entire biocommunity of free-living animals.

On top of it all, free-range animals generate plenty of greenhouse gas emissions; at least one study indicates that free-range egg farms use up enough extra green space, feed and energy to increase their effects on global warming over battery farms more than 10 percent.[26] In contrast, residents of North America who opt out of eggs, dairy, and flesh products will cut their yearly individual greenhouse gas emissions by about a ton and a half. It's important to note that, overall, animal products tend to have higher emissions than food produced from plants.[27] Some dairy products result in more greenhouse gas than some flesh products (cheese, for example, can have a bigger ecological cost, ounce for ounce, than chicken products); so while replacing flesh products with plant products makes ecological sense, the most effective way to reduce the ecological impact of our diet is to go vegan.[28] And this way, we aren't contributing to the huge amount of animal waste and fertilizer runoff used in the monocultures that support large-scale animal agribusiness. How important is this ecological argument? Well, when octopuses try to clamber up fishing lines to escape the water, something's gone horribly wrong. Both agricultural runoff and climate change are causing massive zones in the ocean where animals can't find the oxygen that's normally in seawater, and they've been seen struggling desperately to leave the water to avoid suffocation.[29] When these massive dead zones move (they cover up to 20,000 square miles each), they kill crabs, lobsters, tube worms—all marine beings who fail to escape in time.

Given the peril facing all life due to climate disruption, campaigning for adjustments in the way farm animals are stored before they're killed is fiddling as Rome burns. Animal rights matters. Animal rights is a vegan position, which brings in vegan-organic growing and cooking, and people need to learn this stuff now, not after the wealthiest people among us use all the hospitable land up on farm animals so they "know where their food is coming from." The argument for local and pasture-raised animals is valuable just insofar as it allows the vegan argument to be raised in response. It is imperative that we explain at every chance that the single most important daily change we can make, if we're going to stop deforestation and climate change before it stops us, would be to adopt a completely plant-based diet. Carrying the principled message that society must transcend animal use rather than refine it, vegan activists are as vital in the practical sense as in the ethical sense.

When we instead focus on animals owned by industry, are we turning away from animals who are *not* deemed useful for human purposes? Or those, such as seals, salmon, bobcats, wolves and coyotes, who are treated as targets? What will the end of property status for animals mean if animals who could benefit from that right are gone because we haven't been paying attention, protecting their habitats, and struggling ardently to represent their interests?

Our relations with other animals on Earth do not need incremental change; we need a complete paradigm shift. If animal rights means the right to live on your own terms, not on the terms of the people who have subjugated you, then a true step in its direction could manifest itself in the work to preserve the autonomy of a free-living community of animals, while presenting the argument for conscientious objection to the use of animals as products or entertainment attractions. Preventing acts of violence against deer, foxes, badgers or coyotes in a local community sends an important message to other humans. Continuously reaching out to others and presenting the idea of a commitment to stop using animals has the simultaneous effect of sparing habitat needed by autonomous animals *and* sparing domestic animals from being brought onto the planet as commodities.

Of birds and abolitionists

We've touched on a major trend in animal-advocacy circles: the cage-free egg concept. For several years now, it's been generating a flow of press attention for advocacy groups and egg companies alike. Let's go back and consider the standards devised by the Whole Foods Market grocery chain, with the advice and endorsement of several advocacy groups.

At least one of Whole Foods Market's promises, if kept, would result in a rearing system that purports to accommodate all of a bird's interests in freedom of movement. In early 2005, after the company's "Animal Compassion" standards were announced, a representative of Vegetarian International Voice for Animals (VIVA-USA) told an interviewer:

> Welfare reforms are not anything that VIVA-USA works on; however, I don't think anyone has ever seen anything like what Whole Foods is trying to do. It's nothing like 'let's make the cage bigger.' It's above and beyond that. What Whole Foods is doing, saying that the ducks have to have water to swim in, is just unimaginable. It is what is natural for the duck. People just assume that ducks have these things, but in factory farms they don't have anything like that. And right now, when we are doing our campaign against Albertsons to stop selling their duck meat from factory farms, we are able to point to another grocery store chain that will not allow the animals to be treated badly and all of this is being done because of consumer pressure, because consumers do not want animals to be treated inhumanely. Other organizations, animal organizations, industry groups, have been trying to create standards, but in my opinion, unfortunately, they still seem to be part of the system.[30]

Now, the Whole Foods Market standards don't follow the narrow criteria offered in *Rain without Thunder*. The Whole Foods standards were voluntarily devised by the company, not under mandatory rules or laws. And Whole Foods' corporate standards can be withdrawn even faster than legislation can be repealed. Yet advocates who work for such standards and see them as a precedent could argue that they provide the model for lawmakers to follow. After all, if there is no example showing that industry owners can make certain changes, how would legislators insist that they do? Thus, the advocates of Whole Foods husbandry practices evidently (but incorrectly) believed, at the outset of their campaign, that they were bringing animal-right theory to the table.

Because the scenarios offered in *Rain without Thunder* set out to show how activists might try to erode the property status of animals who stay inside the institution that profits from owing them—a confusing proposal to many—debates have arisen about the criteria and what they mean or don't mean to encourage.[31] The debates will probably continue. But they need not. Donald Watson's description of a childhood visit to a dear uncle's farm offers us a key principle of animal rights. Without having ever seen a caged hen or factory farm, Watson conveyed the message that even the most accommodating animal farm does not erode the property status of animals; even the most idyllic farm does not lie on the route to animal rights.

The farm will fail utterly to protect the bodily integrity or freedom or life of its animals. The farm and its animals are present only because they suit our desires; the animals themselves are bred for characteristics that please us; and the circumstances of the animals, on any farm, depend not on their own interests, but on the attention humans can afford or be bothered to pay. It's of no avail to tinker with dominion.

The shift to veganism...

Means refusing to become advisors on matters of animal husbandry. The key is to ask: "What is the vegan approach to this?"

Could advocates working with Whole Foods Market get change that's not just tinkering with dominion? Let's address the question first by ruling out the option of becoming advisors on matters of animal husbandry. We know the one kind of activism animal enterprises cannot co-opt is the voluntary decision by people worldwide to refuse to buy animal products. So the key is to ask: "What is the vegan approach to this?"

Thus, we might request the replacement of various house-brand products with similarly attractive offerings, while spreading the word that no animals were used in their production. The Vegan Society could be brought into the effort and Whole Foods Market could enter into a trademark agreement and, aisle by aisle, cultivate the sunflower symbol that traditionally denotes the gold standard in vegan certification. Whole Foods Market uses specially designed paper bags as well as reusable bags; any of these could be stamped with the vegan sunflower and a few lines about the history of vegan living, or the value of such living to other animals, the ecology, and the health of people throughout the world.

The overall effect of this initiative would be strongest if selling animals and animal products is something Whole Foods Market can do without, rather than an inherent part of the enterprise. The grocery chain grew out of a local vegetable market. Once the entity became profitable, however, its chief executive's interests changed. Animal products, especially niche animal products, can have quite a high profit margin. The company got animal advocates to endorse its promotions, and can now implement or ignore activists' requests depending on what makes business sense; in any case, animal agribusiness now appears to be an integral component of the corporation's activity. A profile piece in the January 2010 issue of *The New Yorker* reiterates that CEO John Mackey has no intention of removing flesh foods from the aisles, let alone removing all animal products.[32] Recipes and pictures of roasted chickens and baked sea bass flow freely from the corporate branches through paper, e-mail, and social media promotions. All of this suggests that the advocate's energies and support would be more fruitfully offered to projects that eschew animal exploitation and mindfully offer peaceful replacements, although there's room for further exploration of the question.

Again, let's be clear: It's not wrong to want to minimize suffering caused by the use of chickens, ducks, and the other animals people own. Most of the general population will agree. So will animal agribusinesses and the people who buy what they sell. The question is whether we can build a movement around that, and the rational answer is no. Well worth supporting are small companies following a vegan ethic. Such projects, as well as community-based environmental organizations, vegan-organic growers, independent bed-and-breakfasts, schools, health providers and health-food shops, where animal trading is not inextricably woven into the undertaking, offer especially fertile ground for cultivation of the movement.

Speaking of cultivation, let's pause for an explanation of vegan-organic (also called "veganic") growing. Veganic growers liberate farming from animal agribusiness. How? By finding alternative nutrients to fishmeal, powdered feathers, animal wastes and blood. For soil fertility, they rely on clover, kelp, and composts. Free-living animals, like rabbits—worms too!—pass through everyone's veganic garden and add some waste, naturally enriching the soil.

Vegan-organic growers avoid harmful chemical pesticides and weed killers; they use no genetically engineered anything. They painstakingly avoid disturbing Earth's great carbon reservoir—the soil. At the same time, they avoid generating the massive pollution caused by runoffs of chemicals and wastes that so badly damage marine life. The food they grow is eaten locally and in season, and delivered with as little packaging as possible, so it's the most environmentally safe way to offer humanity our nutrients. Natural diversity is encouraged on veganic farms—both to respect individual animals and to encourage a local biocommunity that's resilient to climate changes. What's not to love about vegan-organics?

In any case, regular organic production can't expand to cater for a much larger market; there's just not enough animal manure available because the land area required to feed the necessary animals is so vast. Veganic growers are reminding us that all life ultimately depends on plants, which do not have to be passed through an animal in order to be nutritious. As vegan-organic growing challenges centuries of agricultural practice, and the idea that purpose-bred animals bring ecological harmony, encouraging such work is a great use of energy. And as veganism itself expands, an increasing number of people will be looking for food and clothing materials that have been derived apart from animal agribusiness. So how do we get veganism expanding?

Take note of how some students at the University of Glasgow have proceeded. In January 2008, guided by the campus Vegan Society, the school's catering service acknowledged that high-quality vegan food "appeals to just about everyone" and is "healthy, ethical and planet-friendly" and thus became the largest caterer to gain Vegan Society accreditation. All foods and services registered with The Vegan Society must be free of animal ingredients and animal testing.[33] The University of Glasgow met the criteria, and now displays the sunflower logo to promote an extensive vegan menu. Debut dishes included Thai Green Curry; Baked Squash with Cajun Tofu; and Falafel with Asparagus and Fennel Compote. A menu so attractive, available at every meal, every day, and in dining areas open to the public, predictably gained support at other schools. It's certainly possible for a student population to become vegan; many schools' residential colleges already are. Batten House at Bryn Mawr College in Pennsylvania is a residential college whose members have committed to veganism, based on environmental concerns and the feminist call to end unfair hierarchy. These are accomplishments—without drawbacks—for human health, for our recognition of other animals' dignity, for economic wisdom, and for the climate.

After a person's consciousness is raised, it's helpful to have guidance as to how to actually make the transition into vegan living. That's why advocates in this social movement should publish vegan recipes and cookbooks. And that's why, in January 2008, when a small London-based group called Vegan Campaigns supported 25 people to go vegan for a month, the facilitators matched each participant with an experienced vegan for support. People taking the Vegan Pledge also received basic medical checks, nutritional information, and recipes at no charge. Many decided to stay vegan. So the group repeated the pledge in January 2009. By then, The Vegan Society was doing a Vegan Pledge, providing nutrition advice from a scientist and a registered dietician. The Vegan Pledge crossed the ocean when a group of Friends of Animals members started it up in Philadelphia. First, the group planned a World Vegan Day on the First of November 2009 to share vegan history with the community at Singapore, a completely vegetarian restaurant in downtown Philadelphia. Soon a non-profit project called VegFund approved a grant for the Vegan Pledge.[34] As in the original project in England, each person who pledged was paired with a mentor who'd already been a vegan for a while. The experience gives every contributor the opportunity to get to know people who in turn enrich their lives in unexpected ways. By the time you read this, there are likely several more groups working together to bring the experience of the Vegan Pledge to people in their communities, and there's no way to overstate the benefits of working, communicating, *loving* in this way.

Meanwhile, in a small, coastal town in California, where the big event is the Salmon Restoration Association's annual salmon barbecue, a chefs' school offers something different: Save the Salmon Cutlet with Horseradish Dill Tartar Sauce and Sweet Chili Drizzle—a raw vegan dish. The Living Light Culinary Arts Institute's newsletter explains, "We're participating in order to reach a common goal: educating the public about saving the salmon and raising funds for habitat restoration."[35]

These initiatives are coming together at a time of worldwide awakening to the environmental catastrophe human industry has wrought. In the 1950s, people thought the ability to enjoy consumerism made human beings happy and healthy. Donald Watson was well ahead of the curve. The curve has arrived. Now, we see British hospitals removing flesh products from their menus in order to address environmental damage; they acknowledge that vegetarian agriculture involves far less land and resources than does the omnivore's diet. The city of Ghent, in Belgium, recently committed certain days to vegetarianism in response to climate change.[36] Ghent residents did not seem to know yet that dairy products can be every bit as harsh on the atmosphere and the forests as flesh products are—we need a major shift in what we consider our food, not just a "meatless" diet—but these issues began to emerge with the ensuing media attention.

In 2009, the government of Manitoba, Canada, observing the role forests play in climate, announced a commitment to protect a substantial area of boreal forestland, including key habitats for polar bears, caribou, and Arctic birds. The same year, the British government created the "animals and us" segment of the recommended primary school curriculum—guiding children to develop respect for worms, ants and bees, learn not to stamp on insects, and acknowledge that other beings have needs. As *The Sunday Times* worded it, "The government has decreed that children should be taught not to hurt a fly."[37] Teachers are starting to make gardens a focus of learning, vegan-organic methods are being introduced to schools, and schoolchildren are growing their own salad crops. Everywhere, people are talking about changing things for the better—cutting pollution, focusing on improving train routes as greener alternatives to air and road travel, questioning the use of chemicals, turning lawns into gardens—and the time is ripe for animal ethics and environmental respect to mesh perfectly. The idea that we cannot legislate a vegan culture might well be crumbling under ecological reality. But advancing a social movement means we get this change through voluntary commitments. The best ban of all is the ban each person passes by controlling oneself. This way, instead of being restricted, the individual is empowered.

Expanding veganism through community-based ideas will eliminate cages through the most direct action of all: *eliminating the underlying demand for the cages* as more people agree not to consume animals or the products of their bodies. So we need not focus time and resources on the idea of enlarging containment systems used in the already sprawling agribusiness sector. Instead, we can make every day of our life, every hour of our advocacy, speak fluently for a new paradigm.

Now, when we explain that veganism addresses the cages by working at the demand level (that is, as people are persuaded to stop buying the products, confinement will be discontinued), some might say we're uncaring about the lives of animals currently being exploited. Not at all. Veganism spares animals from being used as resources in the first place and shifts society to a completely new mindset. This is effective direct action, as becoming vegan, in-real world terms, precludes the torment and slaughter of many animals the very day a person commits to it. Helping just one more person to go vegan will spare yet more animals that would have otherwise been consumed. And so on.

At the same time, we can say veganism can indeed make a difference to animals already being exploited. The vegan does care, and deeply so, about the situations of animals who spend their days in institutions because people buy animal products. Not to care, and not to understand those who genuinely want to ameliorate the animals' conditions, would be callous. Harold Brown, who grew up on a cattle farm, has pointed out that the increasing popularity of vegan products will cause sellers of animal products *themselves* to attempt to reinvent themselves for the caring shopper.[38] Of course it's true. The International Fur Trade Federation's 2008 "State of the Industry Report" proclaimed: "Animal welfare is key to the success of the fur industry." When industries face criticism, they are good at defending and repackaging themselves. Thus, veganism does address industrial conditions, because it raises awareness about animals' situations, and industry knows this, and knows that a growing vegan movement is their one serious challenge. The animal-rights advocate should certainly respect those who are working in hopes of improving industrial conditions, genuinely believing it is the best way to help animals. The question vegans are asking, though, is this: Should we, as advocates, make ourselves useful to companies (or, in the case of animal-control schemes, the government) when doing so could help them sell their plans to the public? Or should we make it crystal clear that we don't need to buy what those animal owners sell?

In recent years, to promote the notion of a more humane form of animal control and exploitation, non-profit groups have gone down some troubling paths. One group has presented an award to an animal experimenter who developed a supposedly humane mousetrap (it still kills the mouse); the same charity told the press that eating lobsters would be "acceptable" if the lobsters were electrocuted—and this was no misquote, for the group actually ordered the lobster-stunning machines and paid the manufacturer for a public demonstration of how they kill the animals.[39] A sanctuary group got New York City restaurants to pledge to only serve "humane" veal; restaurants selling veal from calves who purportedly weren't in crates (yet were still yanked from their mothers and still killed) were, in effect, praised by advocates for selling the animals through their menus.

When husbandry rules are modified, out come a flurry of announcements like that on a website I look at as I write (this one for a state in the Midwestern U.S.): "Another Win For Farm Animals!..These days are good days." No disrespect to the activists intended, but despite their best efforts, animal farms cannot be genuinely improved except by being phased out as obsolete. Every bigger cage and every cleared pasture, on a finite planet, means less untamed spaces; and it's in those spaces that animal rights will be found. In those spaces, birds are able to form their relationships, feather their nests, lay their eggs, fledge their young, live and die in their natural time. There, foxes won't be shooed away; they will also be free to live in their ways.

The right to be let alone

It's no surprise that animal rights bewilders people. We humans have, for a few thousand years, taken for granted our position of control over other life. We've regarded this as the natural and eternal way of the world. Being born in a body that isn't human is, in the popular western song, "your misfortune and none of my own."[40] Often, we credit ourselves with knowing what makes life on Earth worth living, and assume other animals are better off living with us than in their own ways. But even when we genuinely try to help, our impact is often not what we expect. Feeding deer during the winter, for example, can inadvertently kill them, by introducing a change in their diet and interfering with the levels of vitamins, minerals and bacteria in their sensitive digestive tracts. Feeding birds through the winter can change their migration patterns, and even their wing shape, making them less able to fly over longer distances. As a general rule, we could allow other animals to find their own paths in the world, as nature has equipped them to do, and as they know best.

The concept of a right to be let alone arose in an 1890 *Harvard Law Review* article co-authored by the future Supreme Court Justice Louis Brandeis. Troubled by the distress caused by intrusive reporters, Samuel Warren and Louis Brandeis proposed a new tort: the invasion of privacy. Their aim was to shield the individual from "popular curiosity" and to respect the "inviolate personality" as "part of the more general right to the immunity of the person." Almost 40 years later, Justice Brandeis wrote of "the right to be let alone" as "the most comprehensive of rights and the right most valued by civilized men."[41]

Protecting that private core of personhood is the spirit that moves people to limit the extent to which reporters and marketers may pry into ordinary peoples' lives, to keep others from going though our diaries or our private papers. Even in these days of *YouTube* and social media, we ourselves want to decide how the world sees us. Respect for privacy is what troubles us when we hear a phone's been tapped; it's lost when individuals and communities are violated during military occupations. It moves us to advocate for detainees. It's assaulted in the ritual mutilations used to maintain a gender-based hierarchy. It's battered when a child's body is violated. It's disregarded in arranged marriages, and in social rules that thwart the relationships of gay people. It's annihilated by slavery, for no slave ever has private papers, private space, private time. And through the course of domestication, a slow form of controlling the traits deliberately bred into animals, it is forever taken away from animals, now and in generations to come. Animal rights would disallow this control, and fully respect animals' interests in their lives and their freedom of movement. For other animals, the "most comprehensive of rights" would mean regaining the freedom from being subjected to our notions of civilization entirely. It would mean the chance to live full lives, on their terms.

Francione states that our institutionalized exploitation of other animals "is made possible only *because* animals have property status."[42] It is true that modern institutional use relies on classifying non-human beings as property, as articles to be exchanged. Yet systematic domination is the deeper problem here. Long before modern conceptions of rights and property, humans domesticated other animals.

Francione states: "The status of animals as property is not new; it has been with us for thousands of years."[43] While that is true, domestication has been carried out for longer still.

And the interest in not being treated as a public curiosity is—note the way our planet's obscure beings are regarded after some explorer has discovered them—rooted in something deeper than what a study of property rights can reach. And if domination is a deeper, broader problem than a change in property status can encompass, we'd do best to look at abolitionism—the call to end the commodity status of animals—as a component of the more comprehensive animal-rights ideal, which in turn means respecting animals' autonomy and their right to be let alone. We must expressly challenge our prerogative to wage war on other beings, move them aside, demolish their spaces.

Francione wrote: "If we are going to make good on our claim to take animal interests seriously, then we have no choice but to accord animals one right: the right not to be treated as our property."[44] To stop treating other animals as property *is* important. Abolition's clearest expression holds that property is a legal construct, and changing the law can change the status, so that an entire class of individuals will be relocated from the category called "property" and over to "personhood"—that is, understood and respected as conscious beings who ought to have the opportunity to play their roles in life. If other animals are to play their roles on their terms, we must still do more than stop trading them and treating them as resources. The broader challenge of veganism involves being mindful of animals' connections with their activities and communities, and cultivating a respect for their interests in the climate, nutrients and landscape, the land, water, and air they require to experience autonomy.[45] Thus, the abolition of property status is a critical component, but not enough to comprise the whole view of animal rights. Respect for a conscious being's "inviolate personality" means more. Most

essential of all is our positive responsibility to ensure that free animals have
the peace and the space to *be*.

> **Abolition is a component of animal rights:** As used in animal-
> rights theory, *abolition* (the diagram's inner circle) means the
> end of treating other animals as our property. This is
> necessary, but not sufficient to ensure the respect
> for animals' dignity that is the point of animal
> rights. Animals freed from human society—as
> individuals and communities—also need to be
> assured the opportunity to experience autonomy.
> Thus, animal rights, defined as living on one's
> own terms, encompasses the interest in not being
> someone's property, but it is more comprehensive.

Evolutionary scientists tell us that species naturally go extinct and
others emerge to fill the gaps; but the current rate of extinction is many
times higher than the normal pace. The work of biologists, notably including
Edward O. Wilson, suggests we must dramatically change course, lest
more than half of all plants and animals be obliterated by 2100—perhaps
many more, when accelerated climate disruption is factored in.[46] Right now,
somewhere between one-fourth to a *half* of the planet's known mammal
communities face an urgent extinction risk.[47] One in three amphibian
communities are at risk of being lost forever; by the time you read this, the
number is likely to be higher. Animal law must respond.

In a macabre sort of way, we might say the animals in those
extinguished communities are no longer being subjected to treatment as
property. In this critical sense it is not enough to be non-property; animals
should have the right to be—the genuine opportunity to live on their terms.
This is why environmentalism can't be separated from animal rights. It's
time for us to give this point its due in the movement's platform.

The idea of animal rights as the right of other animals to live on their terms and not ours brings us a new concept of humanity, one barely imaginable in our current society. What will *we* be when we stop subordinating other conscious individuals and their communities? What will we be when we are no longer the masters of everyone else on Earth?

Business realities

We've made other animals into the spoils of war. Early environmentalists built their ideal of the wild on a battleground; the great environmentalist John Muir's ally was President Theodore Roosevelt, who would pose for photographers with trophy carcasses—the bodies of deer, pronghorn antelope, bighorn sheep and elk, which he called "lordly game" for their impressive antlers. Today's lordly game comes in expensive grocers' packets and on restaurant menus. We're not taught to think about it, but these businesses cater to the social acceptance of domination. We have a lot of history to confront; but then, so has every social movement.

So far, it's a small minority of advocates who are open to seeing the movement's potential to bring humanity to life-beyond-dominion. And because so few have accepted its revolutionary potential and tried to impart this vision to others, it's too early to call animal rights unrealistic. Another world is possible if we insist, and as friends add their voices to the call, we'll form a movement of COs to dominion—conscientious objectors to the long human war on other communities of living, feeling beings. We'll experience resistance. Sometimes, in the course of our daily errands and interactions, we'll be publicly chided for making an issue of it all, and seeming hard to please. We'll be called dreamers for celebrating the potential we see for a new and decent humanity. If only we'd be more realistic about what kind of changes are possible, we'll hear. These remarks function as warnings to activists: Don't get out of line and start taking the movement too seriously. That's why it's easier to instead support the popular campaigns: cage-free eggs and the like. The negative things other people say can become a false barrier we allow to be built in our minds.

We are fully aware that millions of animals are born daily to live their entire lives in misery and to die painfully. As we've noted already, some will argue that if something can be accomplished to lessen that suffering, we should not wait for public opinion to swing toward veganism. But this is self-fulfilling. Who's supposed to swing first? We need to swing, and show it. We need to *actively decide* to reject the invitation into a negative thinking rut. And veganism does work! Just try sharing the principles of vegan living. Let people know the power of a refusal to support corporations that benefit from the use and consumption of animals, and the joy of encouraging others to engage in this peaceful revolution. And you'll see. It works each time another person commits to vegan living, as well over two million people have done already.[48]

It works because it means people need not wait for a company to change its methods or a legal authority to enforce the protection of animals' interests. People are simply making their own decisions to opt out of oppression. Just a few decades ago, "vegan" wasn't in the dictionary. Twenty-five people offered this word in a 1944 newsletter to express a new principle.[49] At first, the word was peculiar to their own ears. People might well have thought they were living in a dream world. Mark Twain wrote, "A person with a new idea is a crank until the idea succeeds." What a bunch of cranks the first few vegans were! But they did succeed, so for us, it's much easier. Today, big cities and small towns have vegan restaurants, and community gardeners are appearing everywhere. People are challenging the use of animals as spectacles and tourist attractions. People are objecting to the pollution and fragmentation of other animals' homes. It is coming together, and as Donald Watson said: Realize that you're on to something really big! We could say that non-human animals already have rights, as far as the people who decline to use them for our ends are concerned. They do have rights, to the extent that we diligently respect their interests in living on their own terms. We needn't wait for lawmakers to hand down rights, or create peace on Earth. We ourselves do it as we create a vegan culture.

The objection "everyone is not going to go vegan overnight" is a distraction. People can and do *make a commitment to become* vegan overnight, and they're more likely to attempt the project when surrounded by daring optimism and positive messages. And individual people make up a movement, one that resolves to organize, to teach, to speak in consistently respectful terms. If the goal is transcending customary domination, then to opt out of exploitation is a straightforward concept to guide our approach in each situation.

And when people tell us that rules against battery cages, or chefs' pledges to stop serving "cruel veal" (the kind that comes from dairy calves confined in individual stalls) are positive steps, we can respectfully explain: If we say free-range veal is an improvement, people will understand our words to mean some veal is not so bad as other veal—in addition to absorbing the degrading idea that a once living, feeling being should be called veal. And some will order the purportedly free-range version, sincerely believing it's important to support the farmers who produce it. This is why suggesting the rejection of conventional cages and crates as a step to the abolition of animal-using industries will have serious, albeit unintended, drawbacks.[50]

Let's strive to be honest. Truth is the one thing corporations can't manipulate. Let's not try to take two positions simultaneously; for example, by claiming in front of other advocates, as many activists do, to promote the vegan movement—but avoiding the word *vegan* and instead lauding better veal or cage-free eggs or a new slaughter method to the public. Watering down our principles (or at least making them sound less certain) is the pragmatic way, we're often told, to animal rights. But is our role as educators to let people know what they can settle for, or what they could strive for? Holding out the easy route is not the respectful approach to the interests of non-human beings; nor is it respectful to those who steadfastly object to animal use. Let our acts and speech reflect what we know to be true, so we can open the door for big changes.

Are we saying something murky, like "Go Veg"—which might be taken as asking people to replace meat in the middle of the plate with a cheese omelette? Or rustling up people who will agree to (and can afford to) pay extra for eggs with certain labels? Through straightforward conscientious objection, we give others a model to strive for. Relatively easy lifestyle changes might create an illusion of progress, but it's entirely possible to eat *more* animal products after renouncing cows' flesh or finding purportedly humane animal products, and as long as people are buying eggs and other animal products, they aren't learning better ways to cook and prepare food. What do we want to accomplish with our days? What if we only had one day left? Do we produce a concerted campaign for bigger chicken confines, or a well-presented vegan cookbook? The cookbook is a real part of politics, a real contributor to animal-rights theory, a real form of direct action for animal rights.

The vegan advocate steers clear of campaigns that purport to extend some measure of freedom to purpose-bred animals not because it's fun to be contentious, but because the only way respect-based activism can emerge is by more people committing to it, rather than giving in to the crowd's pressure to be realistic, understand business, wait for conclusive data, and the like. And overall, there's something self-defeating about lesser evils becoming the regular way of doing activism. Maryanne Appel, a volunteer tour guide for a U.S. sanctuary, writes:

> I visited a natural-foods shop and asked where they purchased their goat milk. I was given the address of a small goat farm not too far from where I lived.
>
> The farmer graciously showed me around her rather small and exceptionally clean and tidy farm. She said she separates the kids from their mothers soon after birth. The kids, kept in a fenced area, cry out, and their grieving mothers call out for their babies. Twins seek each other out among the many kids and find comfort in staying close to one another.
>
> When they're old enough, the females are used for milking. When milk production wanes, so does profit, so they're sent to slaughter at the age of eight—halfway through their 16-year

life span. The males are sold for meat or as pets, so they also involuntarily contribute to the profit of the dairy business.

At this same farm, I saw a dozen baby pigs being fattened for market. They would be sent to slaughter in just three months. The pigs were all very friendly, hurrying over to me and obviously enjoying the attention I lavished on them, unaware of the awful fate that awaited them too soon at the hands of my own kind.

There is simply no kind way to raise animals for human consumption. Humane animal agribusiness is an oxymoron and a lie.

As more people join the global vegan movement, more agribusinesses will attempt (without our help!), in order to stay viable, to improve themselves trying to avert public critiques or to add value to their products; but they'll lose their power to persuade. Eventually, business owners will understand that the market for their products has dried up, and then convert to a more peaceful form of earning their livelihoods. We could say that whatever moves people to shun animal use most quickly is the best policy; yet if that means accepting some form of animal exploitation for ends-justified reasons, we'd be running a very costly marketing experiment—on animals, who cannot give us their consent. And what would we achieve even in the best of scenarios? The popular family-farm ideal is wishful thinking, a nostalgia for the days when fluffy-coated animals scampered over the grass and nuzzled their siblings and parents, under the care of a kindly farmer. But they, in all their fluffy coats, would end up in the same place, a place where rights will never be found.

"I inspected and visited the most 'humane' of 'humane' agricultural operations in my days as a Humane Officer," says Cayce Mell. "I can tell everyone first-hand there is no such thing as humane animal farming or humane slaughter. Exploitation is exploitation and execution is murder no matter how 'gently' it is performed."

So steps to the end of animal use aren't in evidence when people choose organic goat milk or uncrated veal instead of high-volume veal. Fortunately, they *are* in evidence when people learn to prepare guacamole instead of quesadillas, and there is wonderful advocacy potential in the creation of a new way of growing, preparing, and sharing the food that sustains us. As it turns out, the best form of advocating for animals doesn't depend on putting them in the middle of our campaigns: Perhaps it's not being an animal person that puts one on the road to the end of animal use, but being a vegetable person!

And while it's true that many people stop supporting animal agribusiness in stages, often ruling out flesh foods first, the point is to commit to the opting-out, and no category of animal agribusiness is reliably worse or better than another. All of these products are based—none less, none more—on the practice of making other animals submit to us. If we commit ourselves to vegan living, but attain our personal goal in stages, it's of no moment whether we first bid adieu to the hamburgers or the milkshakes, the pickled herring or the egg salad sandwiches.

Invite people to an excellent vegan meal. Imagine stuffed grape leaves, a Mediterranean salad, spinach pies, hummus or tabouli with Greek olives, marinated fava beans and baba ghanouj—yes, indeed, there is a *lot* for the vegan to eat. Preparing vegan food for co-workers is an important way to move things in a liberatory direction. As for restaurants, we can support and strengthen the ones that commit their resources to buying and serving vegan offerings. They are excellent models to their communities. There's a profound calm at my local vegan café. You might dine there for years before suddenly noting why: it's the absence of knives.

If we'd like to do something for the restaurants that do purchase animal products, we should help them establish vegan menus, vegan buffets, and the like. Let's agree to avoid any campaign that claims to improve the confinement and death of conscious beings. Because it's not our role to rate these things. We just can't advance a movement by being consultants on the methods of exploitation, control, and killing.

Not long ago, an advocacy organization praised a restaurant, Chipotle, for its president's vow to "give purchasing preference to suppliers that utilize the most humane method of slaughter available" for chickens—where doing so is "economically feasible."[51] And for this craftily qualified corporate assurance, the restaurant chain made public-relations gains while still selling chickens, and the activists claimed that, by pressing a shareholder resolution on the company, they got the company to do something (although nothing was promised at all). The advocates wrote, "We value our relationship with Chipotle; this was all very amicable." This mutual back-patting, of course, reveals nothing of the animals' perspectives.

The same animal charity devised a plan to send a stock-owning employee to the annual meeting of Hormel Foods Corporation and ask the company to discontinue the electrical stun baths they use on the turkeys that go into products such as Spam®.[52] Instead, the charity wants Hormel to use only controlled-atmosphere killing, which kills birds by putting them into a chamber containing nitrogen or argon, possibly mixed with CO_2, to cut off their oxygen supply. The group has, in the past, offered to drop the shareholder resolution if Temple Grandin, a slaughter plant design expert, would be allowed to inspect Hormel's sites to certify they were using a gas technique.

While some advocates are recommending shareholder protests to obtain corporate change within the system, business reality won't allow corporations to be forced by a small minority of shareholders to make any genuine changes in the way non-human animals are viewed by a culture. Therefore, what the campaigners would tend to get is not transformation, but a way to deliver a series of rebellious messages—and some dividends for the shares. An enormous injustice—such as that which involves enslavement—is not amenable to change by investment. It requires divestment, an understanding that profit-seeking corporations are not suited to grant rights or promote social justice. Investment in and support for life-affirming enterprises (illustrated by the use of the vegan sunflower trademark) is quite arguably the only kind of marketplace agitation that makes sense.

It's a fact: Many advocacy campaigns, and many reporters, mistake the stream of platitudes about humane handling for an animal-rights platform. Campaigns for supposedly more humane eggs in school dining halls enlist students in dozens of schools to persuade cafeteria managers to select the preferred eggs. The ensuing hype used by advocacy management often borders on farce. Press-release writers for humane groups in the United States and Canada have praised companies that buy from cage-free suppliers using catchy terms such as "egg-cellent news for hens" and describing these companies as "putting the chicken before the egg"; and the Royal Society for the Prevention of Cruelty to Animals now has a "Rooting for Pigs" promotion to connect major British grocery chains with the pig-flesh industry to develop labels for their products. Since a 2004 law mandated notations about animal handling on eggs, the RSPCA says, "there has been an increase in the sale of higher welfare eggs as consumers make an informed choice about the eggs they buy. We want to see the same happen for pigs."

But these trendy eggs and pieces of better pig flesh can command more than double the price of competitors' products, belying any claims that corporations are sacrificing on behalf of chickens or pigs. The duties of the corporate officers and directors aren't compatible with accepting certain methods of production as steps on the way to abolition of the industry; the reality is precisely the reverse.[53] When acting on behalf of a corporation, the decision-makers must put the shareholders' interests first, and cannot pursue some other goal to the detriment of the profits.[54]

Some corporations can afford to pursue philanthropy (a word adapted from the Greek *philanthropia*, meaning "loving humankind"); this they see as an opportunity to enhance public relations. The global banking firm J.P. Morgan Chase & Co., with assets of $2 trillion, states that it will "focus our philanthropic efforts in communities where we can best leverage our financial and non-financial contributions."[55] The earthquake that struck Haiti in early 2010 prompted an outpouring of contributions to rescue charities from big U.S. businesses: J.P. Morgan Chase, Morgan Stanley, Bank of America and Goldman Sachs Group, for example, each pledged $1 million to relief efforts. As one writer noted, "the recent mortgage meltdown and controversies over bonuses paid to employees after receiving taxpayer bailout funds" mean these and other corporations "have much work to do to repair their images, and corporate giving in its various forms can go a long way to furthering that aim. Indeed, one of the most important roles corporate philanthropy plays is to show consumers that companies can be good citizens…"[56] As for the animal agribusiness, grocery and food sector, it is pure folly to think that harsh treatment of animals can be effectively restrained by factors unrelated to the mission of commerce: profit. The corporations know it: Once it's agreed that animals can be consumed, the rest comes down to who speaks for how the whole process will be carried out. Arguing over the definitions of "cruelty" and "humane" could go on forever, keeping the animal-protection groups in business for a long time. Husbandry refinements may be framed in the language of welfare, but the ease with which they're subjected to co-option as public-relation moves shows how effectively they provide a safety valve which animal agribusiness uses to prevent rebellion against human control and commodification of non-human life.

We see this clearly in the case of the Chipotle restaurant: the president announced that slaughter methods would not be changed if the price weren't right. Industry people will see the question of slaughter or confinement methods as cost-benefit issues. They'll consider the industry standard in various countries, the cost of equipment, ease of maintenance, staff requirements, efficiency, and public relations, and, if it makes sense to do so, their role in "animal-welfare" leadership—which concessions enable them to claim. And this, to them, is effective management of activists. They will change only at the locations and only to the extent that the change can be profitable. It bears recalling that Whole Foods Market stock hit a new record high the day it announced the hiring of a director for the Animal Compassion Foundation. As one reporter phrased it, "Analysts said the plan to sell more humanely harvested steaks and chicken breasts will help the bottom line of the chain."[57]

After a period of pressure from activists, the Trader Joe's grocery chain agreed to "improve its laying hen welfare policy"; soon, an animal-protection group sent out a press release under the title "Trader Joe's Gives Birds Something to Sing About," containing this explanation: "By converting its private-line eggs to cage-free, Trader Joe's helps reduce the number of birds confined in cruel cages."[58] The implication? Conventional eggs are cruel; but shop at Trader Joe's and your eggs will be from hens who are somewhere out there happy and singing. The reality? Male chicks will lay no eggs, so the producer will just as soon kill them as look at them. Worn-out female birds will meet the same fate. Astonishingly, some advocacy managers have even promoted "cage-free" eggs to India's vegetarians—virtually a whole new market, for the generally accepted definition of vegetarianism in India has long ruled out eggs. The history of the end-the-battery-cage idea has been much worse than a distraction.

As readers who follow the animal-advocacy movement know, the suggestion that abolitionists consider questions in new ways has set off inflammatory exchanges and tense disputes. And yet the questioning is part of what ensures the integrity of a movement. When good ways of conceiving ideas are challenged so they can be better ways, strong contributors will pause, step back, agree to rethink and change the map, then move ahead, treating a sincere challenge as a benefit, and, if possible, regarding the challenger as an ally and a friend. For this is not about winning theoretical arguments; we all learn from each other and from life, and one of the things we learn is how to express and carry out our good ideas in better ways. Seemingly minor and everyday interactions count as peace-building acts that build community and model a vegan outlook. Replacing distrust and competition with peace and mutual support would be a revolutionary change for humanity, and if we have the courage to expect it, we'll work very hard ourselves to cultivate genuine appreciation for the potential and the well-being of other people.

At the annual North American Vegetarian Summerfest (in 2004, to be precise), Michael Klaper, a medical doctor, talked about having in the past been short-tempered but learning to stop, for example, being tempted to press the horn if someone fails to move immediately when a traffic light changes—because the horn blast of impatience isn't vegan. We have a big goal now, as vegans: we're cultivating peace and to do this we need to model it in our day-to-day interactions. Our perspective changes when our goal is something really big, and we should become less interested in being upset with other people as we continue focusing on what we cultivate. Today, we see that to model peace is not a form of passivity, but rather a kind of minute-to-minute activism that takes a commitment. It means we allow ourselves to listen, to be mistaken, to learn, to share opportunities with others, to stay open, and to continue cultivating even if we might not see the full results in this lifetime. This is not easy. John Vyvyan wrote that animal advocacy brings together people whose opinions vary widely; when they come, they agree on "opposing cruelty" but might disagree on everything else. "No cause," wrote Vyvyan, "could ever have stood in more vital need of tolerance and charity among its members."[59]

On that note, I must sadly acknowledge having also seen an abolitionist activist proclaim, in reference to activists who have made bargains with animal-owning industries, "Welfarism is pro-violence." What a provocative and ill-advised comment! Let's think non-violently, and let's check ourselves before we throw mean-spirited accusations around. They do not help the vegan cause.

Confronting the "happy meat" backlash

When we stand back and look at the past thirty years of advocacy, the theme is a general agreement to treat industries as though they could somehow be the locus of the animal-rights movement, with different ways of keeping hens or a rule against dragging cows called a step in the right direction. But a business owner's agreement to place birds in a modified kind of confinement or a government rule to remove the weakest animals from the slaughter line has no genuine correlation to the advancement of a culture beyond domination.

The abolitionist position has won adherents in academia thanks to the important efforts of Tom Regan, Gary L. Francione, and allied thinkers, and they have set out important precepts; but rather than illustrate and refine the abolitionist principle in a limiting way, let us place it where it can do its good work. The movement has been around long enough to know that rights can't be found at the egg seller's factories, sheds, or yards. We now have the continental European model of enormous "cage-free" factories to consider—deplorable prisons from which suppliers continue competing for the best profit margins they can get. We must also know there's no reason that the selling of animal products should be seen as normal. Nobody needs birds' eggs except birds.

John Mackey's Whole Foods Market profits largely from the sales of animal products. Mackey has bluntly declared, "I mean, Whole Foods is a grocery store, and our customers want to—they want to buy dead animals."[60] Whole Foods Market itself helped restore popularity to animal products in places such as Takoma Park, Maryland, where, in 2006, the town food co-op membership voted against safeguarding the term "vegetarian" in its mission statement. The co-op needed to start selling meat, its manager told the *Washington Post*, pointing out the competition from Whole Foods Market.[61] As the reporter put it, "The embrace of food-with-a-face in this peace-rallying, tree-hugging, self-declared nuclear-free zone has become so enthusiastic that some residents wonder whether a counter-counter-revolution is afoot." A local yoga teacher interviewed for the article declared, "We could start to be part of the revolution for lovingly and humanely raised and culled meat." After ten years of being a vegetarian, the teacher went into Whole Foods Market, ordered half a roasted chicken, and found a table, and now "suggests meat eating as a path to karma." A recent addition to the anti-vegetarian rumblings is *The Vegetarian Myth: Food, Justice, and Sustainability* by Lierre Keith, who claims that farming (including vegetable cultivation) brings disease, whereas "no one speaks of 'the diseases of hunter-gatherers' because they are largely disease-free."[62] It asserts that animal fats promote longevity, associates vegetarians with bulimia, rickets, rage and low test scores, and extols "[r]eal proteins and real fats from animals who in turn ate their real food."[63] One of Keith's house guests "stammered in awe" at the cooking. Keith explains, "She'd never had eggs from chickens who happily lounged and hunted and lounged some more in woods and pastures, nor cream from heirloom cows who spent contented lives with their heads in the grass."[64]

An October 2007 *Guardian* newspaper blog article titled "Happy Meat" ("A happy Highland cow on Balnafettach Farm" is the photo caption) shows a cow standing in an old-growth forest, rays of sunshine trickling through the branches and glowing on the reddish waves of the animal's thick coat. The scene epitomizes husbandry improvements that far exceed the norm, improvements activists presumably dream of achieving when pressing for freedom of movement. It's the gold standard of animal treatment. Apparently, the enterprise is sustainable to the profiteer. Potential investors are told "[t]he Highland's proven ability to produce top quality meat without the addition of expensive, high-quality feeds makes this breed the perfect choice for those people who wish to produce beef with natural inputs."[65] Sure, but why are humans taking up the Scottish highlands—where there are no more wolves, and only a few hundred wildcats still cling precariously to life—and breeding animals there for the purpose of selling their bodies? The owners of these "native Highland cattle" claim their farm is "protecting and developing the wonderful natural environment in which Balnafettach is situated." These animals have long been in Scotland, but this doesn't make them native animals; they were bred from a mix of two kinds of stock cows. They are now bred elsewhere in Europe, and they've even been brought to North America.

Along similar lines, Whole Foods Market in London has advertised Penbugle Farm (a photo of the owners' children holding lambs on their laps turned up on the Whole Foods "Suppliers' Stories" webpage), "home to only native breeds of cattle, pigs, sheep and hens." Here is what the Whole Foods website said about the company's animal flesh:

> There was a time when you could walk into your local butcher's shop and find a perfect, beautiful porterhouse, cut

that very morning with you in mind because the butcher (who knows you by name) figured you'd be in looking for something like that for dinner tonight. Think this scene is pure nostalgia? Think again. The meat expert standing behind the counter at your nearby Whole Foods Market is prepared to serve up whatever cut of meat catches your eye in the cooler or case, packaged especially for you and accompanied by cooking tips and sage advice only a real, experienced butcher can provide. We still do meat and poultry the old-fashioned way, when people cared where their meat came from, how it was raised and how it was processed.[66]

In October 2005, Whole Foods head John Mackey was invited to give a keynote speech at an animal-advocacy conference in North Carolina called "The Power of One," described in its promotional brochure as highlighting individuals who have "dared to challenge the status quo and take up the cause of the oppressed."[67] The convention's brochure proclaimed:

> Every Animal Rights Advocate has something to contribute to the animal rights movement. And not just any old something. What each person contributes is something special, something needed. Every Animal Rights Advocate teaches by the power of example.—Tom Regan, *Empty Cages*

Animal-rights philosopher Tom Regan helped convene this event, and also spoke, yet did not challenge the event's surreal message: that Whole Foods Market's CEO represents humanity's power to act for oppressed animals.

Keynote speaker John Mackey's career turned from a Texas vegetable market to the international marketing of cheese and lamb chops. It seems the advocacy style associated with "animal rights" is indeed Singer's husbandry model—alas, exactly what Regan insists it's not. By advocates and media alike, "animal rights" is used as a label for any animal advocacy—

most commonly, advocacy that's disturbingly inconsistent with the idea of respect. If advocates want the media to be clear that "animal rights" means respecting other animals, let us refuse to expect other animals to submit to us; let us refuse to commodify them; and for heaven's sake let us refuse to showcase an entrepreneur who makes a fortune doing both at an animal-advocacy conference!

Campaigns that promote John Mackey's interest in moving from small crates and cages to sprawling, pasture-based farming, as we face the biggest set of extinctions and the most ominous climate indicators in modern history, look nothing like animal-rights awareness. There is simply no benign animal agribusiness. Not for the planet, ourselves, the animals we've domesticated or those we haven't. If, as an animal-rights proponent, one really does care about the situations of all animals, one would avoid pursuing "steps" to offer owned animals full freedom of movement (an impossible goal), and instead:

- Unequivocally promote the vegan movement, while
- Steadfastly defending the autonomy of untamed animals.

The time to inject serious discussion of animal rights into the public discourse has never been riper. Within the coming few decades, extreme weather will mean water, shelter, emergency transport, and other lifesaving provisions will be denied to some living individuals by others. The ones most likely to be cut off from resources are already deprived. The financially poor will bear the brunt; and non-human beings, whose lives have long been deemed of lesser value than human lives, will be killed, consumed, and abandoned in droves in the desperate struggles for safety. So let's be serious about the serious stuff. We should be prepared to explain clearly, in conversations with others, that environmental degradation and greenhouse gases are strongly related to meat and dairy production. *Every kind* of animal farming strips land of oxygen-giving trees to set up grazing pastures, and then uses still more land to produce hay, grain and bean crops for the billions of beings churned out by the whole enterprise.

On the other hand, by growing a movement to permanently boycott the products of such industries, we'll be working to inhibit climate change, rather than letting it approach catastrophic proportions and deciding who gets assistance later. Animal-rights theory can and should be central in humanity's readjustment, and should include finding ways to make vegetarian agriculture a priority in environmental activism. This is not just a matter of responding to environmental crisis, although it certainly is that. If we could respond to the crises before us with a commitment to end our dominance-driven relationships with all of the planet's residents, we could learn a way to stop placing ourselves in crises, and to instead live creatively.

How hard is it for aware people to opt out of animal products in a developed society? Why not do so? Animal agribusiness means clearing landscapes of their living communities. It means the production of feed, immense taxation and distribution of subsidies as well as enormous quantities of water and fuel and energy, artificial breeding, dealing with the waste, the stench, the runoff, noise, diseases, antibiotics, the schooling of veterinarians, the blood and killing, the regulations…And then there's the methane and nitrous oxide. Compared to enduring this, what aware person can say that following a vegan cookbook, or converting to vegetable farming, is difficult? Is there really a good excuse for putting off vegan living?

CHAPTER 5

Objections to Veganism,
and Practical Responses

"**O**ur members are pronounced individualists, not easily scared by criticism, and filled with the spirit of pioneers," wrote Donald Watson on the 24th of November 1944 in the first edition of *The Vegan News*. Bring on the criticism!

First, consider the most common dismissal from people who've not really thought about the issue. They might ask a question, and, without waiting for any more than a sentence or two, write your reply off as your own business and not theirs.

That's fine; just don't push your views on others.

Yes, we know. Humans do have the legal right to exploit other animals. Most people, for much of our lives, can and do look away from hurtful situations, avoiding a reckoning with our complicity in them. Our capacity for wishing each other "peace on Earth" while allowing ourselves to be treated as consumers of institutionalized violence is remarkable.

Virginia Woolf wrote, "The history of men's opposition to women's emancipation is more interesting perhaps than the story of that emancipation itself." Let's apply that here. *The history of our opposition to animal emancipation is more interesting perhaps than the story of that emancipation itself.* Ask deeper questions than your listener has encountered before. Most people have heard about animal suffering, maybe something about the cholesterol in animal fat; they might have even heard about deforestation for feed crops. But they've probably not been challenged to acknowledge their spot in the hierarchy we humans create. If we're conversing with a feminist, or someone involved in any facet of social progress, it's possible to have an intriguing discussion—and perhaps more. Consider keeping a diary of thoughts and discussions. This will help later if you do public speaking or writing. Even talking about veganism and non-human interests—creating a vegan buzz—is important.

In regions far from the equator, some believe hunting other animals really is the least harmful way to eat, and that vegan views ought not be pressed there. Some of these regions' residents also feel strongly about hunting as a tradition. Many are no fonder of multinational animal agribusiness than vegans are, and that's a starting place to build alliances. Hear people out. After all, none of us, except perhaps a few vegan-organic growers, can claim to essentially do no harm.

Animal use has been important to just about *everyone's* culture and family history. And although themselves subjected to prejudice, there are people living in aboriginal communities (homeless people as well) who are committed to animal rights. We are all grappling with hierarchy, so we need to ask how we can respect other humans as well as other animals; these need not be separate questions. The significance of an elk's death to an indigenous community is similar, at essence, to the importance of the body of a turkey (complete with its age- and gender-specific stuffing and carving customs, prayers and toasts) to the majority culture. So we do need to understand the importance of specific traditions to people outside the dominant culture, and at the same time think about how we all comprise the dominant culture vis-à-vis the other members of our biocommunity. Every one of us has a history flowing back through ancestors who, at some critical time, decided that their safety depended on subduing other animals, and our forebears killed off large carnivores *en masse*.

Portrayals of non-Western cultures as settings for the most horrific barbarisms will not always hold up to analysis. It was in the United States that the particularly bizarre idea of cloning pet cats, and then selling the service to the public, became a reality. In truth, people all over the world have been brought up in societies that teach them to disregard the interests of anyone other-than-human. The commitment to relinquish our master role will not come from shaming and shocking each other. It will, rather, involve a change of heart throughout humanity, a shift in the collective psychology, for we are all in this ethical question together. Is the group of primates known as *Homo sapiens* entitled to dominate and use the rest of the planet's inhabitants?

Other objections come from the anti-capitalist movement; one example sounds like this: "Vegans can't help workers escape from selling their skills and time to capitalists, including in the animal-husbandry industry. We need to organize to take over the means of production in order to have the power to start living in harmony with the Earth." But we can create beneficial effects today through our conscientious objection to animal products. Excusing ourselves from fair, decisive action by holding out for a takeover of the means of production is not a fair answer. Shifting control over the means of production will not automatically end race- or sex-based biases; nor will it promote environmentalism or veganism. These have to be dealt with directly. We can begin to live with respect for other animals and the planet now.

This is not to say that we should accept a system that treats the rainforest as a commodity. This is not to say that we should abandon the work for fair distribution of the things we need or the means of producing them. It's important to ask why milk is subsidized, food is dumped, seeds are controlled and manipulated at will by a corporation, and the financially poor are ignored because of their lack of influence in the marketplace. It's important to reject the idea that companies may greenwash their products, that human interactions surround constant profit-making, while we are consuming in one year what the planet takes a year and three months to generate.[1] In truth, we are mounting a key challenge to the system that classifies conscious life as a commodity—one of our current economic system's most violent traits. And as the vegan principle stands for non-exploitation, it expects more of us than a re-directing of our purchasing power from non-vegan products to vegan products. Committing to vegan living today will play an important role in the making of fair ways to produce, and equitable ways to distribute, what we need tomorrow.

Let's turn to the objections we'll hear from animal advocates.

Objection number one: The seduction

People aren't all going to go vegan, so why not get them to make modifications you can see?

This double-whammy first asks: Aren't vegan activists holding the bar too high to get anything done? (One might also be familiar with the cliché "Don't let the perfect be the enemy of the good.") And then, the critic holds out a humane-treatment campaign to distract you. It might not be inspiring at all; but sure, it seems easier to achieve.

Many people, having been brought up in a culture that puts a premium on data and measuring results, want to see and show others the mark made by our efforts. Advocacy groups want to show, with historical data, figures, and consumer research, that theirs is a viable strategy. They want to tally up accomplishments, or just have a lot of campaigns that attract people to become members. Nothing dampens the spirit of activism like someone insisting everything happen for the sake of a strategy, while being willing to associate success with a few months of campaigning for an adjustment to the rules of animal handling, or even clicking an online petition.

We often hear in advocacy circles that promoting cage-free eggs or veal from uncrated calves means that at least people are drawn into more serious advocacy. But at the same time, we see regularly how the hurrahs for free-range handling bring people in the opposite direction. Niman Ranch, a company actually hosted on a guest panel at the expense of an animal-protection group at a conference called "Taking Action for Animals," has been lauded, infomercial-style, through the online Mother Nature Network under the headline "Niman Ranch raises meat so naturally that even vegetarians may want a taste."[2] A smiling rancher is shown in the photo at the top of the article, holding a fluffy-white baby goat up to the viewer. So let us not agree with campaigners who say no harm and only "helping animals" comes through non-profit support of for-profit animal agribusiness. Moreover, people in places such as China or India, where widespread dairy or egg consumption is relatively recent, look to what's happening in advocacy where these products have been around a long time. And what do they see? Yoga teachers who thrill at the thought of eating a chicken; activists endorsing the animal-handling standards where that chicken was bought; wealthy non-profit groups paying to host a ranch bent on wooing vegetarians to "want a taste" of animal bodies.

What would prompt a person to go the other way: from eating free-range flesh, eggs, and cheese to opting out of animal agribusiness fully? We could say it would depend on learning that the conditions at the free-range farm are actually not good. After all, that's likely why the person looks for the free-range label in the first place—to avoid buying from farms where animals are treated badly. But conditions can change, and other sources will advertise themselves to the shopper.

So although some will insist that more people than not will consider going vegan because of animal-handling campaigns, there is really no way to quantify this. And while it's hard to "prove" the effects of any campaign on human minds with measurements and data, we do know two things: These farms take the land and water right out from under other communities of living beings; and husbandry adjustments are, problematically, being equated with animal advocacy the world over. Vegans think as they do not because of statistical analyses. Vegans think as they do because they are committed to justice, to a new way of being human. Advocates for deep social change have always prepared to put in sustained work without measuring or even seeing its fruit. By sticking to our commitment we demonstrate the potential for our ethical ideas to become real. We are the proof.

It's not a bad thing, of course, to set goals; this book will consider how animal-rights activists can set and meet them without compromising principles. It's a fine thing to have one's success noted by others. But animal rights means a whole paradigm shift. It's not about being "perfect"; it's about changing one's cognitive map.

Some people will suggest that animal-rights advocacy can strive for handling changes and still promote a deeper justice, pointing out that in the human-rights sphere, it's acceptable for serious activists to welcome prison reform initiatives. To illustrate this point, we can recall that prison abolitionist Angela Davis has stated that prison reforms are also necessary.[3] Animal-rights proponents wouldn't *disapprove of* true husbandry improvements, if and where they might be possible. (Certainly no vegan I know is expressing a wish that animals in labs, zoos, or farms be miserable and never get any possible respite.) But there's another, more important point. Here, we hold the prison keys. By unequivocally refusing to involve ourselves at all with the system that commodifies other animals, we personally exercise direct power to spare animals from being brought into that commodified existence.

Some will ask: "Won't supporting *both* veganism and industrial concessions help us go further than we would if we said only one is worthwhile?" Well, the wealthiest animal-protection groups will continue working with corporations for concessions. Note that these groups support the use of animals in human society, as long as some minimum standards of treatment are established. The people who are expected to produce these standards will get hired, and will produce them. Many people see such projects as the only viable enterprises, at least at this time. They might see things differently as time goes on.

The call of this book is for people who are right now interested in thinking about what a serious theory of animal rights means for the real world, and how to go about synthesizing that theory with activism. Veganism needs supporters who are serious and fully committed to cultivating a new social pattern. It has needed them since 1944, and needs them as much today. The warning that vegans could be alienating people, and that everyone must travel at their own pace—that's the opportunity for reflecting on how we're delivering our message (are we listening and engaging in community outreach as well as talking and writing?); and, most important, for starting up a conversation about why it takes so long for us *Homo sapiens* to give up our privileges, even the ones that are bad for us and that we could stop indulging in today. We like to think of ourselves as modern. Are we still fighting and vanquishing animals—maybe not personally, but by paying for the deforestation of their habitat and the expansion of our farming? By only permitting them to exist insofar as we can take advantage of them? Continue the conversations; they're important. Most people have never given these questions any thought.

Objection number two: The dismissal

Our fundraiser should be vegan? Oh, right. If you want to be some kind of ivory-tower idealist who makes the movement as small as possible.

This one might be based on an intuition that excluding people is unwise. Yet insofar as it suggests that conscientious objection to dominion isn't a viable movement (or even guidance for a viable event), it frames vegan values as the outlandish notions of outsiders—and that's a kind of exclusion itself. Granted, the advocate usually needs to cultivate allies in advance of suggesting vegan events. But even if you're on your own, or one of a small group, preparing and passing out delicious desserts goes a long way. Good cooks are rarely mistaken for killjoys.

Objection number three: Getting personal

Don't you think you're being too rigid? Seems you are only doing this for your personal purity.

The best way to respond might be to acknowledge that the person making such a criticism thinks you need to be more open to others' perspectives. It's fine to say something like, "You seem to associate my view with dogma, but I'd like to be a respectful communicator. Won't you hear me out?" Then, address this criticism directly. Most vegans aren't ascetics who focus on personal purity. Most are socially engaged. To be vegan is to experience the pleasure of contributing to the well-being of one's health, the planet, and every conscious being alive. A vegan's joy comes from the confidence of knowing one can live according to a vital principle.

In fact, just being vegan (not counting the talks, writing, rescuing, and public picketing or performances many vegans additionally carry out) makes a significant difference. We should do more than eat vegan food along the way to a paradigm shift. Animal autonomy does need defending, and dependent animals do need caregiving. Yet it's worth noting that a vegan, by being vegan, spares more animals a year than most any sanctuary in the world can take in! If the sanctuary is doing something real by helping animals in a hands-on way, then the vegan is also accomplishing something real—and working at the very roots of oppression that makes animals need rescue.

Yes, vegan living does focus on ingredients and materials, but you might point out that taking veganism seriously is an effort for social change—at a level more profound than the term "personal purity" can reach. It's not so much about products and staying pure as it's opting out of domination. Today, we can find "vegan horse riding boots" advertised. Is the material the big question here? We'll ask about the customs that put the bodies of horses under our behinds. Similarly, the idea of vegan cat food only looks at the surface issue: the components of the product. Is it our role to press cats into becoming herbivores? Our real concern is whether the very concept of pet cats makes ethical sense. If we can't bring these matters up with other vegans, then maybe we *are* singularly focused on ingredients at the expense of the overall picture of our interactions with animals.

A related but rarer criticism is: *Your impossible standards are making it worse for animals.*

That one goes further than the "purity" criticism, because the "making it worse for animals" objection assigns blame. The suggestion that adhering to vegan principles makes things worse for animals usually arises when campaigners want the vegan to back a bid to get a different slaughter method, or to praise a company for some (often minor) adjustment in handling methods. It is also the heavy artillery that comes out when you ask for accountability from a group that's gaining an advantage by bargaining away other animals' most basic interests. Rest assured that vegans are not, by adhering to their values, "making it worse for animals." Vegans live as though animal rights were a reality right now, and *thereby bring animal rights into existence* (the central point of Gandhi's famous recommendation that we ourselves be the change we wish to see in society).

In a somewhat less accusatory appeal, some will insist, "If I were one of the animals involved, I would want this [bigger stall, gas-chamber slaughter method, or whatever the proposed handling modification might be]." Such advisors urge us to compromise with the exploiting parties. Now, surely it's fair and logical to say the animals would not want to be in the position of being slaughtered at all. We know they'd try to avoid being harmed; it's manifestly obvious. By extension, it seems logical and fair to say on behalf of other animals that they would appreciate vegan campaigning—that is, they'd appreciate our not consuming them. Not agreeing to victimize them in any way. But to suggest that we are speaking for other animals when compromises are made over their interests (and in reality animals cannot come to the meetings to represent themselves) is troubling.

Moreover, the planet has finite space. If increased space to move would truly be involved, for pasture or a more sprawling design for the buildings, and as we know that predators are eliminated to protect live animals in commerce, then one can't really limit the argument to what the given cow or chicken would say. What about the other animals who are pushed out of the way? What about what *they* would want?

Objection number four: "Vegans harm animals too."

That's true. The gentlest gardener will likely displace some animals. When the buildings in which we live were constructed, many mice and other small animals lost their spaces. Bike components and book glues are not always vegan; the list is long. It's sensible to acknowledge this, but it shouldn't dissuade us from being serious about opting out of exploitation. And it doesn't mean we need therefore accept human dominion over—and selective breeding and breaking of—wolves, wildcats, ferrets, fish, rabbits or horses. Veganism means we strive as diligently as possible to avoid harming and manipulating conscious life, and we do the best we can to ensure other living beings are enabled to thrive in their ways.

Objection number five: "You just don't understand business."

The objection of the worldly person telling us we just don't understand the real world is both common and flimsy. No one understands business better than those who have applied a sober assessment to industry and have decided that supposed pragmatic compromises will either be rejected or co-opted by industry experts, depending on what suits their shareholders. That's business.

Nor is it true that higher prices for animal products leads in the direction of animal rights. It leads to people seeing animal products as desirable items, even if fewer animals are sold.

And are fewer animals sold when the price goes up in some segments of the industry? That argument is unpersuasive, for it's not possible to know how many people are steered away from vegan living if they can afford "humane" product choices (here we might recall our own journeys and the questions we asked: *Do fish who swim freely suffer so badly? Is eating eggs better if I look for the free-range brand?*); and through all of the advertising, the idea that animal products are normal is reinforced to everybody. When we resolve to opt out, to eat something else, our journey becomes truthful, life-affirming, fair, and ecologically sane, and we help liberate our culture from its ties to animal agribusiness. This is entirely practical. On a planet of limited land and water, humanity breeds so many animals into existence as food that the free-living animals are pushed to the margins of the land. But through vegan movements, such as vegan-organic farming, we're showing the way to a viable future for human and non-human beings alike.

Objection number six: The call of the Big Tent

How popular will your activities be if you insist on promoting them as vegan?

Some might object to a call for a vegan event because they genuinely think you're missing outreach opportunities. There's another way to look at this. Vegan get-togethers are inclusive and they are real examples, to everyone who attends them, of the broadening of our ethical community to include every conscious non-human being. Everyone is welcome. The dietary aspect of veganism is perhaps the most inclusive and most healthful ever proposed.

In late 2009, Prince Philip and UN Secretary-General Ban Ki-moon hosted a vegan banquet at Windsor Castle, in order to include people from many religious and spiritual backgrounds—Baha'ism, Christianity, Taoism, Hinduism, Islam, Judaism, Shintoism and Sikhism—and to respect the environment. The *BBC News* offered a copy of the menu, which included a roasted English pear salad, ciabatta bread served with olive oil, portobello mushrooms stuffed with artichoke, red onion and thyme, set on pearl barley and butternut squash risotto with gremolata oil, and roasted carrots, parsnips and beetroot turned with baby chard. As ecological truths become more obvious, we can expect to see much more of this. (And who'd complain?)

Yet people who identify themselves as vegan are being drawn away from their focus. Here comes an announcement for a "Veg*n Climate March"—the event's title inching the word "vegan" back to a less specific vegetarian idea. It's understandable to see an attempt at all-inclusive friendliness for an environmentally important cause. But applying the term vegan with a letter blotted out, so that it becomes merely a short form of vegetarian, hides the crucial message: No animal products are environmentally beneficial. In scientific fact, (asterisk-free) veganism is the proven way to address the ecological effects of animal agribusiness, and we have very little time to address those effects. Figures applicable to the United States show that each person annually emits four tons of global warming gas (in carbon dioxide or its equivalent mix); vegans cut that by an impressive 1.5 tons.[4] Simply changing from some animal products to others won't do this. Fish production goes right up with the flesh of cows to top the list of highest possible all-around energy uses. And milk products are derived from ruminant animals, who emit high amounts of methane—an especially potent greenhouse gas.

It's important to prevent veganism from appearing as an optional variation within some apparently more popular position. Respecting the environment—just like respecting ethical principles—means more than cutting out steak and hamburgers. So the simple, powerful word *vegan* is more important than it's ever been. It already respects vegetarian ideals: Taken from the first and last letters of the word, it brings "vegetarian" to its logical conclusion. More than a diet, it's a focused commitment to social progress. As a result of a most impressive example of peaceful and effective direct action, it's now in every leading dictionary of the English language and a few other languages as well. Let's celebrate this word, enjoy using it, and appreciate the integrity and strength of the people who offered it to society.

From time to time, activists will ask me if there could be a way to get past the strife that plagues animal advocacy. They often follow up by suggesting that it's friendly and helpful to promote both animal rights and better conditions for animals owned by businesses, and ask if cage-free eggs could be a good step to support. Some feel if there isn't any meat visible, we should not be too picky. The Big Tent position seems reasonable to them. Here's why you might decide not to go there—and it's got nothing to do with liking strife. Should we accept all sorts of approaches, including campaigns for husbandry adjustments, as steps in the right direction, we'll wind up in campaigns that lack any public articulation of the goal, leaving vegans to shoulder that task alone. Industry advisors gain, because the animal-rights idea gets pushed aside as advocates sit down to business and give concession agreements their full and immediate attention. The activists who believe power comes from sitting down at the table may be reinforced as their membership rolls grow.[5] Then they boast about belonging to a "big" group, while the activist who takes the animal-rights message most to heart feels the outsider's frustration. When challenged as to whether changed caging or slaughter methods could ever really lead to respect for animals, the supporters of the "big" group call the conscientious objector's holdout stance divisive because, in effect, it's not the view of the majority of society. Well, let's face it: People who renounce dominion over other animals *are* outside the majority. There. Now we've said it.

Seen in this light, we regard a viable movement for a new ethic as having to resist the majority's hydraulic pull. A social movement works to gain dynamic contributors; yet it is not a popularity contest. The minority must work diligently to make its message available, and empower the public to make informed decisions. Expect part of that diligent work to involve *persuading potential compromisers to commit instead to conscientious objection.* Find allies. Talk to them about animal rights. Others might be working for state-of-the-art slaughter techniques or roomier sheds, but this will not raise the legal status of animals. It won't enable us or free-living animals to survive on this precious planet. But an environmental or vegetarian group that takes animal-rights concepts seriously can. The deadline for getting on board such an advocacy platform is now; an ethical and sustainable way of life is long overdue.

Maybe some animal advocates do enjoy strife, but that's not what veganism is about. Veganism is about acknowledging a responsibility. If we are not living according to the vegan principle and imparting to others this same principle, veganism doesn't exist. The people who coined the term "vegan" are no longer physically present, but the word and movement they introduced has become known worldwide through conferences and festivals; and today a university press office can, as the University of Chicago did, issue a release titled "Vegan Diets Healthier for Planet, People Than Meat Diets." Vegan cookbooks now abound; vegan restaurants have attracted top chefs. It's this *vegan tent* we need to keep expanding.

Objections will be many, and people will try to dilute the principles of veganism and even blur the word. We can expect all of this. Those original vegans also faced social pressure. By forming their organizational base for change, they weren't looking for strife, or being unrealistic or anti-social to the vegetarian movement. They were committed to seeking the best of the human potential; and they—barely two dozen people—activated it. Their example is now generally accepted by the animal-advocacy community as positive, without drawbacks of any sort, except that it's thought by some to be a slow approach. Although it might be slow, a lot of things are; and veganism is clearly advancing the position of animal rights. Donald Watson's simple approach to animal rights has been elaborated upon, yet never improved upon.

"If the vegan ideal of non-exploitation were generally adopted it would be the greatest peaceful revolution ever known," Watson said, "abolishing vast industries and establishing new ones" in the better interest of human and non-human animals alike.[6] The change Watson envisioned is revolutionary. Its proponents, to be true emancipators of other animals, would "renounce absolutely their traditional and conceited attitude that they had the right to use them to serve their needs."[7] This means relinquishing our self-appointed role as master over every animal.

No revolutionary idea appears, of course, without attracting people who'd like to blend it into something else. The advocacy sector's Big Tent prefers not to see veganism as a movement, instead referring to it as a "tool" for opposing the "horrors of factory farms and industrial slaughterhouses"— although veganism came not to challenge factory farms, but to challenge animal farms.

Admittedly, the vast scale of animal use and the ubiquity of animal products can be overwhelming. Anxiety, driven by the thought that assaults on animals won't end in our lifetimes, might lead us to ask whether pressing for industry reforms is the best we can do. Reforms or not, suffering isn't reduced when animals are unnecessarily bred or brought into an exploitive system.

A Summary, and a Note to Realists

To sum up the proposal of Part One of this book:

1. Peter Singer's advocacy model has no opinion on domination, and it would allow, perhaps even encourage, still more farm animals to be bred—grabbing space that could be freely enjoyed by animals already living in it. Follow Singer's reasoning to its conclusion to find a world that, in order to reduce pain, can accept even the concept of engineering animals without minds. We must search elsewhere to find guidance for genuine progress.

2. The abolition of property status is important, but animal-rights theory requires more. When human slavery is legally abolished, those held in bondage and their descendants do not disappear; they struggle for civil rights and equality. Non-human beings need a different paradigm. Meaningful rights for them would mean being spared from being brought into human society. This means we need a movement not only to abolish the classification of animal property (thereby ending the breeding of domesticated animals), but to enable untamed animals to exist and thrive independently of humanity's supervision. It is time for advocacy to take stock of all that our precursors in the movement have said and accomplished, to look at the environmental situation that faces the planet, and push the animal-rights question further.

3. The right of non-human animals to live on their terms and not ours conveys the point and the essence of animal-rights thinking.

4. If we can first conceive it, we can organize a movement to achieve it.

The paradigm shift: A note to realists

If one presents the vegan commitment as the answer to the world's most pressing problems, plenty of well-informed people will ask, "Come on, how can we possibly get up in the morning, with the human population growing daily by more than 211,000 people, wars everywhere, polar bears drowning, an extinction crisis, kids and dogs in the global south living in the streets and think this vegan stuff is going to work?" Good question. Recent studies of Greenland and Antarctica indicate widespread ice sheet loss is likely, if not inevitable. The acid in the oceans is beginning to burn the very shells off sea animals. We're now learning of climate change's choking effect on plants, as foliage becomes less able to absorb all the carbon pollution pumped out by human activity.

The symbolic Doomsday Clock, maintained since 1947 through the Bulletin of the Atomic Scientists to represent minutes to the midnight of our destruction, weighs threats posed by nuclear weapons, new developments in life sciences, and climate change. It was first set at seven minutes before midnight, and as of this writing is set at six to midnight. The clock can be, and has been, set back in time, too—in response to political decisions humans have made. The message? Human-induced global warming and war are no accidents. Nor are they foisted upon us by nature, fate, or God. They are the results of human decisions. As long as we're here, we can decide in new ways, and help offer that power to others—balancing our sober discussions with good news, enjoyable walks and teas and great recipes. A serious commitment can, and surely should, be accompanied by a sense of generosity and joy in being alive.

Cormac Cullinan, author of the book *Wild Law*, offers a sound reason to be optimistic about the future of human law and culture.[8] Proposing it's entirely possible to have ecologically respectful law, Cullinan reminds us of the *paradigm shift;* the term, as Thomas Kuhn introduced it in the 1960s, means a transformation in the scientific worldview. Usually, a paradigm shift provides a more coherent perspective than we had before, and this is well highlighted by the example Cullinan picks out: Before the Copernican revolution, everyone took for granted that Earth was central in the cosmos; everything revolved around us. When it became clear that our planet revolves around the sun, we ceased to be the focal point of creation. What had once seemed obvious and eternal was something else entirely: an error of the past. Humanity's perspective changed.

Likewise, the vegan principle challenges an old view that we're central and that everyone and everything revolves, eternally, around us. Environmentalists have discovered how incorrect the all-for-us view is, from a biological perspective. Earthworms and bees and other supposedly insignificant beings are now understood as enormously influential in the biocommunity. Meanwhile, vegan advocates, starting with Donald Watson, have shown that we cannot give animals some kind of moral rank; all are entitled to live on their own terms, bees and earthworms included.

Note that the Copernican revolution wasn't the result of change in increments to the old system. Although some communities understood the news sooner than others, no one was asked to accept that the sun was a little closer to the central point over time. Astronomy charts didn't show Earth moving gradually outward as new editions were printed. So let's not say, "Well, OK, start with eggs from hens who were given freedom of movement." Let's impart the direct truth today. We don't know the tipping point; it could be a small number of people who are working on a problem now, and the next generation could be the one for which everything falls into place.

No free-range continuum is necessary when each of us, and everyone we meet, has the power to commit to vegan principles right now. Nor is such a continuum even possible; to urge people to go from factory to free-range is to forget the reality that planet Earth's land is finite. The spread of pasture-based animal agribusiness uproots free-living animals and snuffs out their lives. It takes a complete paradigm shift to stop thinking of animals as objects and start thinking of humanity as contributors in an interconnected biocommunity. There is a bright-line psychological difference, and not a continuum, between accepting human dominion and rejecting it.

Vegans reject human dominion. Vegans strive to be living examples of people who arrive at animal rights today, by cultivating an attitude of respect for other animals and demonstrating that we can get our hands off them and still live. This means opposing their classification as property and also being mindful of their interest in their lives, communities, and futures on this planet free from our dominion. It's a radical idea; a paradigm shift is radical by definition. It will not happen overnight, and it will be met with resistance (Galileo's books were banned, and the great scientist was placed under house arrest for having accepted the position of Copernicus, which was deemed contrary to biblical authority). But the cultural shift, once the new paradigm is presented and acknowledged, is unstoppable.

When the idea of ourselves as—in Cormac Cullinan's words—the "master species" is understood as an untenable and destructive myth, it will be replaced. By learning to cook and to get involved in vegan-organic farming, many people are preparing for that shift today. It's true that each of them experiences a lifetime of striving, and is—at least at the beginning and possibly throughout life—a member of a minority group in a given place. For a vegan, there's a profound feeling of connection with life, yet a feeling of otherness within society, a lasting sort of non-citizenship. The animals we spare from a commodified life can't pat us on the back or give us a promotion for it. Committed vegans will tell others this truth, then create nurturing social environments where new vegans feel a sense of community, a sense of being in the majority. This will empower us to show others how to think in a new way. The change we cultivate could become apparent relatively quickly in society and the law, and that's good. By most indications, we have little time to spare.

PART TWO:

Enduring Freedom

CHAPTER 6

The Fall

Animal rights is about us all. It's about how we compete, compare, and dominate within *and* beyond humanity.

I learned about domination as a child. The first of us to show up on Earth, I heard, ruined things for just about every being on the planet when we tasted the knowledge of good and evil. After good and evil were pointed out, other dichotomies swiftly followed. They weren't subtle. Humanity was identified as the male and the female, the former to be served by the latter! Also present was an agent of the non-human world: a troublesome serpent. Here is the pivotal passage in Genesis:

> The Lord God said to the serpent, "Because you did this, More cursed shall you be Than all cattle And all the wild beasts: On your belly shall you crawl And dirt shall you eat All the days of your life. I will put enmity Between you and the woman, And between your offspring and hers; They shall strike at your head, And you shall strike their heel"…And to the woman He said, "I will make most severe your pangs in childbearing; In pain shall you bear children. Yet your urge shall be for your husband, And he shall rule over you."

Adam and Eve received leather clothes after it occurred to them to be ashamed of their bodies. Nature knows no indecencies, to paraphrase Mark Twain; we invent them. And the longing to return to the simpler, decent days must have led to the prophecy popularized in art and literature as the Peaceable Kingdom. It sounds like the perfect redemption. Yet it situates peace within a kingdom, and the word, although it's used a lot to mean some general category, suggests yet another hierarchy with a male potentate at the pinnacle. Under this rule, oddly enough, the wolf lives with the lamb, and the leopard lies down with the kid. Risky animals become tame—although this would mean, on the real Earth, obligate carnivores would have to starve to live up to the human ideal.

Having expected the carnivores to cease meeting their needs, humans themselves could, presumably, still slaughter and eat the herbivores; for here we see calf, lion and fatling—an animal fattened for slaughter. And a little child leading them. Thus, this supremely conflicted ideal is wrapped in the fantasy of the smallest human beings in charge of the earth's most formidable animals.

Eden's story can be interpreted in various ways. It could be a challenge to our propensity to detach and oppress, lest we lose forever our real potential, and repeat injustices in multilayered manners, like people walking through halls of mirrors. The construction of opposing categories—human and animal; male and female; reason and nature; native and alien; good and evil—and the building of borders, century after century, defy infinite messages from the natural world that all is interwoven, overlapping, interdependent, subject to the same seasons, threats, and needs. Yet to many of us, the Eden story was delivered as an eternal truth rather than a social commentary about regarding humanity as separated into two distinct classes, with one as the other's rightful master. *Yet your urge shall be for your husband, And he shall rule over you.*

"Explaining the subordination of women to men, a political condition, has nothing to do with difference in any fundamental sense," writes Catharine MacKinnon,[1] who describes the concept of species hierarchy in parallel terms:

> The hierarchy of people over animals is not seen as imposed by humans because it is seen as due to animals' innate inferiority by nature. In the case of men over women, it is either said that there is no inequality there, because the sexes are different, or the inequality is conceded but said to be justified by the sex difference, that is, women's innate inferiority by nature.[2]

Alice Walker has included yet another layer of hierarchy in the analysis, connecting pornography with generations of violence against slave women, describing pornography that treats African-American women as other-than-human, fit to be conquered and made into commodities.[3] Zora Neale Hurston wrote of the "pet Negro" system in which some early twentieth-century elites in the southern United States customarily singled out certain human workers for special gifts and privileges, employment opportunities and scholarships, which complicated race-based inequality and lent it the stability of interdependence, Hurston explained, "and a lot of black folk, I'm afraid, might find it cosy."[4]

This is not easy stuff to contemplate. But the potential of the animal-rights movement hinges on our motivation to visit the deep level at which all oppressions connect, from whence they spawn social injustice, environmental injustice, and the degradation of the ecology and living beings. This is not to say that various groups are the same, or that the kind of inequality they've faced is the same. And as we've seen, the animal-rights argument can't be precisely likened to the movements that enable people to reach their individual potential within a global society.

Animal rights involves freedom from, rather than equality within, a global human society. This means theoretical work is needed to distinguish groups of animals whose existence results from selective breeding (those, that is, who must rely on the care ethic as long as they are here) and those who could flourish on their own terms. To date, with animal rights usually defined as regarding all animals *en masse*, people rarely note that animal rights is not an all-purpose concept. Advocates elide and confuse the needs of selectively bred animals and free-living animals by applying an animal-control model to beings in their natural habitat: for example, by trying to impose birth control on free-roaming horses, bison, deer, or birds.

Conversely, animal advocates have regarded domesticated or captive-raised animals as though animal rights could be meaningfully applied to their situations. This is in evidence when advocates debate whether pets should have the "right" to roam free. A wildcat in a natural setting could be discussed in terms of autonomy unproblematically. But the encouragement of risk as a right is questionable insofar as we have moved animals beyond their natural habitats to serve our purposes, and (through domestication) compromised their ability to cope with that risk.

The popular media can portray animals' dependence as enviable. In a *Christian Science Monitor* article, a group of researchers proclaimed dogs brighter than their free-living ancestors, the wolves. The experimenters tested the abilities of dogs in their natural environment, which, they explain, is the human environment. Their findings suggest that dogs, unlike wolves, have acquired an innate motivation to co-operate with and behave like humans, and make good cognitive study subjects.[5]

And their undomesticated counterparts? Wolves, beings who pay attention to the demands of their own communities, not ours, are vilified for existing anywhere in the proximity of human society, no matter that they can hardly find secluded spaces. In Britain, these gifted survivors of the ice age now exist only behind secure fences; nearly everywhere, their populations are scant, while our domesticated dogs number in the hundreds of millions.

Yi-Fu Tuan has written of 'the human need to associate with animals and to do so on the principles of domination and control, in Eden and in practical life':

> The dream that ferocious animals, on the approach of man, would kneel in docility and thus be a fit companion in a perfect world may be among the most vainglorious of human aspirations. It is not confined to Western culture. Evidences of it appear in other high cultures as well. Wherever man envisages a perfect world, elements of this dream occur and recur. Attempts to translate the dream into reality encounter the problem of how animals can be brought into the garden and made to seem a natural and integral part of it.[6]

The untamed animal cannot gain admittance. Such an individual is viewed as a competitor to subdue, and this has gradually resulted in elimination of animals who would threaten us, and the production of others who will accommodate our desires. Domestication has simply become so customary that few people question it, and most extol it. We speak admiringly of the good shepherd, whom we associate with peace on Earth, all the time neglecting to consider what ultimately happens to the shepherd's flock.

Hard questions would come from a social movement that interrogates our customs of ordering animals, whether they be perceived as food, service providers, guards, or pets. This movement would not begrudge free-living animals their liberty. This approach would certainly present risks; yet it would ultimately safeguard life on Earth—including human life. To observe how our habitual acceptance of the disappearance of untamed life is already backfiring on us, we need simply note how worldwide bee disappearances impact the pollination of plants, including crops. Turns out we are co-workers on this planet, ourselves and the bees and everyone else.

Dominion and defiance

Regarding "the Judeo-Christian idea that human beings have been given dominion over animals," Martha Nussbaum observes: "Although that idea has been interpreted in a variety of ways, it has standardly been understood to give humans licence to do whatever they like to non-human species and to use them for human purposes."[7] Surely, the idea of divinely prescribed dominion over other animals, whether interpreted as stewardship or domination, brings the same results. Often, a particular use of an animal will be blended with scientific authority and assurances that the use involves benign stewardship.

Two Sumatran orang-utans at Zoo Atlanta are trained to play computer games. While the apes win food pellets, researchers at the zoo and Atlanta's Center for Behavioral Neuroscience receive data about their mental responses. "The best part," *CNN* reveals: "Zoo visitors get to watch their every move."[8] Zoo officials say the exhibit will raise awareness about the free orang-utan population, which could disappear in the next decade. In something eerily like a first step in domestication, researchers hope to

teach the free-living orang-utans in Indonesia new eating habits and ways
of finding food. Evidently, zoo experts in the United States—the world's
largest importer and consumer of wood products—believe training orang-
utans to relinquish their own knowledge, habits and traditions is preferred
over training humans to stop usurping their habitat for ourselves and all
the animals we breed into our service.

In a time of unprecedented extinction levels, is it possible to talk of
civilizing animals to death as well as the outright loss of species? Increasingly,
animal commodities are allowed to stay, while animals who aren't amenable
to playing a role within our society are hooked off the world stage. Animals
are also killed off when perceived as dangerous to human individuals
or communities. Bears, coyotes, and big cats all present risk, and have
frequently been tracked with radio collars, and if any of them do harm
humans, they are often hunted down and killed with something that looks
very much like punishment or vengeance. As noted in this book's third
chapter, a few years ago in the western United States, a radio-collared cougar
paused to look at a camper before moving on. Not only was the cat killed,
but the agents brought the head to the scientist who had been studying the
cat.[9] In Golden Gate Park in the hot summer of 2007 a pair of coyotes were
seen, appearing protective, although no one had found out why. When they
followed a dog walker in the park, and injured a dog on a lead, California
officials decided to shoot them. And earlier in the summer, after a child
was dragged from a tent in Utah and killed, wildlife officers with 26 dogs
tracked down, shot, and finally, hours later, caught and killed a black bear.
In late 2007, a four-year-old Siberian tiger was killed after escaping from
an enclosure and killing a visitor at the San Francisco Zoo. These animals
have all committed crimes against human dominion. Geese or deer might
become mildly nettlesome—defecating on golf courses, eating flowers and
standing in the roads—and are thus somewhat haphazardly controlled—
although management might become systematic with innovations such as
attaching GPS tracking mechanisms to deer.

For all our scientific knowledge, humans see ourselves as impossibly special, above biological connections with other life, members of a deceptively insular category. What should advocates' response be? There's a teaching role here, a need for a message that we can and ought to share the planet's finite space with other beings, beings whose own experiences of the world matter. A risk-free planet is not the creation of peace; it is, instead, the imposition of bland landscapes and an artificial sense of order.

Yes, we still see human groups treating *each other* as unacceptable risks; we are still warring over territory amongst ourselves. Arguably, our habit of ranking oppressions has kept justice movements from supporting one another in ways that could better address the harms faced by all oppressed groups. For those beings, human or not, who are perceived as lacking personhood, the harms include harassment, physical assault, even death.

We need a vocabulary enabling us to discuss beings without in every case resorting to the duality of 'human and animal' or even human and non-human. After all, where do we really mark the species boundary? Dolphins have tiny, leg-like limb buds during their earliest weeks in the womb, suggesting an overlap in the traits that separate sea animals from land mammals.[10] The whole concept of evolution indicates that some species develop from others. Thus the term *chronospecies*, referring to various stages in living communities as they adapt through time. And then there are the *ring species*—some salamanders and birds, for example, living in various places, forming a continuum of slight differences all along their range, so that they can interbreed with those next to them, but not with those further along the geographic continuum. Has the notion of the firm boundary between Us and Them helped us construct a group of our own that's rationalized a fantasy: a human prerogative to classify, command, and own all others?

The class warfare waged in this context dates back some 50,000 years, to the time our ancestors moved outside their equatorial lands, armed with blades and harpoons. Humanity's development into a weapon-wielding culture has fashioned our current social structure, and all its pressure to equate domination with success. Our schoolbooks are full of action figures who overwhelm the terrain, its inhabitants, and history itself. As for other animals, today they are objects of a dominion so complete we rarely think of ourselves as vanquishers even as we consume them. Laws constructed by and for the people refer to other animals as natural resources, scientific models, pets, food or entertainment, systematically erasing their own interests and experiences.

Our laws emphasize social control as well as species control, and we ourselves lack even the simple right to move freely across our own earthly habitat. In our quest to protect ourselves and control others, we have covered imaginary borders with real security systems and heaps of corrugated metal, which drive real bodies to attempt escapes, to collapse, and to expire.

Perceived race and national origin have kept various people classified as less than constitutional persons for centuries now—a reality with which the animal-advocacy movement has generally not concerned itself. When lawmakers authorized a 700-mile fence building project along the U.S.-Mexican border, the advocacy group Defenders of Wildlife recommended "high-tech surveillance and communications equipment, enforcement and conservation training for border security and land management personnel, and strategically placed vehicle barriers and fencing where it will be more effective"—but not where it would imperil jaguars and desert bighorn sheep.[11] Were this group and its allies clear about why all lives matter, including the lives of desperate workers and their children, a law poised to severely disrupt habitat would not have been so easily enacted. It's somewhat absurd to think that animals, even those at the brink of extinction, will be respected by a humanity that's so willing to imprison or exclude its own members.

A cruelty-free world?

Our message—that we can and ought to share the planet's finite space with other animals—involves taking a new look at environmental protection. This is basic. Who is going to benefit from animal rights if habitat is not protected so animals have the means to thrive?

Some advocates hear of animals on the brink of extinction and assume efforts to protect endangered communities in their natural habitats will be futile.[12] Some are still insisting that protection of the ecology or biodiversity fails to advance animal rights. And some just seem to think nature isn't very nice. Conceiving the natural world as pitted against many animals' interests, they'd like biologists to devise ways of reducing overall suffering in natural habitats as well as in captivity.[13] They say that challenging species bias would mean intervening to stop some animals from becoming the prey of others—in effect, arguing for transforming all animals into vegetarians. Is this the animal-advocacy movement's Isaiah prophecy, its Peaceable Kingdom? Yes, as it turns out.

In "Reprogramming Predators (Blueprint for a Cruelty-Free World)," utilitarian philosopher David Pearce discusses "the problem of predation" and decides science can deliver a replacement: a "global anti-speciesist ethic to complement an anti-racist ethic". As for the large carnivores, Pearce asks: "Should these serial killers be permitted to prey on other sentient beings indefinitely?" When predators are eliminated (either by extinction or genetic engineering), Pearce proposes, buffalo and zebras would be managed with contraception technologies in wildlife parks. "On almost *every* future scenario, we're destined to play God," says Pearce. "So let's aim to be compassionate gods and replace the cruelty of Darwinian life with something better."[14] Here's the stewardship concept brought to its absurd conclusion. Richard Twine, of Lancaster and Cardiff Universities' collaborative Centre for Economic and Social Aspects of Genomics, does not think David Pearce's position has credibility. "It's a publicity-seeking position, one that discredits veganism overall," Twine asserts. "To disavow all predation (instead of targeting the notion that humans 'by their very nature' must kill animals) is not really an ecologically sustainable position, and is guilty of projecting a falsely painless, edenic perspective onto the rest of nature."[15]

It's a fact of life on Earth as well as a strain on the advocate's emotions that the world's animals often have short, stressful lives. Tom Regan acknowledges: "When it comes to interspecies relations, nature *is* red in tooth and claw."[16] Regan's *Case for Animal Rights* firmly states that the rights view does not, however, urge us to control others; instead, it obliges us to let other animals carve out their own destiny. Animal rights does not boil down to pain relief, and the call to control the lions and bobcats from doing what they do to live shows that at the most striking level. We humans *can* refrain from killing others; and we've developed and can spread the ethic of non-violence. But forcing other animals, including obligate carnivores, to subscribe to vegetarianism would bring no challenge to our dominion and control over other animals; instead, once again, it would prescribe a stewardship model for exerting it.

Meanwhile, back in the present world, this idea that dominion is animal-friendly if it's described as *benign* control leads to substantial overlap between (a) activists and (b) the corporations that sell animals or government agencies that control them as resources. A few examples:

- **Pet shop breeder pledges.** A well-known humane advocacy group asks pet shops to sign a pledge not to buy animals from high-volume wholesalers (knows as "puppy mills" or "puppy farms"). The logical implication is that some breeding methods are not acceptable, but some are. The advocacy group thereby makes it clear that dominion won't be challenged if it's done according to the group's rules. Most people, including most advocates, accept these terms. Should they?
- **Roundups of horses in North America.** Free-roaming horses and burros are routinely chased down and taken from their land, often because ranchers want any land and water sources on which these untamed animals still survive. When the horses are slaughtered, activists protest. Instead of steadfastly insisting that the federal government protect the autonomy of these horses, and their access to the lands and waters they use, the horses' advocates have, at times, helped to promote

roundups and privatization of these horses through "adoption" plans, or encouraged the government to make them disappear in a still more insidious way: by sterilizing them. Controlling the horse population to avoid slaughter is purportedly humane dominion, or stewardship. Most people, including a substantial segment of the advocacy community, have accepted these terms. Should they?

■ **Predator control.** The few remaining wolf, coyote and bear communities of the Americas are under incessant attack by humans in their midst. In the case of these animals, too, some advocates—animal-rights theorists included—have recommended removal or pharmaceutical birth control, claiming it's a practical, non-lethal way to manage free-living animals and less harsh than outright gunning. That claim is highly dubious, but advocates present it, calling it a humane alternative. Should they?

The Humane Society of the United States sponsors tests of experimental contraceptives on free-roaming horses and other animals. Were the subjects of such projects members of human populations (whether deemed native, invasive, or naturalized), questions would be asked about the rights of the communities being managed. Regarding free-living animals under reproductive control, however, the debate has barely emerged.

What has our stewardship done for the planet so far? Within the past century we have aggravated the causes of extinction, torn rainforests apart, and planted vast monocultures. We have polluted the air, water, and ground. We have developed chemical and nuclear warfare, and disrupted climate patterns. In an era of climate change, advancing new ways to think about animal advocacy matters intensely. This could, for the first time, empower us to become genuine moral actors on the ecological stage. And a better development of our discourse could well be what keeps that stage from falling apart.

CHAPTER 7

Barking Up
The Wrong Tree

Guinness had been given to the child of one of my airline co-workers. Marion's parents had not been asked whether their child could be given a kitten. On Marion's twelfth birthday, many months of carefully saved allowance money turned into cat food, a ball, and a litter box. All in vain. The child was given ten days to place the kitten, who'd be otherwise sent to the local pound. Dad meant it. Mother posted flyers at work.

I hadn't seen this kitten, but had my own childhood memories. It hurt to think of the child and the kitten and a tragedy so unfair, the kind that can't be undone. After a week of searching and asking co-workers and friends and friends' parents, I found Shelby—a lovely person who agreed to take the kitten. Alas! Shelby just then happened to receive approval for a long-pending request to work in another city, and decided not to adopt the kitten after all. On the tenth day, I went to Marion's home to get Guinness, an athletic and bright-faced being with grey fur, swirl designs on each side.

Once I'd taken the plunge, and become involved in surgeries and pet supplies, it was a bit easier to take in more cats. The rest arrived in worse circumstances than Guinness had: street-dwellers, all of them. Several had seen their family members deliberately killed. One arrived partly crushed by a car or other object, and underwent multiple surgeries—that is, after waiting several days as I frantically searched for a bone specialist who would work on a feral cat. All have found a loving caregiver. All had relatives much less fortunate.

Many people take in animals until it's impossible to take more without compromising the well-being of the earlier arrivals, or their personal ability to function at work, or the tolerance of their human partners. They make decisions on a fairly regular basis that look something like the lifeboat dilemma. All because we adopted the custom of petkeeping. An offshoot of agricultural domestication that relied on surplus wealth, it began as landowners bred more animals than they meant to consume. Yi-Fu Tuan describes petkeeping as a mark of affluence:

Seemingly far more genteel [than the hunt] is another quintessential activity of high culture, namely, breeding animals so that they turn into playthings and aesthetic objects. This activity presupposes an order of material abundance such that animals no longer need be seen as potential food, or even as sacrificial victims in rituals that have the promotion of fertility as their aim. It speaks of leisure and skill, and the desire on the part of those thus endowed to manipulate the reproductive processes of animals so that they turn into creatures of a shape and habit that please their owners.[1]

Over the past two hundred years, this hobby of the affluent has turned into a high-volume industry. Selectively bred cats, rabbits and other animals are considered commodities, and, as with most commodities, the number of each type produced does not precisely match the demand. We talk of pet *over*population as though some magic number of pets could be bred to perfectly fit the number of people interested in caring for them. Those who are killed are never fully counted, but number in the millions each year. The animals may be, and sometimes are, discarded for any number of reasons. The puppy's holiday-gift newness has worn off; the child has grown up and moved away; the dog barks too much; the cat scratches a chair; the rabbit has a digestion problem and an unexpected veterinary cost is projected.

People may say their pets run the house and exert power in various ways. Their true power, however, is thwarted by hard realities. These animals do not get to choose their mates. Pet animals have no say, ever, regarding the others with whom they'll spend their days, and where, or what happens if circumstances in the home change and someone finds their presence troublesome, in which case their time could suddenly be up. The pets who would rebel and seriously threaten their owners or the owners' children are generally eliminated. Some dogs are played with and walked proudly as babies, then pushed outside the back door and left there, like old tools. Some pet animals never really become pets; that is, they don't live in homes at all. A few are used for breeding or kept as blood donors for their more fortunate counterparts, and a good many are used in research.

Alex the counting parrot was bought in a pet shop like many others. But Alex became a minor celebrity. The African Grey parrot, who, by luck of the draw, would live and die in a psychology lab at Brandeis University, was described in *USA Today as* "the rock star of the parrot world who dominated [the researcher's] lab and her life for 30 years." But, just like a lot of unknown pet birds, Alex was kept inside a cage in a very small room. One observer began describing the bleak experience of meeting Alex for a magazine story this way:

> [University lab workers] Olga and Arlene warn me not to expect much because Alex has been off his game lately. They tell me he knows it's the end of year, and he's getting depressed about that. He's been known to pluck half his feathers out after the party. I take a seat in Arlene's chair by the door while Alex gets ready to sing for his supper. They gather up some of Alex's teaching tools and bring him out of his cage and onto a wooden perch. Almost immediately Alex starts squawking, 'Wanna go back, wanna go back.' 'Wanna go back' means he wants to end the session and go back to his cage.[2]

Then there's biomedical testing, the kind that involves infections or experimental surgeries. Animals typically thought of as pets—birds, rabbits, dogs and cats—are used in laboratories, along with primates, mice, rats, farm animals, fish, and so on. Some animals are collected from pounds; many more are purpose-bred for the lab. The website of Marshall BioResources, a New York company that delivers beagles internationally, touts a happy lab dog, claiming that the "proprietary socialization process" of the Marshall Beagle "yields a dog that is active and happy while in the cage, comes willingly to the front when approached, and is calm and pleasant when handled."

Other animals become guard dogs, dropped off each night in grease-spattered car parks surrounded by barbed wire; an evasive few are left behind bushes, under buildings, and in junkyards, looking for sustenance on a hostile landscape. Refugees from the pet trade are forever out of place. Dependence is bred into domestic cats, who, on their own, typically depend on bins where we discard food. For unsterilized cats, the biologically and socially stressful cycle of procreation is stepped up and usually begins at less than six months of age. For caged birds, escape is normally fatal. About twice during the course of each summer, I'll see along my jogging route a series of hand-made signs imploring for the return of Omar, a cockatoo, or a lost small, green parrot, or some other little escapee who sampled a bit of freedom, alone, in a climate that will soon turn cold. Escapee birds who manage to find each other and carve out a life on utility poles, and even become naturalized in certain biocommunities—as monk parakeets have done in Connecticut and New York and a few other places far north of their native ranges—are subject to poisons, trucks deployed to gas them, or repellents that sicken them.

Humanity has convinced itself that pet ownership is an example of our appreciation for the animal world. Many people refuse to call themselves owners and won't call pets their property. But softer language does not challenge the concept—as retailers have been known to advertise it—of love for sale. So if the discussion on this page seems unusual to your eyes, it is. Petkeeping has largely escaped critique even in advocacy circles. Animal-protectionists can be seen working to impose rules on high-volume pet dealers, while supplying advice on how to find responsible breeders. (And responsible they are—for the unremitting pressure felt by many a rescuer!) Advocates often talk of "companion animals" and their special place in our lives, but does it advance respect to refer to pets as our animal companions? Or does that term carry a subtle message, not altogether fair and accurate, that these beings entered our personal lives through a mutual arrangement? The Collins dictionary defines companion as a "mate, fellow, comrade, associate." Does that honestly describe animals bred as pets, when in reality the human decides whether to accept a specific domesticated animal into the household? Collins gives a second definition: "person employed to live with another." The dog or cat does "live with another" but cannot make independent decisions as employees usually do. Even a beloved pet is still unfree, and does not seem to fit either classic definition of companionship.

Were we to agree that selectively breeding cats, dogs, rabbits and other animals compromises their dignity, could we then resolve to ask our culture to kick the domestication habit? We know many pets are dearly loved. But our personal feeling for our pets doesn't undo the reality that petkeeping requires other animals to submit to us. We can allow the animals in our homes plenty of leeway, but we, not they, decide just how much freedom they have. So, at the same time as we love them for who they are, we can challenge *what* they are as a collective, and ask why we humans developed whole categories of beings deliberately made vulnerable to us—to any human who wants to breed or buy them. Questioning the custom of petkeeping guides us to ask about other animals' true natures, rather than the natures we've imposed on them.

Vegan advocacy groups don't condone the custom of breeding animals to be pets, although these groups do recognize that their supporters open their homes to animals who are already born. And they understand vegans might therefore be in the position of looking after carnivorous animals and thus be tied to businesses from which we would otherwise be disconnected. Particularly difficult is the question faced by sanctuaries that take in abandoned carnivores. In a typical day, the Exotic Feline Rescue Center, a refuge for captive tigers, ocelots, and other big cats, will process and distribute 3,000 pounds of animal flesh to the cats.[3] Flies are burnt to death in large traps. The cats will be captive all their lives, relying on support from people who pay an admission fee or stay at the guesthouse or attend charity auctions. The cats can't live in their own ways in Indiana, so they're neutered, like domestic cats. When I reviewed the group's website in early 2009, many of the names of the resident tigers and leopards resembled names given to pet animals: Tigger Boy and Tuffy, Cuddles and Sassy. A magnet in the online gift shop had this caption:

> If you've ever been to the rescue center, than chances are pretty good that you have heard of Max. He is, without a doubt, the cutest and sweetest tiger I know! Too bad, he keeps on growing. We have put his cute baby face on our car ribbon magnet to promote the center.

The refuge, while surely well-meaning, seems zoo-like in its willingness to attract support by advertising the babyhood or vulnerability of its residents.

Rights versus dependence, revisited

It's consistent with the animal-rights view to look after animals who must rely on us, either because they are domesticated or because they're captive, denied the chance to forge bonds with their communities and learn the skills they would need in their habitats. These animals are refugees from human institutions, and it would be unjust to ignore their needs. Their welfare should be defended; that's why the animal-rights advocate champions no-kill shelters and refuges, financially and otherwise supporting their capacity for caregiving.

Today, pounds kill animals if a disease is believed to exist in the system, or simply to make room for more cast-off animals. Worse still, popular advocacy condones, promotes, and even carries out killing. A person in the United States who decides to get a job advancing the interests of other animals might receive an offer to work with a trainer who teaches killing techniques. Are you prepared to *kill* animals?

Killing is one of those things that the advocacy community was formed to stop. Yet two animal-charity employees were sent to North Carolina in a van stocked with sodium pentobarbital, where they killed dogs and cats, puppies and kittens and then tossed their bodies into refuse bins behind a Piggly Wiggly store, in a case that riveted the U.S. media in the summer of 2005. The bodies of cats and dogs had been found dumped on the same days the employees collected animals from shelters.[4] One of the employees was a 24-year-old trainee. Dead animals were found week after week. The 19th of May. The 2nd of June. The 9th of June. The 15th of June. A total of 92 dead cats, kittens, dogs and puppies before the two employees were taken into custody. At a press conference to respond to the coverage of the cruelty charges, the group's president didn't condone dumping bodies into a parking lot waste bin, but nevertheless felt it appropriate to proclaim that "euthanasia is the kindest gift to a dog or cat unwanted and unloved" and that for many animals, it is "the only loving touch they have ever felt."[5] Of course, the dead do not suffer. But neither do they get a chance to do anything else.

With the exception of the way they disposed of the animals' bodies, the two employees were following a policy of systematic killing put into place by the president of a non-profit which annually facilitates the demise of thousands of animals.[6] Why did these advocates agree to an assignment that involved them in killing, for example, a mother cat with kittens, who had been cleared for adoption by the shelter's veterinarian? Nothing speaks more clearly about the failings of the animal-charity sector than the activists' acceptance of killing as fitting into the advocacy framework. One doesn't claim to advance human refugees' rights and then go and "clean up" a crowded refugee camp by killing off the migrants there, no matter how supposedly humane the killing method is.[7] Yet homeless dogs and cats are refugees—from the system that subjects them, by the millions, to our whims. And when we see a great bulk of the animal-advocacy community agreeing to call this practice euthanasia, how can this be explained? Advocates are told it's the reduction of suffering—that animals will have a worse death if they don't personally do the killing. Will our culture's perception of non-human beings as replaceable commodities change if *advocates* believe they must kill?

We must not kill. If a significant number of people in various communities refuse to go along, and concerted opposition to killing arises, pressure will be put on the beginning point of the pipeline; that is, breeders will have to stop plying their trade. The day pounds and non-profit groups refuse to kill dependent animals, but insist on having the resources to properly care for them, will be the day adoptions of existing animals become a top priority, and towns will learn they've run out of room for breeders and traders to set up shop. That will be the day the exploitive businesses can best be challenged. The movement has begun to arise in places such as South Lake Tahoe, California, where rescuers have pressed for a ban against retail sales of pets. That's not a ban on all pet breeding operations, but it lays the groundwork. "I'm happy when some animal-control group or pound has the courage and decency to become open-door and no-kill," says Ellie Maldonado, an activist in New York City. But to cultivate a society that refuses to kill systematically, we'd need to phase out breeding, says Ellie. "Killing will always be the other side of breeding, and that's a reason to reject petkeeping entirely."

Some advocates instead want to transform domesticated animals into rights-holders. The *News & Observer* of Raleigh, North Carolina published an article in March 2008 with the headline "New Class of Hairy Lawsuits Asserts Pets' Rights."[8] "Once considered mere property," proclaimed the article, "animals are being invested with legal standing as they're increasingly being named as partial beneficiaries of estates, subjects of lawsuits and victims of abuse." Part of the push has come from animals' rise in prominence in people's lives, the article explains, with people "routinely spending thousands of dollars to give a cat chemotherapy and sending dogs to day care, therapists and groomers." A Duke University law professor is cited as saying animal law disputes revolve around questions about the inherent rights of animals.[9] But only domesticated animals are mentioned in the article, and to be domesticated by another species is to be under control. So caring for a dog is not, in itself, about animal-rights theory. The idea of a pet with rights is an oxymoron. Of course the animals in our homes, like all conscious beings, have moral significance; they have interests in their lives, their relationships, and their futures. They have personalities. But the *case for animal rights* would be made on behalf of any animals who could, if not captured and used, live their lives on their own terms.

Perhaps the most frank—and frankly troubling—view of pets appears in a book called *Dominion: The Power of Man, the Suffering of Animals, and the Call to Mercy.* Author Matthew Scully insists on the correctness of our authority over other animals: "It is our fellow creatures' lot in the universe, the place assigned to them in creation, to be completely at our mercy, the fiercest wolf or tiger defenseless against the most cowardly man."[10] The fierce wolf and wildcat are precisely the animals we have subdued and fashioned into pets. Having summarily demoted these once-autonomous animals, Scully deems the term *pet* "exactly right in capturing the creatures' utter reliance on our good will, and indeed their sheer, delightful uselessness apart from mutual affection." Scully sees pets' dependence as "the whole point, the fun of it."[11]

Let's take a close look at Scully's claim. Is it fun to be expected to mate at the whim of others, or to be taken away from one's siblings and mother at birth to an unknown destiny? Not long ago, a New Jersey resident was found after having been trapped for nearly three winter days in the parking garage of the home, warmed only by a space heater because this person's cocker spaniel lived there. It wouldn't be much fun to live alone in a parking spot. But it's legal—or if it's not, you can bet no one will know unless the dog's owner gets into a fluke situation and a news story is done. Moreover, the habit of pet owning certainly connects with humanity's domination of these same animals in other ways, such as having them do work for us.

And what about the process of domestication itself? Is it fun to be a Peke-faced Persian, whose eyes and sinuses may be so deformed that they require antibiotics for life? Many breeds of dogs, cats, and rabbits have serious health concerns, and the extreme cases are examples of what is routinely permitted once we accept domestication. But people who see us and our relationships from a profit-based perspective aren't talking about that. The American Pet Products Association says U.S. residents now spend more than $40 billion annually for live animals, pet care and boarding services—not to mention pet food, much of which constitutes yet more profit for animal agribusiness. The malls where pets are bought and sold have replaced land that once belonged to free wolves and wildcats. Were there ever a case of cultural cognitive dissonance, this is it. We're using benign terms like "companion" for the beings whose fates hinge on the character of the person who happens to walk in that week with a pen and credit card. This doesn't make us a fun-loving species. It might provide opportunities for children to learn to care for a living being, but at the same time, it makes us forget about a deeper justice, a deeper way of caring, and fairer ways of having fun.

Another confusing idea where domesticated animals are concerned involves the "farm animal rights movement." One is introduced to this concept as activists send e-mailed alerts declaring, "Of all the animals in the United States facing cruelty and exploitation, those raised and slaughtered for food make up the vast majority." To help the largest number of animals, we're told, we must get involved in farm animal advocacy. That calculus leaves out vital factors—such as other animals, the ones who for so long lived in their own ways, who get pushed off the land for these farm businesses. There are more *whole communities* of animals being wiped out in the United States today than within any other country's borders.[12] Do these vast disappearing communities of animals, made up of innumerable individuals who are doing their best to survive around us and go about their lives, just not count?

Perhaps we'll be told there's already an environmental movement focusing on free-living animals. In reality, however, environmentalists rarely see non-human beings as appropriate rights-holders. That's a key reason environmental laws so often miss animals' interests, and are so weak and easily repealed. It's a lot easier to make loopholes for mansions, resorts, roads and farms if animals are just part of the landscape, rather than understood as conscious beings in their own right, living beings with individual personalities, aware beings to whom that landscape is home. How can free-living animals ever have a chance if we may create property rights in the lands on which they live, and they are not seen by us as having any such protections at all? As we widen our roadways and expand our shopping malls, how on Earth can they live?

Untamed activism

Dominion author Matthew Scully does not shy away from exposing and questioning harsh treatment of animals, and yet decides that the tame animal is "the most natural of all, displaying qualities hidden within its own nature that only human kindness can elicit."[13] We humans have a tendency to repackage domination as kindness as well as progress. In a parallel fashion, many writers and activists view animals used for therapy, or parrots who can count, as displaying the best in other animals, inspiring advocacy.[14] Rare is the writer who will ask us to pause to examine the reality that tame animals are everywhere enlisted in the most arduous, most dangerous work. Or ask us to consider what happens to dependent animals when people must struggle to feed themselves—the case with about a third of the world's human population. Attorneys specializing in animal law, one New York City paper reported, say they focus on one of the "noble tenets of their profession—representing and protecting the most vulnerable."[15] The vegan principle asks us to do something else, something quite daring: to imagine a world in which humans stop breeding vulnerable, tradable animals onto the planet. The vegan's expectations are optimistic, necessary, inspiring—revolutionary.

The financially well-off segments of human society are now outnumbered about four-to-one by the animals we breed to eat, and we spend billions annually on pets. We lose sight of autonomous animals. We need to readjust the focus. When reporters discuss what they call animal-rights issues, they're usually considering animals who can never have rights at all. Chickens used as restaurant meals, for example, or beagles in labs. When animal-law theorists write and speak, they usually do the same thing, advocating better rules for zoos, farms or pets with a frequency that's surprising once we stop to notice the phenomenon.

One student at a Washington, D.C. law school wrote on a blog about how we "might conceptualize the potential rights of companion animals" and decided that, because humans have bred such animals to depend on humans, we should have a corresponding duty to treat them as legal dependents. The blog entry offers an example of what this would mean: a dog would have a "right" to a daily walk.[16] The student likens this to the situation of children, who have needs and a corresponding right to have those needs met. But the comparison doesn't really work. Children are not bred to be commodities; children are rarely locked in or chained to a house. Most of those who endure maltreatment, thank goodness, have a chance of being heard and helped by teachers or others in the community. Eventually, children grow out of dependency on their caregivers. The blog entry also posits a right not to be sold or forcibly bred—which would end pet shops. "If a person wanted a pet," the entry adds, "there will always be 'unwanted' dogs, cats, and other animals who can be adopted." If there will always be such animals, and they will always be in homes, of course they will still be associating only with those who own those homes, and if they reproduce, it would only be with the animals chosen for them. Bottom line: They will still be dominated. (And is it reasonable to think no one will still be making a profit off of such a situation?)

"Again," the blog goes on, "this system would require serious monitoring. It would also require the standards to be set by people who actually have the animals' real needs in mind, rather than by people who are more concerned about the convenience of the animal's human caretaker." Despite the language of rights, this scenario is another form of regulation. It does not go to the root of the problem: the human entitlement to have and to hold other animals, to keep them tame, and thus forever vulnerable.

From time to time, humane charities, co-workers and friends tell us horrific stories of abuse of dogs. There's an Internet group called *I Love Oogy*. It's open on a popular social networking site for anyone to join. Should you receive an invitation, you'll see a white face, barely a dog's. A head slanted down in an odd angle, one ear missing, one eye lower than the other, a skewed lip. "Oogy is a dog who was abused as a puppy and used as bait for pit bull fighting," the group's page explains. "Tied to a pole and left to die, he was fortunately rescued and now is a loving pet to a family in America... Oogy appeared on the Oprah show, which showcased the cruelty of dog fighting and the horrific conditions he faced."

Oogy's face is a shocking portrait. It's reprehensible that someone would do such a thing to this trusting being. And the people who adopted Oogie merit our gratitude. But the animal-rights perspective goes deeper than questioning why certain people have hurt certain dogs, and deeper than preventing cases of abuse.

Modern animal law practitioners are still focused on prosecuting animal cruelty cases like Oogie's. In many parts of the United States, aggravated cruelty is a felony, punishable by up to two years in prison, if a defendant intentionally kills or seriously injures the animal. The animal-law experts also help the police arrest alleged abusers. But the key question, from an animal-rights perspective, would be: How can we challenge the daily domination that allows incidents such as this to arise over and over again? Oogie is physically deformed, and that's obvious to everyone, but the animal-rights advocate knows people will see Oogies's portrait as disturbing, and see portraits of normal dogs as, well, normal. Every pit bull terrier, every dog bred for fighting, for guarding, for being a child's birthday gift, for being carried in a celebrity's arm, is an animal who became that way because breeders have produced dogs to fit human beings' specific desires. An animal-rights perspective would question that. In every situation, we can consider the claims being voiced, then ask: Where is the domination in this picture? Look under the surface of the image, and we can understand that making wolves into malamutes, poodles, or pit bulls is the underlying, daily distortion of their being. It allows people to impose just about any type of treatment, from the most indulgent to the most horrific, upon these and all other kinds of dogs.

Pet ownership is sometimes defended with the claim that pets benefit from a symbiosis with humanity.[17] But what would we have to do to a wildcat or a wolf to get such an animal to curl up under our sheets, or stand up and beg for food? Baby wildcats and wolves are playful and docile to their parents, and most people want cats and dogs who keep that childlike essence. So the making of pets has meant selectively breeding animals through a process called neoteny, generally meaning the animals keep the traits of baby animals, and are easily handled by humans. Most full-grown dogs bark or yap, which very young wolves do. Yorkshire terriers retain their baby teeth. This juvenilization causes animals to rely on human care and follow human direction all their lives, etching dependency into their cells.[18] Along the way, a great many animals have been weeded out; the details, as you might imagine, have nothing to do with endearment.

Confined for life

Domestication, it must be admitted, is a complex subject. But when we humans systematically apply artificial selection through breeding, the claim that we're acting symbiotically is far-fetched. And when the Kennel Club registers dogs bred from sibling pairs or mother-to-son matings to match breed standards, ever more severely altered body shapes are created.[19] Chihuahuas may weigh just four pounds, and with more body surface than body itself, these dogs struggle to keep warm; it's facile to say wolves "evolved" into these states, or that they're results of some ancient agreement between the dogs' ancestors and ours. In the summer of 2008, in the documentary *Pedigree Dogs Exposed*, the BBC examined the physical deformities of pedigree dogs, who comprise the majority of the seven million dogs in Britain. Up to a half of all cavalier King Charles spaniels must endure life with syringomyelia, a painful condition which occurs when a dog's skull is so small the brain gets pressed out into the spinal cord. A veterinarian told the BBC: "If you took a stick and beat a dog to create that pain, you'd be prosecuted. But there's nothing to stop you breeding a dog with it."[20]

Boxers have high rates of heart disease, cancer, and epilepsy. West Highland Terriers suffer from skin and lung disease. Labradors and other large dogs may develop hip dysplasia, and Weimeraners are prone to a canine form of spina bifida that can prevent their back legs from moving separately. Pugs are subject to dislocated knees, seizures, breathing problems, and progressive blindness, and bulldogs need special surgery to give birth. All of these disabilities are systematically created and perpetuated though selective breeding. Pit bull terriers are especially likely to be sold for fighting. People decry dog fights as a particularly hideous form of cruelty—but often hesitate to say the breeding of these dogs is at the root of the trouble, and needs to stop.

Yi-Fu Tuan observes the way early French poodle barbers applied a topiary art to the hair of an animal, and that goldfish, bred as playthings and interior decorations, may be developed to have stunted bodies, or eyes protruding so far out of their faces that the eyeballs sometimes hit the sides of glass bowls or tanks or get sucked out by other aquarium fish.[21] Lately we've seen a trend to create such beings as Ragdoll cats—who, as the name suggests, are so docile they seem to have no opinions of their own, and, according to the Cat Fanciers' Association, will run to greet you at the door, follow you and flop on you—and teacup dogs, small enough to carry in a celebrity's glittery handbag. Yet another trend is "micro-pigs," pigs bred to be much smaller than standard farm pigs and advertised as the latest celebrity pet craze. And we haven't seen the worst of it yet. Now, the *New York Times* tells us, DNA tests are being developed in order to develop dogs with a certain shade of hair, or dogs who will cock their head endearingly when they look at us.[22]

To talk about the rights of such beings to be treated in certain ways would be to miss the most important point. We can care about them, we can think of them as individuals, as persons, and we can even create enforceable rules to ensure they're looked after, although there will be a limit to what laws can do when they're designed to protect beings who are allowed to be kept constantly in private spaces. But it would be euphemistic to talk of rights for animals bred as pets. These animals are as far from the life of the wolves as they can be. What can we give them that's respectful, except to stop bringing them into being as adjuncts of our lives? Non-human animals do not themselves construct rights; we do. Perhaps the question of animal rights ought to be reversed, and examined with regard to ourselves: Should humans have the right to domesticate other animals, make them dependent on us? Should we have that entitlement? Why?

We should note that the notion that some can be engineered into playthings of others has affected humans as well as other beings—not only to draw a parallel, but to see all of this as resulting from the desire to dominate. Yi Fu Tuan notes that royalty of the Italian Renaissance made attempts at selectively breeding dwarfs, who were popular additions to palaces of the aristocracy.[23] Dwarfs—I use the term to retain the terminology with which Tuan described the way such people were observed and displayed—are simply biological variants. As the field of disability studies asserts, people who are smaller than average should neither be disparaged nor erased. Deliberately bringing someone into existence, causing someone to be born with an unusual stature for the purpose of entertaining others, would involve a serious lack of respect, and a "rights" movement in such a context would be an unjust distraction from the core issue. Were people deliberately bred into existence their interests should be respected, and rules could be enforced for such a purpose, but the unfairness of the entire situation would be the real matter.

Where purpose-bred beings are taken from non-human communities, they are physically stunted and trapped in a dependence on us, and the idea of extending "rights" to them misses the point utterly. Any rules that help to phase out such breeding, however, from mandatory neutering to ending the breeding of animals as pets in a given place, could be considered within the sphere of animal rights, because, from the big-picture perspective, to reject pet breeding is to respect *wildcats and wolves* enough to resolve that they should not be selectively changed to suit us. This distinction— that animal rights is meaningful only insofar as autonomy is protected or augmented—needs to be made expressly. When we are talking of domesticated beings, a care ethic is appropriate; but talking of pets' or farm animals' rights is confusing.

I do not mean to pick out extreme cases when critiquing domestication and ownership—although extreme breeds would, in a genuine move for animal rights, be the most appropriate ones to insist that kennel clubs stop promoting and breeders stop breeding first. Yet all domesticated animals, even though they may be happy in a caring home, may also be transported as freight, forced to breed, legally traded away or even killed should they become inconvenient. Similarly, horses owned by the people best able to care for them are still left in metal trailers during hot summer show days, as is happening somewhere even as you read these lines. Even in the best of situations, domesticated animals need their owners to meet their basic needs, and if they give birth, their young will experience that same need for care. Some outlive their owners and may face an unceremonious end at the pound or be thrown out to fend for themselves. The offspring of abandoned dogs and cats gradually change their physical traits and will tend to live and move in their own groups: They are described as "stray" or "feral" and their interactions become closer to the habits of their free ancestors; and yet they survive mostly by raiding human refuse bins, are commonly targeted through municipal killing policies, and never turn back into wildcats or wolves. Matthew Scully portrays the alienated state of domesticated cats and dogs as a source of human amusement, likening pets to "ingratiating foreign visitors to our world...comically out of place, pretending to fit in, to be one of us, trying not to be found out and deported."[24] This is no comedy. Domestication of animals into pets not only takes these animals out of their own world and puts them into our houses and businesses, but physically alters them so that they, like domesticated cattle, are forever exiled from their free-living state.

As noted in Chapter Three, abolitionist animal-rights theory has largely bypassed or left unclear the vital point that free-living animal communities, as long as they and their habitats exist, could benefit from legal rights—not cats or dogs or cows. Most of our theorists give scant attention to free-living animals, their lives and their communities, while spending many pages on details of industrial conditions, and analyses of advocates' reactions to those conditions, thus reinforcing the problematic sense that there's a connection between animal rights and human industries. As we've already seen, some animal lawyers believe that achieving rights for pets makes sense, and this misunderstanding is reinforced when abolitionist texts place dog and cat illustrations and examples in their texts. Gary L. Francione, who argues for animal rights (specifically the right not to be property) for animals who are sentient, has stated that abolitionism would "require that we abolish—and not merely regulate—our exploitation of nonhumans and that we stop bringing domestic animals into existence to serve as means to human ends" and indicates that "domestication cannot be justified";[25] at the same time, when discussing whether apes should have legal personhood, Francione's writing could be read as suggesting that dogs should be considered for that recognition:

> Perhaps it is time to take a closer look at the entire enterprise of linking the moral significance of nonhumans with cognitive attributes beyond sentience, rather than trying to determine whether some nonhumans have such cognitive attributes or have them in a way that makes them sufficiently similar to humans to merit moral and legal personhood…Is there anyone who has ever lived with a dog or cat who does not recognize that these nonhumans are intelligent, self-aware, or emotional, even though they are more genetically dissimilar to us than are the great apes?[26]

Without question, dogs and cats have moral significance. I wouldn't hesitate to say they are persons. But the trouble with using *dogs and cats with whom people live* in this particular picture is that some readers will not be entirely sure whether Francione's view of abolitionism means pets as well as great apes could and should have rights. Perhaps it's better to explain that ordinary observations show the self-awareness of a free-living bird or bat. For the end of domination, and, within it, the abolition of commodity status, could be real for a bird or a bat.

Autonomy is central to animal-rights theory and activism. It's time to talk about this.

Enduring freedom

When we train vanilla vines to stop growing higher than the human waist so we can easily pick their pods, we're forcing living beings to adapt specifically to needs of our own. While this kind of activity indirectly affects the lives of conscious animals other than ourselves, it does not seem disrespectful on its face; it does not seem like violence, as the plant we train isn't conscious. But it does show our habit of changing the natural world to suit ourselves. And we systematically treat animal beings in the same way we treat vanilla plants.

Yi-Fu Tuan says "the desire to dominate or patronize is too deeply embedded in human psychology to disappear altogether." Tuan cites the treatment of all subordinates:

> Dog owners like to order their dog to fetch and see the animal trotting off in obedience. But it is a pleasure available to all who have human subordinates at their disposal. The boss says fetch—though, of course, he uses more polite language— and his subordinate goes to get coffee or a multimillion-dollar contract.[27]

Patterns of domination and subjugation, and hierarchical ideas about species, are indeed deeply ingrained in human thinking. If we say it's not possible to change ourselves, whether we're right or wrong, by saying so we thereby perpetuate the power structures humanity has constructed. The first step to achieving change is conceiving it, and that's what the vegan proposal has done. Donald Watson didn't accept humanity as-is, and neither must we. Watson said we do not know yet the benefits humanity could experience by committing to the ideal of non-exploitation, but by doing this we would cultivate the first civilization that merits the name.

Each of us, and everyone we meet, has the wonderful potential to commit to this now. It means taking a tremendous risk, formulating a new psychology that says outright: We have felt dominion is our birthright. We have warred on Someone Else to make dominion our social reality. Now we can challenge ourselves to change, to cultivate respect, for each other, for the greater conscious community, for the ecology and the life force that sustains us. Donald Watson saw this as the greatest task of all religions, and the true test of Christian principles. Watson was an agnostic, but recommended the relinquishing of our dominion as the greatest challenge the human spirit has ever conceived. Here was a person who withstood the pressure to go to war; one of the few who took "thou shalt not kill" seriously. Instructively, Watson would not disrespect others who did what *they* deemed the morally required things—whether that meant going to war with the hope of stopping atrocities, or getting inside labs and taking animals out of the cages in which other people had trapped them. But Watson saw the need for human change at a much deeper level. We can talk about just wars and we can plan undercover rescues for a long, long time. The deeper question is how to transcend the desire to dominate that is now so deeply embedded in human psychology. How to stop making the guns and the cages.

An intricate web of habits is spun from the desire to dominate. And what of Tuan's second factor, the desire to patronize? We've discussed in detail how petkeeping has largely gone unchallenged in the animal-advocacy field. And most advocates aren't even asking if farm animals are something a culture that accepts animal rights would have. Ever noticed pictures of activists nuzzling animals, or happy little farm animals staring up at us from the pages of vegan pamphlets? In a vegan culture, we'd have no selectively bred birds, pigs or calves, happy or not. Law professor Cass R. Sunstein indicates that anti-cruelty laws—that is, laws that prescribe minimum standards by which we treat other animals we selectively breed, such as those that forbid a farmer to maltreat a horse—signify a "minimalist" framework of rights.[28] The tendency of law experts to frame animal rights around domesticated beings suggests a willingness to accept captivity, as long as the animals therein are not treated as "exclusively" our instruments or as "mere" objects.[29] But as MacKinnon has suggested, we do not mitigate our dominion over other animals by extending them some level of comfort. Arguably, no domination is more complete than that which appears to be exerted without pain, without force.

Rodeo shows are widely denounced by advocates while more genteel equestrian pursuits and indeed the breeding of horses go virtually without comment. Some animal protectionists point out that riders in genteel equestrian events pet their horses after a performance; in contrast, rodeo riders would not pet a bronco, calf or bull. The epitome of the genteel performances is the dance of the white Lipizzaner horses, bred into being by the Hapsburg family that ruled Austria for several hundred years. Today's Lipizzaner shows, sometimes presented in the middle of a gourmet dinner (something of an upscale twist on exhibiting trained dolphins as part of dining events), are meant as displays of Baroque-era aesthetics. The show is called the purest form of classical dressage, but it could also be called a stylish circus. At all levels of equestrian entertainment, a few horses satisfy the aesthetic, and the rest must be disposed of. Equestrian training is the antithesis of respecting the interest of the individual, which would, in turn, entail respecting free-living horses wherever they remain and letting them be; yet the Lipizzaner website pretends to know that horses *wish* to be under human dominion and control: "The law of dressage—for it is a law—is a law of nature perfecting the natural." The site waxes poetic about the horses' *voluntarily offered obedience*. Until we forced them to be obedient, however, it was not a reality; horses didn't come looking for us to do it. An animal-rights theorist should be capable of envisioning ourselves as part of a humanity that looks beyond these habits. To start, we can honestly acknowledge our own training. Many advocates come into the work because they feel strong emotional ties to animals; and of course love and caring is better than exploitation, and it's often needed. But do advocates think about whether they genuinely want to pursue a world in which free animals exist and flourish?

CHAPTER 8

"Let Them Be!"

I t is our urgent task, whether we are animal-rights advocates or simply residents of a planet facing ecological degradation and extinctions, to question the notion that animals who aren't commercially useful should be hooked off the world stage as the collective known as *Homo sapiens* (along with our entourage of purpose-bred animals) relentlessly expands. The disappearance of free animals at our hands may well be rooted in our ancient fear of other animals, for we primates are the age-old prey of large carnivores. At some point we managed to ordain ourselves Top of the Food Chain by killing or controlling those who would prey on us or on the animals we use as food, and by doing so, we've removed virtually all of the risks posed by animals who could physically overpower us.[1]

Our ability to reorder the planet's life, in turn, means the deer, moose, and other prey animals who live near us have fewer natural predators, but leave it to the head honchos to begin imposing control on them too. One of the ways we control them is to license people to shoot them dead with arrows or bullets. We have manipulated them so badly that they are now undergoing a strikingly rapid form of selective breeding. By stalking trophy animals—the elk, deer, and others with the most impressive horns or antlers, the ones who'd be best able to survive if we weren't seeking them out—we've been pressing evolution backwards.

Alberta, Canada is home to a population of bighorn sheep with thick, curving horns. Those with smaller horns aren't so eagerly stalked by humans, and get far more opportunities to mate. A thirty-year study of the sheep of Ram Mountain, carried out by biologist Marco Festa-Bianchet, observed their horns gradually becoming smaller. Atlantic cod on the east coast of Canada now breed at five years of age instead of six (when they're more vulnerable to human capture)—and the shift has occurred in only two decades. Since nets began capturing only fish of more than a minimum size in the 1980s, the average body sizes in numerous communities of fish have also shrunk. Columbia University biologist Don Melnick notes that artificially selecting animals in the wild—in effect, breeding them—limits gene diversity and can result in the end of a species.[2]

Still another way to control these free-living communities is to make sure they can't bear young. Of course, hunters would want to avoid this. But animal protectionists, hoping to save animals from the suffering that hunting imposes, hope to see contraceptives emerge as the preferred way to control populations of free-living animals—birds, deer, burros, and bears—that get too numerous for people's comfort levels.[3] Defending the autonomy of free-living animals (and, by extension, the integrity of their habitat), Priscilla Feral, president of Friends of Animals, has long asked difficult questions about practices such as the addling of goose eggs, and other methods of birth control, prompting me to give these practices a hard look. Contraception *might* involve less physical pain than another form of animal control, but does involvement in the manipulation and control of animals mean unintentionally accepting the human agreement that animals simply must be kept in check if not used as food, clothing, entertainment, or objects of curiosity?

Fertility control: Its history in advocacy

All animals would be free-living animals in a society that accepts animal rights, so there is every reason for the advocate to appreciate their autonomy rather than remove it. Yet by the late 1970s, animal-protection advocates had developed visible interest in reproductive control of free-living animals. The philosopher Peter Singer, having been asked whether we should prevent lions from eating gazelles, replied:

> ...I am fairly sure, judging from man's past record of attempts to mold nature to his own aims, that we would be more likely to increase the net amount of animal suffering if we interfered with wildlife, than to decrease it. Lions play a role in the ecology of their habitat, and we cannot be sure what the long-term consequences would be if we were to prevent them from killing gazelles. (The way to do this, I suppose, would be

by eliminating lions, perhaps by sterilization.) So, in practice, I would definitely say that wildlife should be left alone.[4]

But Singer added: "If, in some way, we could be reasonably certain that interfering with wildlife in a particular way would, in the long run, greatly reduce the amount of killing and suffering in the animal world, it would, I think, be right to interfere."

Two years later, in the much-heralded *Animal Liberation*, Singer would write:

> If it is true that in special circumstances their population grows to such an extent that they damage their own environment and the prospects of their own survival, or that of other animals who share their habitat, then it may be right for humans to take some supervisory action; but obviously if we consider the interests of the animals, this action will not be to let hunters go in, killing and wounding the animals, but rather to reduce the fertility of the animals. If we made an effort to develop more humane methods of population control for wild animals in reserves, it would not be difficult to come up with something better than what is done now. The trouble is that the authorities responsible for wildlife have a "harvest" mentality, and are not interested in finding techniques of population control which would reduce the number of animals to be "harvested" by hunters.[5]

Similarly, twenty-five years later in the book *Introduction to Animal Rights: Your Child Or the Dog?*, Gary L. Francione decried the efforts of government agencies to promote the stalking and killing of free-living animals, recommending contraception as a better approach,[6] and stating: "As a general matter, wildlife agencies are hostile to nonlethal alternatives to hunting, such as contraception, which has proven effective in controlling the size of deer herds but decreases the availability of deer for hunters to kill."[7]

But is it acceptable to control populations of deer as long as there are no shots, no traps, no blood? Shouldn't the bodily integrity and reproductive freedom of animals matter, and matter greatly? What happens when you combine expanding space for farm animals with the idea that free-living animals can be made to disappear when humans deem this correct? Consider the actual effect: animal advocates want to rule out cages of a certain size and secure freedom of movement for farm animals, and, at the same time, promote birth control for animals who now move freely over the planet. More space for agribusiness concerns, less free animals in wild spaces. Sounds like a sure-fire prescription for the end of animal rights.

A 2008 article in the *Globe and Mail* presented appalling news about the government's annihilation of wolves in British Columbia, Canada. Of note was the reporter's awareness that forced sterilization is indeed part of British Columbia's war on wolves: "Reports on how many wolves are being shot, trapped, sterilized, and otherwise hounded out of existence under predator-control programs in beautiful B.C. aren't readily available. When they do occasionally surface, it is a reminder of just how grim the battle is that is being waged out there against wolves…"[8] A welcome but rare whiff of resistance in the mainstream media.

Tom Regan's *Case for Animal Rights* urged us: "With regard to wild animals, the general policy recommended by the rights view is: *let them be!*"[9] These three little words go right to the core of the theory, and they free the spirit of activism. Thus, as for killing, terrifying, or purpose-breeding animals, logically the general policy is: Don't. And as for making free-living animals sterile, the general policy here too would be: Don't. Instead, we'll need to control our own numbers, our own tendencies to encroach. This will mean learning to respect the environment not just for our health or aesthetic satisfaction (or as some vast storehouse reserved for our later exploitation), but because it's home to other living beings.

I was one of a small group of activists in my community urging Swarthmore College (founded by the peaceable Quakers, as it happens) not to go ahead with the school's planned deer kill. We asked the school administrators to try a variety of natural landscaping answers, but most of all to dedicate themselves to moving beyond the view that free-living animals need to be controlled. As Tom Regan put it, to *let them be!*

Some advocates who got involved with this case urged the use of a contraceptive substance that affects deer immune systems to cause infertility. Porcine zona pellucida, or PZP, is made from the membranes of pig ovaries, and it causes an immune response in the body of the target animal that attacks that animal's own eggs. It's being offered as a way to control deer, birds, bison, elephants, horses, bears, and other non-human animals by preventing their future offspring from ever appearing. Most of the activists I've asked don't think imposing contraception on a community of free-living animals represents the animal-rights position. They would personally prefer a hands-off position, they have told me, but feel backed into a corner by authorities from state game commissions and federal park officials who see shooting as the easy way to manage animals in their sphere. They believe killing is the worst thing that humans can do to deer and other animals. Fair enough. What I think we need to say, though, is that our human penchant for being in charge of all other animals allows everything, *including whatever we think is the worst thing*, to be imposed. And that's why any advocate should step back from pharmaceutical deer control initiatives as a valid answer. Is the question itself (what do we do about too many animals) valid? Why should the animal-advocacy community add yet another weapon to the arsenal humankind uses against the other animal communities of the planet?

Decision-makers will use those vaccines only in the most selective ways. State game commissions market hunts, collect fees from hunting permits, and can more easily pay salaries wherever there are a lot of deer running about. The state of Wisconsin alone has a billion-dollar hunting industry.[10] So it's something of a conflict of interest for state game officials to agree to birth control as a means of lowering the deer population; they'll only do this in narrow circumstances. But in any case, there's no reason to accept their assertion that the deer are unacceptably out of order. Why must the deer be ordered? Some will argue it's not realistic to think we can take a hands-off position with free-living animals. I've heard the argument, in animal-rights circles, that animals are "moral patients" and it's unreasonable to say we won't intervene. But this needs to be interrogated, lest paternalism be mistaken for a rights position. Actually, it's entirely realistic to think that human intervention generally causes as many problems as it sets out to fix. We can indeed adopt a hands-off position, and use this hands-off position to stop the expansion of animal agribusiness—insist, that is, on letting the deer and the free-living horses be, drawing a line, pushing back. So ranchers and developers stop taking the every bit of land they can exploit. We can indeed adopt a hands-off position, and insist that the imposition of pharmaceutical population control on free-living animals is off-limits, and that the states must stop taking the big cats, wolves and coyotes out of the equation.

Without a whole paradigm shift, animal rights means nothing. Pharmaceutical solutions mean more careers in the labs, more forms of animal control for the official repertoire. And relinquishing the animal-rights view in a series of emergencies in town after town isn't going to save deer and other animals. When is someone actually supposed to tell the authorities "no"? When do we begin questioning the road construction, the McMansions? Press for contraception as the residents and businesses press for roads and malls and soon deer will be gone from the spaces that once belonged to them. Contraception will clear them off invisibly—as we humans take their land out from under them. In the meantime, these pharmaceuticals wreak havoc on the deer's biology and significantly change their social interactions.

If we are developing an animal-rights theory about challenging domination, we need to bring the theory to the table, and try to give activists the support they need to get it done. It could work. It's fair enough for a caring pragmatist to ask us, "So what do we do in the interim, until the time humans become more aware? How can we present the reasons clearly to these landowners and officials, then present alternatives?" The key is to be absolutely realistic, but not give up the message of respect. We know killing is going on; but that does not force us to give up presenting ways humans can live without eliminating the bears, the free-roaming horses, or the deer. It's not just about keeping the elimination bloodless. Some might view the goal of the animal-rights movement as the end of suffering, and think birth control is less cruel—and somehow imagine the deer would want that. But this notion has nothing to do with allowing animals to live in freedom, on nature's terms.

And as the caring pragmatists are now seeing, even if they have accepted birth control for free-living animals as a lesser harm than bloody killing in the short term, the overall effect could be, on some level, more insidious than bloodshed. Pharmaceutical birth control is now being tried on free-living animals on federal lands, where hunting is ruled out by law, as an adjunct to deer-hunting plans, or on animals—horses, for example—the hunters don't usually pursue. When deemed scientifically proven, pharmaceutical fertility control could be offered wherever and whenever we humans believe it efficacious. Imagine one group of people, wanting to stretch out over more space, imposing sterilization on another group. It's not hard to think of an example of humans doing this to each other. It would never be justifiable on the terms that otherwise the first group would shoot instead!

Tom Regan was one of the philosophers who urged a contraceptive plan for the Swarthmore deer. So here again, Regan's written words didn't guide the activism in the field. Can we talk? *Let them be!* isn't a bookshelf platitude; it shouldn't be left to turn yellow in the pages of *The Case for Animal Rights*. It should be applied. It should defend Swarthmore deer. When we see that the state game commission, which has been arranging for the killing at Swarthmore, receives revenue as it licenses deer stalkers, trappers and anglers, it's not surprising that the commission has backed the too-many-deer view at Swarthmore. Advocates can point out the bureaucracy's conflict here. Were the commission funded from the state's general treasury (not hunters), surely the administrators would be less keen to project the idea of an overpopulation of ravenous, hazardous deer than they are today. A worthy legal project in any state would be to push back against these agencies, beginning by changing their revenue source, for example, through a ballot measure. But probably the last thing advocates need to do is buttress the view of an overpopulation of free-living animals or offer new ways of thinning the herd. Respect for other animals' autonomy fits with the answer that most closely mirrors the ways of the natural ecology, and other animals' capacity to adapt to it.

The guiding principle of the animal-rights philosophy won't be a vague prescription to help animals or to reduce suffering; these ideas often become rationalizations for animal control. The guiding principle of our philosophy is to respect their autonomy; so we resist the temptation to meddle in the reproductive lives of beings who haven't asked for it, and can't agree to it. This does not mean doing nothing. This does not mean we're ivory-tower talkers who don't care about what's actually happening to animals. In today's political climate, and under the environmental laws constructed largely in an era when other animals and the environment were thought to exist simply for our pleasure, it takes stamina and a whole lot of engagement with people to advocate for animals' interests in living freely in their habitats; it takes focused attention to navigate through and within existing linguistic, legal, and social contexts, yet deliver a coherent message. It's something we as advocates can get used to trying, and help each other try. And as we work at this, we keep learning about how to let other animals be.

What might they want from us, other than that?

What other members of Earth's biocommunity *need* from us is a robust movement to defend what natural places remain, before the entire planet turns into housing developments, office parks, malls, and farms. The activists at WildEarth Guardians tell us some 98 percent of the waters and lands of the western United States is under the yoke of animal agribusiness; they are working to reclaim it, for prairie dogs, Chiricahua leopard frogs, and other groups of animals at risk. We can see that a new emphasis on animal autonomy would strengthen environmentalism, because the ecology will be critical to this animal-rights movement. It will be important to value plants, the health of oceans, and the integrity of the landscape, as part of the vital interests animals are deemed to have. Our collaborations with environmentalists will, over time, strengthen the animal-rights position in turn.

There will be difficult questions; doubtless you've thought of a few as you read this. Once we agree in principle what animal rights should be and then implement it, cultivating a society that can outgrow its drive to conquer and kill and force others to be of use to us, we then decide the most peaceful approach in specific situations. Some will involve conflicts we might have caused or aggravated between living communities, given our outsized population and the ways we have already changed the face of the planet. The key will be mindfulness, so as to steadfastly avoid reinstating the primacy of humans over the other animal communities. At the same time, we can ask people to make this outsized population an issue, to talk about limiting our numbers, and to consider real reasons why adopting (or educating and caregiving) is every bit as fulfilling as bearing children. Initiatives to secure financial support or tax breaks for prospective adoptive parents could be a step in the right direction.

Wedge's thin edge? The case of the primates' communities
Most everyone seems to think all apes remind us of ourselves, so one would think the other apes should be considered persons by now. If legal rights theory means similar cases should be protected equally, what's taking so long? And other apes could really do with some privacy in this world. Yet we seem chronically unable to let them to have it. Today, many communities of non-human primates are susceptible to being wiped out except insofar as their members can become a useful underclass in our society. We are fascinated by their physical similarities to us and what that might be able to tell us about ourselves, so we subject them to an endless stream of experiments that involve activities relevant to human culture, such as

counting money, operating keyboards or playing musical instruments, weaving, drawing, and using human sign language. We have followed them in their forests, provoked aggression among their groups so we can watch the action on television, sent them into space in our capsules, raised them in human homes then stuck them back in labs when the experiments ended. Weirdest of all, we rationalize confining them for life to test the question of how much respect they might deserve from us. But we saw in the case of Alex the African Grey parrot what happens when animals impress us by meeting our expectations.

An article in *Science Daily*, under the bubbly headline "Nurtured Chimps Rake It In," called the Chimpanzee Cognition Center at the Ohio State University "the first to demonstrate that raising chimpanzees in a human cultural environment enhances their cognitive abilities."[11] Unlike apes who receive less human interaction, chimpanzees raised in the research project will choose the right rake to reach a food reward. The researcher claims that the study offers comparisons with the formations of attachment and early education for human infants and children. These chimpanzees have been used as instruments to others' ends, carefully trained to respond to what humans want; and they—those most likely to serve as control groups for psychological studies geared to benefit human beings—are presented as the superior examples of apes. The headline and linguistics of the synopsis suggest something's in it for the apes, and the bargain is fair; it apparently escapes the writer's attention that the chimpanzees cannot accept such a bargain. And rare indeed is the acknowledgment of the loneliness captive apes might feel, the loss of space and time of their own, the loss of creative interactions and natural risks that arise in a free life. What if we could know their perspective, rather than imposing our own?

It was 2006 when two high-profile animal-protection groups waged a series of legal attacks on a struggling Texas primate sanctuary that offered lifetime care for the Ohio State chimpanzees. These groups staged exposés of the sanctuary, ensuring it was seen in the worst possible light. Evidently, the activists approved of the lab situation. An eco-feminist professor called the Ohio State University room where the chimpanzees had been used in cognition studies their "comfortable home."[12] In a twist of bitter irony, the activists who pressed for the sanctuary raid, and who would eventually round up animals and decide which animals would be sent to a pound, which would go to zoos, and so forth, accused the sanctuary of treating the animals as "property" for trying to hold on to them. Given the current legal reality that animals *are* property, and that is the only ground on which the sanctuary could argue against their removal, the sanctuary was placed in a Catch-22: either argue that the private refuge held title to the animals or not argue at all. Had the courts agreed that the animals shouldn't belong to the sanctuary, the precedent would have been useless, if not downright detrimental, to the advancement of a genuine animal-rights position. Had the lawyers involved brought a case against an institution that *uses* animals, and pressed the argument that the animals weren't the institute's property, a serious abolitionist case could have been made against the use of non-human apes and other animals.

In early 2006, Spain's governing Socialist Party considered the idea of forbidding the use of non-human great apes in harmful experiments or on stage. Activists pressed on, with a high-profile, international signature effort. "Spanish Parliament to Extend Rights to Apes" was the headline of an article distributed by Reuters on the 25th of June, 2008. It was fifteen years after Paola Cavalieri and Peter Singer gathered together a collective of writers to propose basic rights for chimpanzees, gorillas, and orang-utans in a book called *The Great Ape Project*.[13] The activists promoting the Spanish proposal cite the book as their inspiration. How refreshing it will be to have a legal system respect any conscious beings beyond the ones who use lawn mowers and credit cards!

Representatives from Amnesty International denounced the idea, observing—correctly, of course—that the rights of many humans in the world are yet to be respected. Objections came even from some animal-rights proponents, who seem to feel apes shouldn't jump ahead and receive from humanity the privilege of personhood before other animals are included;

still others have simply written off the apes as ecologically doomed.

Much work must be done before our society (and our movement) understands how domination of any group affects all, how decommodifying life will energize all social movements—why animal rights and our personal rights are never in competition, but always connected. The best reading of the ape personhood idea is not that activists want to privilege certain non-human beings. The key message is that we humans should remember we are also primates, be fair about that, and go from there: being fair to other groups, spreading outward and accepting core similarities, core needs, as humanity's awareness and law evolves.

A less comprehensive beginning, but still helpful, would be a formal recognition that non-human primates are exempt from the animal-husbandry rules of the federal Animal Welfare Act. Consider this: Would you be grateful that you were being used in some kind of experiment, possibly forced to procreate or raise the young of others—if it were all done according to the procedures laid out by something called a "welfare" law? Like humans, the other primates of the world shouldn't be transported and kept for testing, and the law could readily acknowledge this. At least with respect to the great apes, the demand for fairness has already been heard, for example, in New Zealand and in Spain; both governments have worked on rules to forbid experiments on non-human great apes.

The best possible outcome from the Spanish resolution would be the start of a robust movement to defend apes, other primates, and all other conscious beings in their untamed habitat, where all should have the simple right to live as they will. This would be a boon to entire biocommunities that need us to stop breeding cattle and logging ancient forests and extracting everything we can get our drills into. Respecting the lives of orang-utans would necessarily mean respecting not only the great apes, but other primates in their areas (nearly half of all communities of the world's primates live at risk of extinction due to our hunting and clear-cutting) and tree frogs too—all animals of the palm forests that need us to put down our logging machinery. Apes' rights could be the way to confront that logging now.

A case that argues carefully along this path could have the ability to gain legal rights for primates without reinforcing hierarchy, or at least without reinforcing it any more strongly than defending a group of humans under assault would do. Social change often comes about through single issues, which in turn raise general awareness of others, and I am not persuaded that the fear of perpetuating a hierarchy should invariably dissuade us from ensuring that a specific community is liberated from assaults and can pursue its own way in the world. Reasonable minds may disagree on this point, but those who argue against pushing for primate personhood should clearly explain what stops their argument from also opposing the extension or preservation of basic rights that human groups are deemed to have. Human rights, too, result from struggles specific to a certain group of primates!

As for the real-world case for non-human personhood before us, will Spain's laws reinforce or diminish the concept of basic rights? Unless the proposal both ends captivity (including captivity in supposedly comfortable labs and zoos) and protects habitat at the same time, Spain's animal-rights victory will be illusory. In Spain and generally, advocates measure non-human interests in terms of sentience, and pay scant attention to freedom, autonomy, and community, and so it is in this case: While keeping apes for circuses and television spots will be forbidden under Spain's penal code, keeping non-human apes in Spanish zoos (where, at the time of this public discussion, more than 300 live) will remain legal. *USA Today* described Spain as having resolved to "give great apes, such as chimpanzees and gorillas, the right to life, freedom from arbitrary captivity and protection from torture."[14] Who will decide what captivity is arbitrary? Will human law make zoos a component of "animal rights"? Granted, some zoo directors genuinely want to protect threatened communities of animals. But are we justified in making ourselves other animals' masters and keepers when we say we're helping them? What are we doing to release them from reliance on care and on rescue?

Apes who are already captive, and cannot safely return to their lands, should not be exhibited, but should instead be offered private refuge at a sanctuary prepared to meet their needs, where the employees and volunteers advocate for non-human rights. In Spain, two sites have been called sanctuaries, but they allow public viewing and carry out cognitive research on the non-human apes. To take rights seriously, the influential *Homo sapiens* of Spain have a responsibility to make the region safe for true refuges—places off-limits to cognitive testing and exhibiting.

Detainees

Challenges to the use of primates are a recurring motif in Europe. Britain's Parliament condemned the use of non-human great apes in scientific experiments in 1997; Lord Williams of Mostyn called for the end of the custom as "a matter of morality." European advocates are denouncing tests on primates taken from their habitats, aiming to secure a timetable for ending the use of all primates throughout Europe. Recently, Austrian activists approached the European Court of Human Rights in their quest to have Hiasl, a chimpanzee, declared a legal person. Uprooted as a young chimpanzee from western Africa for Baxter's pharmaceutical labs, Hiasl was eventually released to a Vienna animal shelter, and a group called the Association Against Animal Factories has sought a court-appointed guardian to help keep support money in Hiasl's own name and shield the chimpanzee from being sold. "It's hard," said a *New York Times* editorial, "to see the harm in that."[15] Agreed, of course. But what the editorial tells the public is that this request doesn't disturb the status quo. Organizer Martin Balluch explained: "We argue that he's a person and he's capable of owning something himself, as opposed to being owned, and that he can manage his money. This means he can start a court case against Baxter, which at the very least should mean his old age pension is secure."

A secure pension might ensure a human worker is fairly treated, but it's got nothing to do with animal rights. Yes, money is needed in this case, for the sanctuary where Hiasl resides has fallen into bankruptcy. Yet if Hiasl obtains personhood in the European Court of Human Rights (or any court of national or international law), it should mean that *future Hiasls* have their habitat, life and freedom protected so that they can flourish autonomously in their own lands—not that they get a secure pension and can sue a pharmaceutical company. Legal expert Eberhart Theuer, who is advising in the case, argues (correctly, in my view) that Hiasl should be considered a refugee, for whom a formal legal guardian should be granted—in the same way representation in an emergency situation has been accepted by the European Court of Human Rights in a number of cases before, notably when persons who could not express themselves needed to have their rights safeguarded. Once that is achieved, Hiasl should certainly be assisted financially, in order to secure lifetime care. But the point would be to stop bringing non-human apes into the human world rather than getting them a panoply of "human" rights. Catharine MacKinnon notes the ways we "project human projects onto animals, to look for and find or not find ourselves in them"; whereas the key question for the animal-rights advocate is "what they want from us, if anything other than to be let alone, and what it will take to learn the answer."[16] Do they want better treatment from us? Or to be free not to be treated in one way or the other?

More generally: What is the logical conclusion of building an animal-protection project around better husbandry? It likely means increasing pain relief—an idea that could go along just fine with a world of animals all living in captivity. Domestication might afford animals longer lives, safety from predation, better disease management, and protection from nature red in tooth and claw. But would it be what other animals want from us?

Creating non-human rights starts with identifying, to the extent possible, the fundamental interests of the beings involved. This isn't a matter of contriving palliative responses to the conditions that surround animals already made into objects of trade and study. Retirement is a false offer. Other primates don't come into our society, willingly work, and then retire. Rights would shield them from being brought into our society at all.

Hiasl's case and Spain's rights proposal have been followed by reporters the world over. But only the United States of America continues the large-scale use of non-human apes. The country that warehouses hundreds of apes for use in biomedical and cognitive experiments is in no hurry to extend justice to them. The Chimpanzee Health Improvement, Maintenance and Protection ("CHIMP") Act, signed by President Clinton in 2000, removes "surplus chimpanzees" from U.S. labs when they are "no longer necessary" for biomedical research—thereby saving money for the government's whole research enterprise.[17] Although it accepts and codifies the human prerogative to experiment on chimpanzees, this law was condoned by a coterie of U.S. anti-vivisection groups, including Peter Singer's volunteer-based group GAP, named after *The Great Ape Project*. And any apes removed from labs under the law can be used again for "non-invasive behavioral studies"—as though it's anything but invasive to keep a group of apes' bodies, daily experiences, and relationships completely controlled by their human keepers.[18]

Jane Goodall, author of the opening chapter in *The Great Ape Project*, testified before Congress in support of the CHIMP Act, calling the warehousing agreement a "sanctuary." Hearing chair Michael Bilirakis noted that the National Institutes of Health didn't want a law that would put chimpanzees completely off-limits to researchers; sanctuaries, Goodall answered, don't rule out "a small operation"; the "really cruel thing" would be moving them from a more spacious area into a small cage for testing.[19] But the really cruel thing is how people made up an ostensibly humanitarian law to enable and regulate the warehousing of chimpanzees at the discretion of the research community, which it benefits financially.[20] As this law's language fails to acknowledge non-human great apes as anything but commodities, the law obstructs the freedom and dignity of non-human apes.

What can change the status quo now? Courts should be pressed to consider non-human primates as rights-holders. In North America that project has yet to begin. The lawmakers are now considering a law that would be called the Great Ape Protection Act. Its text cites the apes' intelligence and susceptibility to psychological trauma. If enacted, it would end invasive research on some apes. Invasive research would include that which might cause injury, distress or fear—but not "close observation of natural or voluntary behavior" of an individual. This suggests that putting apes on display or subjecting them to cognitive experiments, which researchers go to some lengths to portray as voluntary, will be condoned. The federally funded site holding the apes who are moved out of labs in accordance with the CHIMP Act has been exhibiting them in an arrangement with the Louisiana Tourism Bureau. For the objects of exhibitions and observational studies, their space and time is never really their own. The relationships that will be made or broken for them will always depend upon the decisions of others. Even the bonobo ape Kanzi, who gained celebrity status for learning to express thoughts in human language through a keyboard, might be let out of the laboratory setting only to wind up on a leash. Researcher Sue Savage-Rumbaugh discussed the lead as a tool of necessity, albeit one avoided as long as possible "since the more freedom Kanzi had, the more he encountered and elected to talk about at the keyboard."[21]

For too long, animals have been plucked out of their own spaces and stuck in labs, zoos, and roadside shows. And now, people are making labs and zoos out of the habitat itself. The Great Ape Project headed by Singer hopes to involve Spanish communities with the Jane Goodall Institute in Africa.[22] In Uganda, together with the Walt Disney Company and the United States Agency for International Development (USAID), the Goodall Institute markets forest-dwelling apes by "habituating" them for tourism. The Goodall habituation project is cited in promotional literature from an outfit called Magic Safaris, which also boasts of a rehabilitation site on Uganda's Ngamba Island where chimpanzees confiscated from poachers are placed and "fed four times a day and this is a spectacular moment for visitors. Good photo opportunities as well."

The Magic Safaris company explains that the process of habituation involves two years of manipulation. Once trained to accept humans, the chimpanzees are subjected to "a continuous day-by-day focus. Problems can occur..." Forest-dwelling chimpanzees have also been habituated for research. Some tourism makes benevolent claims: The companies are, they say, focusing public attention on the effects of logging. But contrast the views expressed, quite recently, when an isolated human tribe was reportedly spotted in Brazil. The director of Survival International said such tribes will "be made extinct" if loggers get their land, yet the integrity and privacy of the people is so respected that debate raged even over taking photos of "uncontacted" tribes to prove they exist to stop logging. When a BBC journalist signed up for a tourist trip to make "first contact" with a West Papuan tribe, Survival's director Stephen Corry objected, "Tourists could threaten these peoples, especially through the risk of bringing in disease." If the filmed encounter was real, said Corry, "the tour operator and tourists should be ashamed of themselves."

But of course filmed encounters with previously undisturbed communities of chimpanzees have gone on for decades, and people are not ashamed; they are, in contrast, rewarded with grants and fame and television contracts. We should keep writing, keep doing, and hold advocates (for human and non-human rights) accountable for their arguments. The struggle for human rights and the struggle for others animals' rights do share a common thread: they happen within the same struggle to transcend systems of domination. How do we proceed? Of all the ideas we could pursue in our time on Earth, giving it our best shot for animal rights would mean working mightily to protect Earth's remaining safe havens, to stop expanding roads and resorts into mountains and forests, and to convert ranches back to wildlands. We can do this for our local parks and forests, and we can support those who do it internationally. For those apes and other primates who cannot go back to freedom, because their adjustment to captivity has erased their ability to cope in their own habitats, the best we can do is to support private refuges. For those who do still have freedom, our demand for their right to keep it must be unequivocal and unrelenting. The struggle for their personhood must be taken more seriously, so that the protections offered to animals—as Swedish advocate Per-Anders Svärd puts the point—don't become like dried raisins from the once juicy grapes of rights.

CHAPTER 9

Victims in Pictures

We live in a visual society, it is said—even a tabloid era. Animal advocates are hardly immune to this influence; indeed, they are sometimes known for taking the fullest advantage of sensational themes. Many activist strategies rely on celebrity appearances, showy exhibits, sexually explicit campaigns, and shocking imagery. One group's biographical blurb on the social media site Twitter offers "Sexy celeb supporters" and "antics" along with "shocking videos, vegan recipes & more!" It's that old recipe for attention: sex and violence. And violence… Can anyone who spends significant time in animal advocacy avoid the photos of atrocities, the horror-show incidents?

Yes, some graphic videos have shown people what goes on behind the doors and walls. People can be deeply affected by the images—including to the point of taking action, or changing the way they live. What I'm concerned about here is the tendency to push this effect so that it becomes yet another form of use, or to sound alarms when a method of use is visibly "barbaric" or a company is "notorious for extreme animal abuse" or manipulated research data. According to the rights view, egregious abuse is not the fundamental wrong; it is the use of the animals, and not the abuse, that is the basic wrong. Where domination is acceptable, atrocities are always possible; challenging dominion itself is the way to true, lasting change. Many people will miss this point when confronted with pictures that overload their senses and emotions. I have watched visitors at vegetarian festivals, particularly those with children, rushing past the stalls that display graphic posters and bloody videotape.

Probably the best chance of prevailing on the public to unravel the now-entrenched practice of animal testing is to explain the importance of a vegan commitment. Persuade people to become conscientious objectors to dominion and systematic control, starting with the personal commitment to stop, to the extent possible, consuming animals' flesh, skin, wool or hair, or any kind of secretion from their bodies, or commercial products tested on them. In contrast, campaigns against the particularly bad practices of a single company will project an uncertain message. Is the point that a farm or lab or animal-control agency should clean up its act and follow the rules? That the use of certain animals, or certain methods of controlling them, should be ruled out? Or is it something deeper? And wouldn't the spread of a vegan movement be exactly what we need to foster the culture that would renounce the worst companies and actions, rather than just move the activities to another location?

For those who can bear to view them, images of sadism and severe wounds may evoke outrage, but the outrage is often directed at rogue employees who flout the established handling practices. What if the activity could arguably be carried out in a bloodless or less painful way? Does the graphic picture explain to the audience that such use would still be ethically problematic? Does it open discussion about whether the animals should be subject to experimentation or bred for our consumption in the first place?

Activists usually answer this concern by saying they have to get the public's attention on any grounds they can. And yet to be ready with gory handouts doesn't mean one is ready to teach respect for conscious beings. We've already mentioned an activist group known for killing animals systematically. The same group produces endless shocking visuals. So using shocking images doesn't mean subscribing to a respect-based philosophy. Perhaps the reverse is more plausible: using shocking images to create an effect easily becomes yet another pervasive form of exploitation. Mindful of the ambitious beggar pinching a child to draw tears when a potential benefactor walks past, activists should ask serious questions about use of an animal's pain to attract support. A rescuer of cats and dogs famously killed some in front of a television audience, saying the sight was meant to raise consciousness. An anti-dairy activist has talked of constructing a slaughter plant open to the public, designed as a theme park, including a petting zoo, and regular announcements that animals are about to be killed. (Not only has that idea caused revulsion even in the advocacy community; it also seems to accept that if animals were simply around to be petted, everything might be right with the world.)

When one animal-protection group applied for a permit to dump pig manure and urine in front of Ohio's legislative buildings, while transmitting sounds of pigs screaming as they endured mutilations without painkillers and bringing "three hogs in 'narrow metal crates' to the statehouse as part of a factory farm protest," one advocate commented, "Apparently, the message here is that it is okay to let [an animal-advocacy group] use the animals to teach the rest of us that it is wrong to use animals."[1]

The body and the brochure

Catharine MacKinnon has called for a new way of understanding animal advocacy, observing that the primary model of animal rights to date misses animals on their own terms.[2] Do advocates' portrayals of non-human animals tend to present the idea of individuals and communities living on their own terms? Any survey would answer with a resounding "No." So where and how should animals be pictured so as to not inadvertently reinforce their vulnerability and our authority over them—in short, to avoid re-exploitation?

The answer is the case for focusing on free-living animals, those who could benefit from our recognition of their right to be let alone. This would align our imagery with our goal; it would acclimate people to the idea of animals living free. Consider the animals used for fur. They are usually individuals who could live full and free lives if not for the trade in their hair and skin. In our interventions to inspire people to let these

Photo: Advertisement created for Friends of Animals by Atlanta-based Tedco Worldwide, running in *Rolling Stone* and other magazines, addresses fur trim. Beneath the thoughtful gaze of the lynx, the caption, styled as a coat label, asks: "If you believe genuine fur trim comes from scraps, where do scraps come from?"

animals be themselves, we can portray them as the powerful and energetic beings they are. We need not treat them as abject victims; the very point of such an intervention would be to enable people to imagine their dignity restored to them and desire freedom for them.

Responses to images of dignity and freedom will vary. Activists are accustomed to associating advocacy with pictures of despair. When added up day after day, how can the pictures of agony be anything but disempowering? Could it be that these pictures also invoke a feeling of despair, even helplessness, in a potential advocate?

Many people over the years have told me that the photo collection in the middle of Peter Singer's *Animal Liberation* haunted them, even if they don't recall anything written in that book, and Singer's layout has been emulated often (although it appears its effect was limited—even on Singer, as noted in Chapter Two). I've read quite a few comments like this one: "The faces need to pull at the heartstrings and SOME element of how the fur is PROCESSED must be included in order to reach people. I think a picture of a hundred caged animals preparing for death would be a stronger message and infinitely more effective." But a different response comes from Ellie in New York City:

> Imagery of a free-living animal is more powerful, because it clearly speaks for the right of non-human beings to belong to themselves. In contrast, focusing on how animals are processed may open the way for bargaining with oppression or claims that fur can be obtained in more humane ways. Viewers who see the gaze of a strong, calm lynx are encouraged to reflect on the idea of a dignified individual, rather than avoid—or, in some cases, perhaps even be titillated by—portraits of pain.

Ellie's desire to focus on freedom rather than bargain with industry makes sense as part of a vegan movement. As we noted in Chapter 2, Leslie Cross wrote that veganism "possesses historical continuity" with the anti-slavery movement, and further explained:

> [V]eganism is not so much welfare as liberation, for the creatures and for the mind and heart of man; not so much an effort to make the present relationship bearable, as an uncompromising recognition that because it is in the main one of master and slave, it has to be abolished before something better and finer can be built. [3]

If it is important to advocate well for Earth's other conscious beings, through a liberation of the human mind and heart, how the "present relationship" is depicted matters greatly. Descriptions completely bypass the opportunity to call for liberation if the viewer understands them as revealing extreme neglect or maltreatment of animals rather than a critique of the hierarchy, the captivity, the domination. And as Ellie further notes, images can also amount to a failure of respect for the people who receive them, or become replicas of violence.

Barbara Sitomer, the owner of Gone Pie Vegan Bakery in New York, says, "I think the peace I believe in has to be reflected in my way of life on every level. Even visual." What seems to have an effect on a particular person may still be questionable, for Barbara points out that the way we reach out to others reflects who we are, and there's importance in acting consistently with our own being, and our own commitment. And does violent imagery offer people creative ways to seek peace? Or do the images instead make the feeling of living in a violent world even more pervasive?

Although in certain circumstances, arguably, a visual documentation of the worst facets of war has been genuinely essential, few of us feel encouraged when we watch something that induces emotional paralysis. Nevertheless, there are advocacy conferences that show bloody films almost ritualistically. I asked one person on a social media network, distributing a link to a bloody video, how it felt to actually watch the film. I said I couldn't bear it, and wondered if we could expect others to do so. My correspondent answered,

"I totally understand. I've yet to see it all the way through myself. When I first saw the undercover videos in it, I almost passed out." Philadelphia-area animal advocate Matthew McLaughlin said about the same film: "So much time is spent going into disturbing detail about what leads up to the death. By the time the death comes, the death seems like a relief for the animal and is a relief for the person watching it."

A post on the online networking forum Facebook announces: "Skinning LIVE ANIMALS 4 their fur! I need 2 find 10000 ppl sickened by this." Attempting to design a campaign or a community around a regular diet of blood and every imaginable suffering probably won't attract most healthy people to our cause. That reality is often forgotten when groups excuse sensationalism, sexism or any kind of insensitivity to human experiences by insisting such advertising brings a lot of attention, and thus supporters. We have no way of measuring how many people that insensitivity chases away from the same cause.

Ultimately, people are mostly likely to become and stay vegan not because they're shocked or scared by advocates but because they're persuaded by words that explain what the justice issue is all about. Not just the pain, not just the torture—the understanding that animals in situations where they're apparently well cared for and thought of as a natural and attractive part of the scene need to be re-thought.

Some worthwhile efforts (such as the campaign to end fur farms in Ireland that keep mink and foxes) have used undercover footage of fur farms, but the images were likely superfluous. Ireland's anti-fur groups, notably the Coalition to Abolish the Fur Trade (CAFT Ireland) and Respect for Animals, have had other campaign ideas going for them: their supporters have carried out protests outside Dublin fur sellers and distributed pamphlets in every fur-farming county to raise awareness and tackle the demand side of the issue.

People sometimes ask whether exposing extreme examples of maltreatment made human domination and ownership of *other humans* end faster. Whether the image is understood in a justice-based context is likely the most important factor. Particularly egregious treatment of enslaved humans in the United States did draw some humane—not necessarily abolitionist—responses; a classic analysis of this dynamic was presented by Judge Leon Higginbotham.[4] Early eighteenth-century South Carolina lawmakers dealt with extreme neglect or maltreatment; they were concerned with preserving property interests in slavery, not in challenging it, and they expressed special concern that some owned people had run away "for want of a sufficient allowance of provisions."[5]

Going back to the premise in *The Case For Animal Rights*, extreme maltreatment is wrong, of course; but it's not the fundamental wrong. Justice is hardly advanced by providing sufficient provisions for people to survive inside the system of slavery. Ensuring "sufficient provisions" and adjusting animal-handling methods doubtless can and will increase or decrease certain acute forms of distress and decrease the impact of disabilities; yet, as we've seen, an owner who provides sufficient provisions for non-human items of commerce is not attending to the animals' "welfare" but rather ensuring optimal methods of housing, transporting, handling them. Professionals in the fields of animal agribusiness, owners of pet shops, dog trainers, lab technicians and biomedical research specialists all apply certain methods of handling to suit the relevant kind of use; and these handling methods should not be misunderstood as an effort to ensure or improve the well-being of other animals.

Industries *cannot* manipulate the truth: that the captivity, the domination itself is the wrong. So the advocate's description of animal use should consistently challenge the domination itself, even where the conscious living beings are kept in good shape. Keep in mind too that the industries that use animals also know how to use the effects of images the viewer understands as revealing neglect or maltreatment.

Matthew McLaughlin told me how it felt to watch a film that purports to advocate for animals by way of presenting a steady stream of grotesque depictions of animal suffering. Matt notes how animal agribusiness has used these images to neutralize animal activism:

At Whole Foods Market yesterday, I saw milk from a company named Traders Point Creamery, which describes its dairy cows as "the girls" and announces that the "happy herd" just loves to be milked. The company's website is evidence of the effort that's gone into making their place of business resemble a family farm. It almost looks like a resort. They give tours of the place where people can see cows grazing in fields. They have videos that show the milking. Because they look nothing like the animal advocates' shocking videos, Traders Point benefits from those shocking images, and so does Whole Foods Market. The attempt to get people to stop consuming animal products through emotional appeals using grotesque images isn't going to work any longer.

Similarly, shocking photos of carriage horses in accidents have prompted calls for the tourist industry and its permitted routes to be more carefully restricted, but it's the powerful image of a horse running free, juxtaposed against a harnessed horse, that can inspire people to think about who the horses are without our driving or riding them. When the horses currently used are released to sanctuaries, the activist is asking that the industry be ended, and that horses living on the land on their terms are protected. The connection is made between what's being protested and what emancipation would actually be.

In the case of dairy cows, we're not asking that they live like the animals on Donald Watson's uncle's family farm. We know that cows on this supposedly idyllic farm have their days numbered until the point at which they outlive their usefulness to us. For most of the male babies born to "the girls" at Trader's Point, this day will come very soon indeed. Traders Point Creamery is Death Row.

Combine people's tendency to look away from horrific images of abuse together with their willingness to believe in rosy depictions of animal use, and the case is strong that the drawbacks of gory photos often outweigh the merits. If we are going to transcend a domination-oriented culture, it's most important that people see animal use itself, including use with the highest standards of handling, as disturbing, and know that animal welfare—well-being, that is—can only be honestly respected if animals are not caught or raised for us to kill or skin or ride or drink from, if they are not forced to submit to us at all. Again, the key point is the one thing industry can't manipulate: *Let them be!*

A recently distributed video, reportedly made by undercover activists, shows a chicken processing plant. Click the video screen, and a narrator begins, "What you are about to see is beyond your worst nightmares." One online commentator juxtaposed it with a representation of "good slaughter" and concluded with these words.

> Bottom Line: Eat pasture-raised animals that have not suffered for your dinner. Choose grass-fed cows. Choose the eggs of free-run chickens and not the product of stressed-out battery hens. Animals need not be treated as prisoners of war to allow us to eat meat. And remember: Organic does not mean humane. Choose happy meat.[6]

Advertisements from the industry might attempt to tell us otherwise, but animals need to be treated as prisoners of war to allow us to eat meat. They are confined, and they are slated for death, and when the owner is ready to dispose of them, they are killed in a place as far from happy as things get in this world.

And do slaughterers change because they see violence? If terrible imagery of animal blood and distress just by itself led to changing people, slaughter plant workers would be a nation of vegetarians. Do vivisectors change just because they see what really happens? Are the heartstrings of fur trappers tugged when they take in images of writhing bodies? Repeatedly witnessing a violent act can harden a person to it. A spokesperson for the American Meat Institute, discussing slaughter regulations, said, "The fact is, you could be absolutely, 100 percent in perfect compliance, but if someone is not used to seeing the slaughter process it would be unsettling." Some people get used to animal slaughter. Including of the human kind.

Adolf Hitler was one of sixty-five million soldiers who fought in the First World War, an instance of mass slaughter, generated by nations, in which nine million human beings perished—thousands each day. Hitler had to crouch in the trenches and endure the wet and cold and mud, the hunger, the constant artillery barrages, the sight of dismemberment and death of hundreds of comrades, the stench of their decaying bodies. Over four thousand in Hitler's regiment alone were killed. Hitler lay in a hospital bed, blinded by poison gas, when the war ended in November 1918.[7] One might expect, writes psychologist Richard Koenigsberg, that Hitler would have then condemned and renounced the slaughter of human beings. Instead, Hitler lived and died in a state of denial. On to the Second World War. Five hundred thousand German soldiers died *each month* during the first four months of 1945, the most concentrated known example of slaughter of humans by humans.[8] But that wasn't what made Hitler notorious.

To this day, soldiering is considered a dignified undertaking. We are all taught to respect and perpetuate the ideal of the nation, and think of it as real, noble, and inevitable, even though, as Koenigsberg says, "nations kill a lot of people." Our warfare against other animals is also widely considered inevitable, and perhaps even noble. We decry the atrocities, but not the customs that cause them to arise. Many organizers work to make human supremacy humane—all the while saying modifications in industry are important because "the world is never going to go vegan." Our thoughts, and the words we select to express them, have consequences. People's desires are influenced by messages they receive from their friends, relatives, media outlets—and us. Living a vegan life, and thereby bringing about animal rights person by person, community by community, is not too difficult unless we choose to listen to defeatist messages. It takes no special power to be vegan. Vegans are just regular people who decline to participate in violence.

We know living peaceably is a good thing. What do we do with this knowledge? We can purport to make war ethical by working out its rules to forbid torture and other atrocities, and the wars will continue, and no matter how they are regulated, we shall have torture and atrocities. Another response is possible, through conscientious objection. We could decide now that war, like slavery, is deemed unconscionable and obsolete. War could be rejected. Systematic violence against other animals too could end—but first we must decide that we want it to end.

Our privilege to look

More than our emotional state can be affected by injections of horrific imagery of animals into the public sphere. The imagery can also shape our perceptions of non-human beings and their daily lives on Earth. Consider a poster, commonly seen, of a monkey amputee with a visibly distressed facial expression, partially wrapped in gauze. The more it is shown, the greater the likelihood that viewers will, to some extent, associate monkeys with pain, confinement, and objectification. Some people will have no idea what the natural life of a monkey would be.

Do the activists who show this picture, year after year, know who this monkey was—or anything about the way this monkey would live, who and where this monkey would have been, if not subjected to human control? Photos of animals as abject victims of cruelty and slaughter do not tell us who these animals were or are; but they do reveal truths about how we view those conceived as others.

Even as I write this paragraph, I receive an advocate's alert about chimpanzees in Spain. The alert features a photo, but it does not depict a chimpanzee; it shows a macaque monkey. As I look at the photo my thoughts turn to a monkey who passed away not long ago after living many years at the Primarily Primates sanctuary in Texas. The thumb-sucking infant, eyes sewn shut from a sensory-deprivation experiment, was taken from a lab in a clandestine rescue, dubbed Britches, and famously filmed. Funds have been raised through the use of this helpless baby's pictures for years; this is a case in which images were used with little regard for the individual pictured, for the money was not applied to the care of the real monkey who appeared in all the films and pictures, campaigns and book covers. Many don't know if Britches is alive or dead (the currently available online reference *Wikipedia* incorrectly and inexplicably tells us the monkey was sent to Mexico), let alone ask how to give financial or campaigning support to the Texas refuge that provided a permanent home once the advocacy group had done its filming.

Perhaps the tendency to objectify can be more fully understood when we consider how human victims are viewed, and how we would personally feel to see our own suffering pictured for a cause. My work has brought me into immigration law—specifically, migrant and refugee issues—as well as animal rights. For some time, online subscribers to certain refugee discussion lists would receive a photo of a child and mother, the same photo, from various fundraising websites. How does a refugee feel when encountering those pictures, those same emaciated human faces, from the first, second, and third fundraising appeal? How does a refugee feel to see refugees portrayed over and over as mouths to feed, while the fundraising campaigners who use the images have no idea what their lives are like or what their talents are? The essence of refugee migration is political or environmental upheaval; it displaces engineers, window-washers, musicians, doctors, linguists, writers, wanderers, mechanics and ambassadors—and people who have played a variety of those roles during their lives. Maybe the child and mother whose faces keep appearing, if they are alive somewhere today, are highly skilled people; in any case, these refugees are more than their victimhood. And this mother and baby themselves, did they want to be shown to the world like this? Did they give permission? Do any of the groups who ask for donations by using these people's faces have the slightest idea who these people are?

Whether they're meant to raise funds or to move people to join a campaign, pictures may inadvertently subvert respect for beings, or whole groups of beings, who are represented as helpless, perpetually needing rescue. And it's not political injustice itself but rather the worst cases of starvation or torture that these pictures tend to project as the wrong. Surely part of this kind of campaigning involves shortcutting: The activist who uses shocking pictures and employs emotional words that require no thought (a high percentage of alerts include "cruel" or "horrific" or "barbaric") can get by with limited preparation and educating, and that can be convenient when membership drives, a petition full of signatures, or fundraising take over as goals. People have become used to substituting shrill adjectives and bloody posters for persuasion through actual discussion. This fails to respect the audience, and it fails to accord genuine respect for the individual or population whose interests are at stake.

Even the gentlest, most painstaking and studious advocacy films interpret others' lives through the camera's lens. To represent animals, to watch them, is so normal for us that we generally do not question our privilege to look, and to do what we like with the images. Often, the photographer or videographer was a passive witness to a harrowing event, infusing a disturbing element to the very process of obtaining the imagery.

Psychological impacts of violent imagery

At times, sensitive, respectful minds will disagree about the precise line between advocacy and objectification. But we should agree at least on one point. Because imagery of exploited animals is, on some level, another layer of use of the animals in those images, and because of its real impact on the human audience, the ethical use of such imagery requires serious care and thought.

Picturing aggression and terror can play a role in the cycle of violence, according to some who study the issue. The advocacy group Human Rights First has taken note of a "startling increase in the number of torture scenes depicted on prime-time television in the post-2001 world"—and also notes that real interrogators sometimes take cues from what they see on television and films.[9] They believe that a proliferation of victimization images sets the stage for situations in which exploitation is absorbed, perhaps replicated, rather than seriously confronted. The issue will doubtless be debated, but caution here makes sense for people working for a peaceful humanity. Being young usually means being especially impressionable, and young people who become drawn to today's model of animal activism must deal with powerful emotions that can be magnified by a sense of belonging to a group that offers highly disturbing imagery, often connecting violence with sex, in websites deliberately designed to win young adherents.

Verbal descriptions can persuade the listener and simultaneously challenge the communicator to engage in discussion rather than use and replicate ready-made photos taken during the course of exploitation. Consider the impact of these words, from New Jersey musician and peace activist Sharleen Leahey, who speaks of why vegetarianism should be inclusive of living individuals caught in the dairy industry:

> My friend Carol and I went to see a friend while I was playing in upstate New York. We ended up visiting a farm. I got to hang out with some boy calves who were sucking my fingers because they missed their mothers. Carol and I talked later and were both sad because they were being sold off to some bleak fate. We both agreed that should not be happening. I can't get those calves out of my mind . . . Their softness and their innocence. It haunts me.

The authentic voice of a sensitive person who has experienced a changed worldview is the most powerful form of communication the vegan movement has ever had.

And consider the positive power of a cookbook, a vegan restaurant, or a garden. Invite people to consider a new perspective with a straightforward, dynamic, creative kind of empathy. Why? Imagine someone trying to convince ourselves of a position quite unlike the one we now hold. With what kind of appeal would an advocate draw us? Vegan education at its best describes the oppression, but does not leave a vacuum; it immediately guides people to a fresh, attractive, and fair way of life. Because successful movements aren't so much against something as *for* something. If you're for more than opposing the things humans do to animals, if you're *for* the right to live on one's own terms, then you want to show pictures of free animals. And humanity doing positive things, such as eating and sharing luscious food.

This is more than just positive thinking, although it is that. Unlike the push to eliminate the worst conditions in institutions of animal commerce, veganism asks us to envision an entirely new paradigm. It involves organizing spheres of voluntary co-operation, to arrive at a society that respects life. It is about declining flesh and milk-based groceries, wool and other products of animal agribusiness—and accepting or providing hearty, healthful, naturally beautiful food and clothing, which is, to the extent we can achieve, free of unfairness. To advocate vegan principles is to address *all* conditions of the farms, feedlots, killing floors and *all* oppressive customs and businesses (including the most visibly atrocious) at once, by showing people how to spare animals from ever being bred for human purposes in the first place. Veganism—defined as a movement of conscientious objection to deliberate exploitation of aware beings—spares animals from being dominated. Portray it as refreshing, life-affirming, and at first, people will ask why there are no hanging cows, squeezed pigs, or bloodied birds in our brochures; but little by little, people will catch on. No one will avert their eyes upon opening the brochure. Vegan restaurants will gladly stock it, as it won't put patrons off their meals. And people will gladly give copies to children and people they meet in the course of their daily errands.

Granted, access to the disturbing visual reality can help us to understand the full impact of an injustice; as a salient example, withholding images of soldiers' caskets may allow the public the comfort of averting their eyes from the results of war. But whether one should show the mangled corpses inside is another question entirely, a question demanding care and respect when applied to scenes of non-human death as well. Wouldn't a photo of Lobo, caught in Seton's traps, have been superfluous? Was Seton's story not descriptive enough, genuine, profound, gruelling, haunting, maddening enough? Were Sharleen Leahey's words about the fate of the calves who tried to suck the singer's fingers really not enough to convey the full impact of an injustice?

This is not to say we should strictly limit ourselves to the spoken and typeset word—which themselves can be used for demagogic purposes— and make no use of graphic imagery. That recommendation would be simplistic, whether for human-rights or animal-rights advocacy. I once heard a story from a wonderful teacher of linguistics about a particular use of what we might call graphic language. The professor, as a rule, didn't swear. Unexpectedly, on a certain day when the professor's colleagues were being impossible regarding an important and irreversible decision, they heard, from that most scrupulous tongue, a four-letter word. The impact was immediate: absolute silence; then, an agreement to consider a change of course. Perhaps this is the attitude to take regarding pictures that tell a painful truth about non-human animals' situations. So as to respect, and not to degrade, the animals for whom one hopes to gain attention, such photos should be used only when and insofar as they must—as the occasional curse that shatters an otherwise gentle articulateness.

Yes, such decisions become complex. That's precisely the point: we should tread carefully here. Animal advocacy is not the replication of spectacles. Images of real lives should not become props, distorted into public attractions and fundraising tools. We are looking to model the interactions that would take place in a society in which gentleness is valued; and where the information we have to impart is startling, the recipients should first be adequately prepared for the experience. Ask: Is it objectification? Do the activists know the stories of the subjects portrayed? Is the picture a shortcut; and would the communication be more respectful (to the viewer or to the individuals pictured, or both) if presented in written form? If the activist really did witness the scenes, are people who are already sensitive to the issues being emotionally drained by seeing various scenes of unspeakable sadness? Is part of our public message, even if an unintended part, that being a worthy activist means being inconsolably depressed? Do a search for vegan users of Twitter, and you might find someone whose profile picture is the dead pig head and guts spilling out. Facebook turns up dozens of profile pictures of animal activists drenched in fake blood. And the other day, when I was joyously supporting my local vegetarian restaurant, a person came in wearing a t-shirt that pictured a monkey, trapped in a restraint chair and being cut into. My appetite disintegrated. I felt the same way seeing this person in the vivisection t-shirt as I feel when someone has walked into the restaurant wearing a fur coat. Details about how animals are or have been used in research are important to make accessible, and yet the image of vivisection at the vegan buffet, where people were not able to grasp what it meant or learn what to do, was jarring and gave off the vibe of the vegan who's ruining someone's meal. And a vegan meal at that! The public, the activist community, and the animals for whom we strive to advocate, could all do with a positive vision of animal rights.

Becoming good students of human nature

Most activists only observe one type of violence, that of physical battery; but there are other types of violence, including emotional violence. If we are serious about getting our message across, we must be good students of human nature, observes former dairy farmer Harold Brown. "Humans, like all beings, spend nearly all of our time keeping pain, suffering and cruelty out of our lives," Harold has said. "We seek safety, comfort, companionship, shelter, good food—just like all beings. Yet for thirty-some years, the movement has been delivering a message of pain, suffering, horror, shame and guilt."

And then there's the issue of where the shame is directed. I recently received an invitation to join an Internet group called "China should be ashamed, they treat domesticated animals shamefully." Activist groups present their members with graphic descriptions and photos of the horror of Chinese fur production, especially if dogs or cats are used; slaughter in Middle Eastern countries is often especially reprehended. Regarding the production of horse flesh in the U.S. for the European and Asian markets, we do not hear of the "barbaric" ways we treat horses in North America.

Rather, we hear about the foreign-controlled slaughter plants. Horses are not eaten in North America, but horses are still made into commodities, consumed and discarded after use.

Until the 1980s, the people of China ate only small rations of animal flesh, and virtually no dairy products. Today, Chinese families can celebrate birthdays at McDonalds, and China is the world's third biggest dairy producer, behind the United States and India. According to Xinran, a journalist and the author of *What the Chinese Don't Eat,* the demand in China for dairy products is a result of the image of affluence and physical abilities connected with Western lifestyles.[10] In this way, Western culture has, if anything, broadened the forms of animal use across other continents. Moreover, the Western demand for meat—U.S. residents on average eat four times as much animal flesh as most of the world's people and more than 40 times as much as the residents of Bangladesh[11]—deforests immense areas of land and devastates natural habitats for free-roaming animals. The animals displaced by deforestation—undomesticated animals—are living right now as though the animal-rights principles, involving respect for non-human dignity and the autonomy, were accepted by human culture; and yet, ironically, the continual disappearance of these animals' communities is ignored by the animal-protection advocates who concentrate on influencing the husbandry standards for farm animals. And are the self-identified environmentalists noticing the conscious beings in that environment? Or are they mainly focusing on some vague idea of a clean backdrop for humanity? When will the "green" people and the vegan animal-rights proponents combine their knowledge and strengths?

Perhaps we can all sit down, have a nice, cold drink, and talk about this. In a time when the environmentally conscious are, in cities and towns internationally, setting up networking occasions known as "Green Drinks," activists throughout the United States have followed a successful tradition begun in New York known as "Vegan Drinks." Everyone is welcome; no resource-costly animal products are served on any bar menu, and the samplings on the bar menus have been delicious. Who would balk at roasted seitan tacos as they share conversation over their pitcher of pomegranate sangria? Here one learns about the finer points of vegan living: Most wines, many beers, and some alcohols are refined through such ingredients as gelatine, or isinglass, which is derived from fish bladders. Some have carmine among the ingredients—a red dye made from the crushed bodies of beetles. But not at Vegan Drinks. Some attendees enjoy a root beer, recalling that early vegans including Donald Watson did not drink alcohol at all. While teaching these facts in an enjoyable setting with exciting food, the Vegan Drinks idea can be a way to raise funds for a local animal refuge, in a relaxed setting. The value of enjoyable social activity as a model is probably underrated. What's true in Donald Watson's time holds true, for many people, in ours: the most difficult aspect of being a vegan is excommunicating oneself from occasions where people meet to eat.[12] This can only be alleviated by the spread of veganism.

People eat animal products and don't think of themselves as "omnivores"; they still set the standard, and many do not like to be reminded that there is another way to live. Omnivorous living cannot be the standard any more. It is time to start thinking of completely vegetarian food as the norm—and as welcoming rather than isolating. Rather than asking about vegan alternatives to this or that menu item, rather than asking a restaurant to bring in "vegan options," let's start talking about vegan *offerings*. Let's imagine and create a culture in which animal agribusiness is properly understood as a custom of the past, and vegan living is embraced as the way to sustain our world. Let's work with restaurants to increase the availability of interesting and fully vegetarian offerings at social gatherings at which people meet to recharge their batteries and exchange ideas.

Activists need friends, and friendships are often much too scarce in the larger society in which the activists live. Dean, a vegan living in central England, points out that activism should include respect for activists themselves, not only the work we provide: "Some see me as a commodity to come to demonstrations and things they believe in. I believe in them too, with all my heart, but need friendships too. Otherwise, animal rights and veganism seem like a shallow excuse for living. There's no point in this without friends."

Dean is speaking as an individual, but of course there's a big world out there, full of people who might like to work for a better humanity; most of those folks are not longing to join a movement that's geared to accomplish as many displays of defiance as possible. Many capable minds will sense that activism is not a calendar of actions, but the cultivation of ethical progress.

Peep-show attractions

In addition to (or sometimes combined with) a regular fare of horrifying imagery, sexual objectification is now on the menu offered by popular advocacy. It would be nearly impossible to research the animal-advocacy movement and avoid imagery of barely clad television celebrities. Many times, we've been assured that sex sells. But genuine social change is not about perfecting a sales formula; it's a transformed way of living. This cannot be achieved through marketing tricks.

When advocacy splits humanity into two groups and trades heavily on the objectification of one by the other, the organizers are, arguably, engaging in the cruelty they are so quick to ascribe to others. The routine use of objectifying images creates stress in the sphere of advocacy and in humanity's social atmosphere in general. Young, barely clad models are now practically everywhere in advertising, notes a fashion and culture columnist, who adds: "It tells us the fashion industry has run out of ideas, and has resorted to trying to shock us into paying attention. Rather than liberating, it is merely oppressive, telling us we do not look the way we should." [13] The same theme haunts popular animal advocacy. Recently, an animal-protection group's vice president came to a dinner presentation to tell others how to be effective activists. I attended the dinner. The audience was told that effective advocacy uses nudity, celebrities, and—best of all—nude celebrities. The speaker reported that animal activism used to be thought of as a "touchy-feely girly" issue, but, fortunately, has lately drawn more men.

The local activists were apparently expected to clap and agree, as though they had not just heard something senseless and bizarre, not to mention strikingly misogynous.

A commentator for the Internet-based magazine *Salon*, Carol Lloyd, observes that in these mean-spirited times, with advantage-taking being the mode of social interaction, some animal advocates are compensating for their untimely or unpopular interest in non-human beings' situations by being "tough and a little mean" and thus retaining an aura of "cool" in another way—by encouraging sexual objectification. "Although historically feminism and vegetarianism have often been aligned," writes Lloyd, "now every movement's on its own—each competing for eyeballs and dollars."[14]

And that's not good at all. Thinking about use of sexism to advertise animal protection, advocate Deb Smoot expresses sadness that we can't work together to improve the lives of one group without demeaning others. Smoot, who once worked in the field of law enforcement, recalls the unremitting calls from scenes of violence in sexual relationships, and the terrible challenge of finding support:

> Like all shelters, the ones who cared for victims of domestic violence were always striving for funds to keep the shelters open. I often heard this group of social advocates decrying the money or time that people were donating to animal shelters; as if compassion and consciousness-raising in one area of our life should be in competition with any or all others.

Some believe burlesque activism attracts young people in a generation that likes female celebrities who adopt such a style. It is, of course, tempting to reach out to people on their current level by holding out something meant to attract them at first, then develop the message better. Sometimes that is acceptable; but sometimes not.

Let's look at how reaching people where they already are *is* wise.

The teachings of the Buddha include a story about a parent who hastens children out of a burning house by calling them to see some new toys (although the parent has no such toys). The frantic parent is, of course, blameless for presenting a false attraction when the point is to save the children from death. A serious animal-rights proponent knows we are in a burning house. Glaciers, the sources of our rivers, are melting. Water and food shortages caused by climate disruptions in major growing regions are expected to turn millions of humans into environmental migrants within the coming decade.[15] Enormous amounts of water are used and trees are felled unnecessarily by animal agribusiness. Is it acceptable, then, to use environmental arguments to bring people to the ideas of animal rights? Of course it is; and this would hardly be a false attraction. The human factor in climate disruptions poses a severe threat to ourselves and all other living beings. The animal-rights discussion should come to the fore of all the discussion of "sustainable" gatherings and products. And we see them everywhere these days: promotions for sustainable animal agribusiness or sustainable meals made with local vegetables and flesh of pigs, cows, or fish purchased from small farms or local waters. Often, people who organize these promotions do not know why the concept of respect for other animals is relevant. They want to talk about sustainability, not animal rights. Yes, it is important to meet these organizers where they are: to acknowledge their concern about a topic of great importance, and to move them from there to the question of whether human domination is sustainable. Is it not the human custom of conquering the Earth and its conscious beings that brought us to a sustainability crisis in the first place?

London activist Donald Leung points out that the people we meet do not just act based on self-absorbed ideas. They are capable of love and caring at least for themselves and those close to them; and that means they can care about other humans, animals, plants, rivers, forests and the world. Talk to them first about what they are already open to appreciating, says Donald:

> To speak from a point of positivity rather than negativity,
> I believe, brings positive, enduring results. The opportunity

then arises for people to be open to the moral issues. To argue initially only serves to widen the chasm between you and them, so you have to shout for them to hear you. I enjoy when people ask me about the animals or I can humorously express the truths of what goes on behind dairy and egg farming, especially to vegetarians. Comedy is interesting because it is deep-felt accord and understanding, in contrast to an argument, which is one view in opposition to another. A person may be neutral but by beginning in argument you are polarizing them against you. If your true intention is to bring about an awareness and belief in veganism it is more effective to begin with accord, I believe. Do you care about the planet? Yes. Do you care about your health? Yes. Do you believe that milk produced by mothers should be for their children? Yes. Does world hunger concern you? Yes. The cost and quality of food? Yes. Well, then...

Donald points out that it's hard to deny the relevance of veganism to anyone personally. And all the while, Donald recommends excellent food: "As people are eating vegan the awareness and sensitivities to other beings will emerge. I wouldn't want to deprive them of that by guilting them into ignorance or deciding a singular point of entry into the vegan universe for them."

In short, there's nothing contrived about bringing environmental discussions—or health concerns, or deliberations on social justice—together with the message of animal rights.

It's great that people get into veganism from where they are, and if they stay on the track a few years they'll begin to see these as interwoven threads. People appreciate integrity and want to be known for having it. People enjoy bringing new insights to others. Creativity and caring and altruism make most people feel good. So those who come into veganism to defend the ecology will learn that this is not separate from an expanded sense of their moral community; neither is complete without understanding the other. But it is an entirely different matter to suggest that we should meet people where they are by waving in front of them images that exploit a gender hierarchy. First, this is gratuitous. We can find ways to bring animal advocacy to young people without subverting their self-esteem and best inclinations. And that brings us to the most critical reason against the "sex sells" argument: Using someone as an object and a lure when the very point of one's movement is to get beyond treating beings as objects must be wrong. "Sexy" demonstrations in animal advocacy usually objectify one class of humans for the entertainment of another—and the press. It can hardly be ethical to lure people with attractions that perpetuate oppression, and it is unconscionable to do this as a systematic form of activism in the name of a fairer society. Finally, the use of images of scantily clad volunteers, interns, and employees suggests to the outside observer that advocacy groups would treat their own members as lures. Animal-rights advocacy is still discussed by the public as having cultish tendencies; the exploitation of activists just reinforces this conception.

"The world's first vegan strip club" recently emerged in Portland. The owner told local media, "We put the meat on the pole, not on the plate."[16] The venue was once a completely vegetarian restaurant, one that was becoming unprofitable. After the management got busy "throwing some boobs up," boasts the owner, customers appeared. Yet veganism was started to represent and achieve—as Donald Watson put it—the ideal of non-exploitation. The owner's crass message is a striking example of what author Carol Lloyd points out as a sign of these mean-spirited times.

We need not sell veganism, and we cannot sell it. Respect is not a commodity. Cultivating it takes patience. We know change does not easily happen in a social system in which nations compete, corporations compete, academics compete and advocacy brands compete in a global economy, when strategy consumes much of our life's essence, when people are seen as units to be measured according to our ability to consume. In such an atmosphere, altruism is devalued. But art can remind us of the capabilities within each of us. It can also show many people, in a way that touches the collective spirit of an audience, the truth about the domination and use of any conscious beings—that domination is domination, and its various manifestations must be understood together to be understood at all.

Along with the pickets and hunger strikes, which have been used in activism with inspiring effect, drawing the respect of people in decision-making offices as well as people on streets, the arts are also part of a balanced life in a social-justice movement. Art nourishes us, and balanced living is important for advocates to project. To address the injustice of the animal circus, for example, advocates can create acrobatic shows. Face painting, music and outstanding food is what makes many people want to be part of the buzz they find at vegan festivals. Lisa Levinson, Zipora Schulz and Jim Harris conceived the Philadelphia-based "Public Eye: Artists for Animals" in 2005. The group plans local dance performances, puppet shows, and art exhibits that raise public awareness about concern for animals. In November 2009, at the Essene Market & Cafe of South Philadelphia, the Artists for Animals Kids' Club presented a hands-on vegan cooking class with chef Rachel Klein (turkeys' interests were discussed), and a holiday art project.

For people of any age, art can inspire our personal capabilities and our sense of connection with others. Creative acts of social justice, Rebecca Alban Hofberger has written, offer what works of art offer. "They inspire us, make us think in new ways, and birth new beauty and dignity in our world."[17] Likewise, works of art can be everything we could ask for in a creative act of social justice. *Playhouse Creatures,* written by playwright April De Angelis, was commissioned and first performed by The Sphinx (Women's National Touring Theatre) in 1993, at the Haymarket Theatre in Leicester, England.[18] This extraordinary theatrical work could have just as well been supported and offered as part of the animal-rights movement. Admittedly, it was promoted in a way that put me off at first: "a rollicking bawdy story, full of rude hilarity, earthy comedy and heartbreak..." But I took a chance because performances by Upstairs at the Gatehouse in London, where the play was staged, are always remarkable experiences. I was not to be let down. The promotion was actually a clever commentary on the circumstances addressed in the play itself. *Playhouse Creatures* is set in the 1600s—when, for the first time in English history, female actors were allowed to perform on the English stage. It was not acting skill so much as titillation that kept these newcomers in demand. Oyster vendors and prostitutes entered the stage, where the expectations were every bit as crude as those they faced on the streets—although the sexual requests might now come from the king of England—and a hint of advancing age or pregnancy would threaten not only their access to work on the stage, but also their lives.

The playhouse used to be run by the father of the elderly Doll Common. Doll can still smell the bears who were kept in those days, trained to dance on that same stage. Occasionally Doll even sweeps up an old tuft of fur. Doll still remembers the sound of the bears moaning at night, licking their fur where the irons cut in.

One bear rose up in rebellion, ignoring the whip, continuing to lunge, rising up, slashing Doll's father's chest. Doll screamed, "No, Dad!" as the bear's teeth were wrenched out.

If one bear gets away with it, Doll heard, tomorrow no bear will dance.

Why, Doll asked, do you whip them? The bear rocked and screamed on the bloody floor.

Doll's father answered: The bears dance, and we eat meat. Never question it again. Doll never did. The blood on the floor gradually turned from hot to cool.

The curtain falls.

CHAPTER 10

The Campaign Plan:
Bringing Animal-Rights
Theory Down To Earth

S o here we are, committed to vegan goals. But we also want to defend specific animals, to intervene, just as we'd do for human rights causes. We can't wait for animals to ask us to help; we must affirmatively step up to intervene on their behalf. How do we go about it?

Assume we want to intervene in a specific case of injustice, or establish a campaign that defends animals' current autonomy and dignity. And we'd like to do it in a way that advances the emancipation of animals from property status—which is, as we have observed, a crucial component of animal rights. It's not always easy to tell if an activist's intervention does this, or if, instead, it entails the regulation of animal use. Here is a pair of guideposts to work with, to make the assessment easier.

1. "Let them be!"

First, ask: Does it let them be? Could the community of animals live in their ways, not ours, if the intervention on their behalf succeeds?

Intervening to stop a local deer hunt or fox hunt, for example, will satisfy this criterion. Ending fur sales in shops in a particular city, or ending a specific seal kill, would be a step on the way to this goal. If there were no fur shops, whole communities of animals currently being sought for fur could live on their own terms without being stalked and trapped for their skins.

I have noticed some animal-rights activists attempting to get people to stop talking up a ban of fur in Ireland—because the ban wouldn't stop people from using other animal-based materials. Defending fur-bearing animals is single-issue campaigning, some activists assert. If people just swap their fur for leather, what's the victory in that?

The term single-issue has become a handy sort of way to write off the efforts of advocates who try, often successfully, to take a stand in certain places. These advocates act locally, but they very well might think holistically, and say so. Nevertheless, the question about fur as a limited issue is not without merit, and we must answer it. A key point to grasp is that fur and leather are distinct industries. The use of leather, and the domination within it, shouldn't be dismissed, and leather is more than a by-product, in the sense that it represents a significant part of the profit from the sale of a cow's body; yet the use of the cows' skin will fall away as humans kick the habit of breeding cows into agriculture. Fur (and the so-called exotic skins—of reptiles, for example) can and should be distinguished from leather; the product is usually snatched from free-roaming, undomesticated beings. In other words, fur takes away the coats and the lives of animals who could have lived free. In this industry, animals are either trapped in their habitat or they're bred on properties of farmers, caged for life. The frustration of captivity leads to self-mutilation and psychotic conditions. Fear of strange noises causes cannibalism. These farming practices should have ended long ago. The taking of a free beaver's life, too—no matter how pleasant the animal's life had been to that point or how carefully the killing is done—violates and ends the individual's life experience. We can and should stop interfering in these animals' lives.

So we have distinguished two groups of animals: domesticated animals such as cows who shouldn't be here; and animals such as the fur-bearers who should and who can have what we call animal rights: the ability to live on their own terms. Vegan persuasion does address the cows' situation. In the case of fur, intervening to end hunting and trapping can essentially liberate animals and their whole communities from our dominion. Both types of actions are vegan actions when we take the broad view of what vegan means. Both types help us to strive for a complete paradigm shift that rejects domination and accepts respect as the hallmark of our world-view. Of course, convincing people to go vegan does bring about respect for fur-bearing animals (as vegans don't wear fur or hunt or trap); and yet it's possible that individuals and whole communities of fur-bearing animals will be wiped out by the time the convincing is complete. We need not turn away from animals under assault when there's a chance we can spare them from harm and let them be. This should be obvious: Advocates can defend animals such as foxes without fearing that they've shirked a duty to speak for all animals at once. Of course, when an observer looks downward, the advocate would certainly be prepared to say, "Yes! Those are canvas shoes I'm wearing!" (Extra points if they're made of recycled inner tubes.) And just as in the case of a hospital or town that puts a stop to flesh products, these anti-fur interventions provide opportunities for discussions in which people talk with each other about the whole idea of respect.

In late January, in response to a campaign organized by Friends of Animals, Olympic-bound figure-skater Johnny Weir committed to "changing the genuine fox fur on my free program costume that I will use in the 2010 Winter Olympic Games in Vancouver, B.C., to white faux fur." Some abolitionist writers have advised us to avoid or shun this kind of organized advocacy that defends free-living communities, and to do only "vegan advocacy": pamphleteering and blogging. Their perspective might be that targeting specific situations could imply that other types of animal exploitation aren't as bad. But advocacy at its best is a blend of things. How can we let Arctic foxes—who, along with polar bears, the only other mammals hanging on to life near the planet's northern pole, already face so many threats—be left to trappers while we wait until everyone's won over by vegan pamphlets? How can we know that deer (and by extension coyotes and everyone in their biocommunities) are being run out of town only a few miles from where we work, yet bury ourselves in pamphlet writing? *Do* write vegan pamphlets, of course, that deal with the roots of preventable harm. Do go out onto the street corners with vegan food. Do help produce cookbooks, or books such as the one you're holding now. But remember that the freedom of the Arctic foxes is a quintessentially vegan idea. Avoid that tragedy that unfolds when animal writers neglect real communities of animals just outside their office windows. Imagine the same advice being given when it comes to human rights. Imagine someone telling us not to say anything about, say, genital mutilation, or the children forced to work on chocolate plantations of the Ivory Coast because they are "single" issues. We might not be able to get involved directly with such issues, but at least we show support for those activists who do get involved.

Another criticism, returning to the Irish fur production ban, has focused on the monetary compensation from the government to the business owners. A question has come up over whether the owners of closing fur farms will take the payoffs and set up shop outside the country, or use the money to start up other exploitive businesses. These concerns are warranted, but they don't mean the ban is worthless. The concerns underscore the need for activists to carry on with broader vegan education and explain to people why the fur ban is only a part of that overall movement. It would be better, of course, if there were no payoffs to the farmers—and certainly it would be a mistake to agree to compensation in the form of immunity to lawsuits for the companies during the phase-out period. But government-provided job training or even actual monetary compensation shouldn't be a reason to avoid campaigning for a ban.

If veganism has, as its founders defined it, historical continuity with the abolition of other systems of enslavement, it's worth noting that President Abraham Lincoln seriously considered a buyout of human slaves for $400 each under an "emancipation with compensation" proposal that would have had the states abolish slavery. The idea was the product of a time when the war, which had been raging for a year without a predictable end, drained $2 million a day.[1] Buying the freedom of an estimated 432,622 slaves in Delaware, Maryland, Kentucky, Missouri and Washington, D.C. would cost $173,048,800—nearly equal to 87 days of war funding. Activists often think money is never contemplated in abolitionist achievements but real situations are rarely so simple.

It is excellent news for foxes and mink wherever their captivity and exploitation ends. Wherever this occurs, the human desire to use animals as a commodity or an object of violent sport is relinquished, and the interests of mink, foxes, lynx, rabbits, raccoons and coyotes and beavers are afforded respect. If we end the fur trade in a given region, whole communities of animals are free from being resources and can instead live on their terms. Our decision to live fur-free, then, lets fur-bearers live *their* way. It allows us to *Let them be!* The ban should, as noted, be coupled with public outreach (using a variety of methods from leaflet distribution to music to theatrical performance) that implicates people and challenges the demand, so that fur isn't simply brought in from another place.

Cows, being purpose-bred, can't live their way; and, as suggested above, it's likely that their skins will be used while their bodies are exploited for milk and flesh. Addressing their situation means converting our farming from animal agribusiness to crops for direct human nutrition. Both forms of activism—ending fur use *and* promoting vegan living—count. In other words, just as proposing that people be vegan is important, defending undomesticated animals' freedom is also important. Take the broad view of what veganism stands for, and you'll be intervening to defend animals' lives and autonomy.

In 1985, North American advocate Alice Herrington wrote to lawmakers with a creative argument that turned inside out the U.S. Supreme Court's 1842 decision that all free-living animals belong to the people.[2] Herrington noted that commerce is the first step to human-induced extinction; that the states had, with that awareness, ended the trade in bird plumage; that the trade in animal fur had surpassed the trade in plumage; and that states similarly ought to discontinue all sales of fur, thus shutting off the market. Herrington's argument was that no free-living animals ought to be commodities; if they belong to the people, it is in the sense that the people, in turn, belong to a biocommunity. Interventions that end the use of skin and fur in any given place would be on track to bringing closer the day we live in harmony rather with than dominate that biocommunity, just as each vegan restaurant brings a vegan culture nearer.

One might raise the objection that Herrington's legal challenge entrenches property status, and the objection would have merit. We understand "wildlife" has been made into legal property, and the unfairness that contains. Nevertheless, the idea of banning fur because most people want to, and because putting animals into the stream of commerce leads to extinctions, is both intriguing and bold. Today, with an area of study that perceives non-human personhood, combined with what we know about extinctions and the way human actions are comprising an assault on evolution itself, nothing but a century of custom stops us from saying we'll relinquish our right to treat other animals as commodities. The law that made free-living communities our property and took their territory away could be changed to respect the environment as home to other animals. Indeed, in some way or another, it's time for our law to do this.

In the book *Speciesism,* Joan Dunayer argued that other animals should have some form of property rights of their own. Let's discuss whether some kind of protection along that line is necessary if they are going to live on their terms rather than live (or die) on ours. Maybe so. For other animals are in quite a bind if only one species, the *Homo sapiens,* keeps property rights and no one else does. Today, our property rights take precedence over the very habitat animals need to live and carry on their communities. Who hasn't seen a local green patch marked with a "for sale" sign, the stake of its resident animals be damned?

As for non-human beings' claim to their own environment, the general idea has already been accepted in some places. In 2004, Britain's environment department, in order to comply with a ruling from the European court of justice, decided to spend millions of pounds turning territory that was highly valued as farmland on Wallasea Island back into marshes, so that birds could have the ground for their winter stays.[3] Global warming is contributing to the gradual loss of land for the birds, and if the birds' interest in their habitat were not protected, these animals would lack feeding areas.

When addressing issues of preserving habitat, we find there are some legal initiatives worth supporting. Restricting dumping or discharge of pollution into beavers' habitats, or keeping pollution or boat traffic away from whales, manatees and other marine animals can enable these animals to carry on living without their bodies and waters being assaulted by human factors.

In 2010, California's government stopped permitting imports of turtles and frogs for food markets—turning off a trade that brought in more than two million animals a year. Activists had historically argued, to no avail, that live animals in markets endure terrible conditions and that they are cooked alive. But when people pointed out that some of these animals are bought and released, and then kill native pond turtles, the commission acted. The resultant "environmental" provision can be seen as advancing animal rights (both for local pond turtles and for the animals who'd otherwise be taken from territories of their own and transported to a bleak end in a food market); if it could be applied to imports for the pet trade as well, the scope would make it a notable legal change from an animal-rights perspective. And a good legal challenge would involve stopping border walls from being built. Border walls deprive us all—whether wolf, jaguar, or human—of our natural ability to move across the surface of the planet on which we were born.

This is not to claim that environmental laws as now written are animal-rights laws. Obviously they are not. But if we are going to take steps on the way to animal rights, this is the area of law with promise and potential. Environmental law can and must begin protecting habitat, because the lives and dignity of the planet's residents depend on it.

Animal rights will only matter for animals who live to benefit from the concept. This is why it's so important for theorists to notice and confront the destruction of the ones who are living right now as they would live if our culture accepted animal rights. Other animals must have space, with its natural food, water, and foliage, to perpetuate their communities. We shouldn't keep taking this away from them. We must make this issue a priority in our work. As our numbers rise and we spread out, our belief in our supremacy means they are being wiped out. The animal-rights movement obliges us to consider the territory and reproductive rights of other animals, and what we must do in accordance—including limiting our own population growth.

As we've seen, any rules that help to phase out the breeding of animals as pets could also be considered aligned with abolishing the treatment of animals as commodities, because these would spare *wildcats and wolves* from being selectively changed to suit us, and at the same time reduce the size of our homes and yards. It's imperative to avoid buying anything at stores that sell animals as pets, whether birds, goldfish, rabbits, chinchillas, cats, dogs, or snakes and various reptiles. And treating sugar gliders or skunks as pets? Domesticating new species of pets should always be opposed. Human communities need to appreciate the importance of letting these animals be, in their original homes, instead of domesticating them. Regulating high-volume pet breeders (including operations known as "puppy mills" or "puppy farms") by instituting rules such as how many times a dog could be made pregnant, or how much access to exercise a dog would get, would fail the respectful advocacy test. Banning high-volume pet breeders *entirely* could be an abolitionist intervention if it were part of a conscious effort to challenge the entire custom of petkeeping. The moment anyone suggests that some breeders are responsible business people, even with the excuse that some people will go to breeders anyway, the case for respect is lost. If an organization claims to be "banning puppy mills" yet part of their advocacy allows for helping members find breeders they are playing it both ways on the domineering custom of pet breeding, and we can say that the campaign is not attentive to the dignity of wolves and wildcats, and other free-living animals. Seem far-fetched? It's just a new way of thinking. Try it as a habit. Ask: What does the way I'm intervening say about the autonomy and dignity of other animals? At once, you'll begin talking about autonomy a lot. If we are ending the practice of horse-drawn carriages in a certain city, we are mindful of, and we prompt others to think about, how an untamed horse lives. If we are ending circuses' use of non-human performers—consider a Bolivian law now in effect prohibiting the use of both undomesticated and domestic animals in circus performances—we are mindful of big cats' interests in living untamed and unconfined. We prompt others to think about this, and also about whether animals should be domesticated for our amusement and a host of other reasons, including, as Yi-Fu Tuan wrote, to be turned into playthings and aesthetic objects.

Laws are the rules a society believes should be normal, right, and conducive to good living; so, ultimately, laws are only meaningful and lasting to the extent that people agree with them. In the best of cases, people govern themselves in order to model respect. Barbara Schmitt lives in Evergreen, Colorado, where the presence of deer and elk is accepted and enjoyed. The traffic stops on an hourly basis to let them cross, and their bugling at all hours is a part of life. When, in September 2009, a person was reportedly attacked by an elk, the warning was simply not to approach a bull elk. "I'd love it if every wildlife-tinged area would adopt this locale's policy," says Barbara, while acknowledging that this attitude of acceptance has not been enshrined in law. In places where deer, elk, and other animals are under attack, Barbara supports legal changes that will protect these animal communities; at the same time, Barbara engages letter and op-ed sections of various newspapers in order to cultivate respect for animals—something our current laws have failed to do.

In short, this first guidepost says: Use caution when asked to get involved with industries that use animals; learn about how to defend the animals who are still living, as far as possible, in their own ways, animals who actually could have rights.

2. Accept no substitutes!

We already know that changing the handling rules in industries that use and keep domesticated animals do not represent an animal-rights campaign, and can directly thwart animal rights by taking up more space that could have been natural habitat. (Keep in mind that free-range or cage-free campaigns go backwards in other ways too. What about encouraging healthy hearts? Does it make sense to separate respect for people's health from the vegan cause?)

The second guidepost prompts us to ask: Is it really the end of exploitation—not a rearranging of the wrong? Demanding a different kill method for a restaurant supplier would not pass this guidepost. There are a thousand things we could be doing: opening a vegan catering service, getting vegan meals in schools and hospitals, starting vegan-organic gardens in schools and hospitals, bringing vegan foods anywhere from urban libraries to rural rest stops. Why would we toss away our time to monitor, plead with, threaten, cajole, or bargain with fast-food restaurants over cage dimensions or slaughter methods used by their suppliers? Setting animal-husbandry standards is not the job of anyone advancing a social movement. Humane husbandry and slaughter is an oxymoron and a lie. The best position to take regarding animals killed for menus is simple and straightforward: conscientious objection. Once we've committed to veganism (and thus simply withdrawn from the practice of selectively breeding other animals, making them over to our needs), we can really talk about animal rights, which undomesticated animals can have.

Now, let's say our intervention is happening on behalf of animals in their habitat, so we've easily passed the first guidepost. Our campaign seeks to let animals live with their autonomy intact. Still, how do we decide if our call is abolitionist? Is, say, organizing to end one deer hunt a form of regulating dominion, or is it a genuine animal-rights campaign?

It is genuine if a community of deer would be safe from human control when the intervention succeeds. But avoid accepting the idea of deer as a "problem" and agreeing to one form of hunting weapon over another, or to hunting if the space is big enough (there is no such thing as fair chase), or to pharmaceutical means of control instead of killing. The general rule is that a population of free-living animals will self-limit, and humanity hardly has standing to use the "too many" claim against others! Avoid accepting population reduction of deer, bears, birds or other autonomous animals—including if it is done by certain experts rather than regular old hunters.

In June 2009, Alaska's government, apparently in the interest of keeping more moose around for humans to catch, decided to allow trappers to use bait and snares in order to cut the bear population by more than half. One reporter stated that an animal-rights group—yes, the paper used that term—was concerned because private trappers would be involved, not state agents.[4] To raise the objection that the wrong group is trapping the bears is to call for a rule change, but we (unlike that reporter) can immediately see it does nothing at all to promote respect for the interests or the dignity of moose and bears in Alaska. The group's position indicated it would accept domination and death.

Another campaign that would fail the Accept No Substitutes test was announced in 2007, in a press release titled "New York First State to Ban Electrocution of Animals for Fur."[5] A state politician said, "It is reassuring that this inhumane practice will be prohibited in at least one state." The end of the demand for fur clothing and accessories would definitely be aligned with the view that animal commodification should be abolished, and by letting communities of fur-covered animals live free, it would mean animal-rights progress. But banning one particular slaughter method—because, as the press release said, it is "one of the most inhumane and painful methods," and because this technique is not accepted by the American Veterinary Medical Association's "guidelines for euthanasia"—does not respect the dignity of other animals. It's a handling regulation. The press release also said (are there flags of a brighter shade of red than this?) even industry trade groups do not sanction electrocution and "the only method of euthanasia approved by Fur Commission USA is bottled gas, either pure carbon monoxide or carbon dioxide." Here, the advocates are lending credence to the industry. One campaigner praised politicians' "leadership in protecting animals from this horrifying fur factory farm practice" as Senator Frank Padavan described the law as part of the "fight to ensure all animals are treated with the highest standard of humane treatment and care." So the killing of animals for fur continues in New York, but with more detailed regulations, and according to standards preferred by industry representatives themselves. Gassing is expressly condoned. Mink, foxes, chinchillas and rabbits aren't respected when lawmakers and advocates deem a particular killing method appalling. Their degradation will only end when people begin to adopt vegan principles—when they are appalled by the thought of killing itself.

Stopping one kind of human assault on animals where no other method is condoned, and where the community of animals could experience freedom from human control, could be aligned with a respect-based goal. A prohibition of aerial gunning of wolves in Alaska would uphold an already-existing federal ban on aerial shooting (countering the notion that federal law makes airborne hunting acceptable if certain legal arguments can be fashioned); and it would end a war on wolves (who can go about their lives in freedom) without substituting another form of assault. While it is true that some opportunistic trappers do manage to catch wolves without aircraft, killing from the air is the one way to wage a systematic war on wolves in snow-covered Alaska. Of course, the activists should never suggest another form of stalking or catching wolves would be more humane.[6] The campaign should be understood as part of a continual project to cultivate respect for wolves and all other free-living beings in their biocommunity. Some will argue this point; but the general principles are sound. Wolves can experience living on their own terms, so the abolition of their use as com-modities and the realization of animal rights for them is possible. Stopping a state-run system of assaults on them is well worth doing, just as stopping a government's war on any community is worth doing. We must make it clear that we accept no attacks on wolves, or on the other animals who live in their midst. We are willing to intervene in *any* harmful human assaults against them, to the extent our resources will allow us to do so. Part of this must involve education so that more people help us to pool such resources. Then, when it can do good, we should be willing to spend those moneys to prevent violence and subjugation.

The big picture: Focusing on a hospitable world, vegan principles

What other initiatives would be important along the way to the ideal? We need more neuter-and-care networks for feral cats while we respectfully, gently ensure that their colonies wind down. Thinking about how commu-nity architecture could shelter such animals, who are not fully independent of us, would be important. Consider, as an inspiration, the example of Operation Cockney Sparrow in the East End of London. It's a project to turn inner-city housing to bird havens.

From time to time, we'll be faced with local matters involving animals not connected with agribusiness: bullfights, dog races, a proposal to use animals in experiments. And the issue will be a matter of simply stopping the form of use outright. I picked up a newspaper on a train and read that an Austrian animal-advocacy group stopped an experiment involving pigs being monitored as they died under an avalanche. Is this a single-issue campaign? If it is, we can be glad it was run. Yes, vegan education works at the roots of exploitation, without drawbacks, but that does not mean we should avoid caring about individual circumstances. In my view we can and certainly should address specific forms of oppression and specific communities under attack, while always putting our work into the larger context: *confronting domination*. Were the activists asked if they eat pigs, I hope and expect that the answer would be no, coupled with an enthusiastic call for vegan living.

What other local matters need attention? It makes sense to end contests: involving the catching of fish, for example, or horse tracks. Some U.S. states are legislating against dog racing, and it should be ended. Rather than demanding racing dogs not be fed diseased animal flesh, rather than insisting that the dogs must be out of their cages for a specific number of hours a day, instead of prohibiting the use of dangerous steroids in racing dogs, the involvement of vegan advocates in these practices will shift the public conversation to whether we ought to have the right to amuse ourselves using other animals, and will ultimately end the demand for racing animals to be bred. A campaign that only asks to keep horses out of races until they are a certain age might seem to be a "prohibition" of racing certain horses, but of course the horses in such a case would continue to be bred and used as playthings and objects of profit. The starting time for races would change, but the custom of racing horses is condoned by the rule itself. Ask for something really important: an end to horses in racing, vehicle-pulling, jumping, riding. Be bold. If we challenge the breeding, breaking and training of horses for human uses, we are standing up for the horses and burros who freely roam the land—and some of these animals are still trying to do just that. Defending their land and autonomy is true animal-rights advocacy.

Highly important regional activism involves projects that ensure green connecting spaces for free-living animals, and a public-relations effort to support better trains and buses, instead of permitting the construction of yet more intrusive roads. Aid for dependent animals in natural disasters would make sense; but most of all, vegan education would connect us with the root causes of major climate disruptions that potentially affect all animal life. It would be impossible to overstate the importance of making vegan principles (and cookbooks, so people know how to apply these principles in daily life) central in all we do.

As noted earlier, legal personhood could be granted to other-than-human beings by the courts (and legislators would then get to work with provisions required to ensure this). But as we've also noted, courts move slowly, and this book is written at a time when the U.S. Supreme Court is busy extending the rights of personhood to corporations, with animal rights nowhere in sight. Even when judges do extend their respect—which would occur one case at a time, respecting one after another class of animal beings—we'll still need a vegan movement because it's the only way we can address domestication. It makes no sense to go into court and demand legal personhood for purpose-bred animals. Thus, veganism is the broad-base approach to abolishing animal use and even transcending human supremacy. Courts can be fickle, but we can empower ourselves right now and model what a human being would look like if animal rights were a reality—by being vegan. As the idea spreads, it incrementally abolishes exploitive industries. Depending on our abilities, there are various ways to take these steps: We can set up a speaking or leafleting event. We can get vegan cookbooks into our local library or bookshop, and review books that have a vegan outlook. We can convince a restaurant with a few hold-out items, such as dairy desserts or cream, to become confidently animal-free. We can pressure retirement funds to divest from animal agribusiness. We can start a garden, and share the results; or we can set up a pool of buyers for a veganic grower. Encourage people to join a group that takes veganism seriously. Work to ensure the Vegan Society's distinctive sunflower logo, which denotes serious, unchanging, international standards of veganism, becomes widely sought and used. All of these acts will lead to a cohesive, coherent movement.

A focused social movement prevents advocacy from squandering energies by reacting or lashing out in all directions at once; it reduces fatigue, despair, or confusion. Forming networks to pursue the vegan idea could succeed. The idea has been succeeding already, person by person, multiplied by the many others who will in turn know each newly committed advocate. As this movement grows, one by one, all of the issues related to human domination will be affected; all forms of systematic use of other animals will be addressed.

This change will come as animal advocates ourselves embrace a fresh perspective, and with it, new kinds of communication. Our acts and words will inspire us to think of ourselves and other conscious beings in new ways. At its most worthwhile, animal advocacy will be capable of imagining and projecting the dignity evident in free communities of animals thriving in their habitats, as well as the dignity that resides in the soul of all vital movements for rights.

APPENDICES & KEY DEFINITIONS

Finding Your Animal-Rights Theory: A Workshop

A culture that subscribes to animal rights would accept certain basic thoughts. To start, it is not our work to filter pain out from Earth's living community; we accept that pain is a natural survival mechanism. Pain caused by our domineering conduct, however, must go. So we'll focus on the idea of humanity controlling ourselves, and refraining from removing animals from their habitats and selectively breeding them, and we'll take action to end the subtler, insidious forms of selection we cause through, for example, aggressive stalking of other animals, unjust resource use, exploitation of habitat, and control of free-living beings' fertility. Other animals will have respected interests in not being enslaved, and their autonomy will also be respected affirmatively.

As people (or groups, which are made out of the interactions of people) who commit to cultivating a society that accepts animal rights, where do we actually start? How do we go about planning our actions?

First, the goal-setting itself—envisioning the world we work to see—is a vital action. On the way to that goal, what we're doing to show others exactly what we have in mind is also important. This way, they too can envision it, even if they encounter us just once. Together, what we do as a movement will then be a way of *performing* the goal. We show it by acting it out.

What happens next? Prepare to hear the voices of strategy objecting, "Although I have differing views on the means to the end, I am certain that we do have the same goal in mind." That's a normal response. It's so normal that it might just start making sense to you. But say your goal is to get to Toronto, and someone says, "Jump in with us, we're going there too!" So you board the bus, and notice that the driver is holding a map with directions to

Nashville. Now, if these folks want to go to Nashville, that's their decision. You could wake them up if they don't know they're on the wrong bus. But some—maybe even the whole busload—might answer, "Although we have differing views on the means to the end, we do have the same goal in mind; one day, we'll be in Toronto!" Well, then, leave them free, and get yourself on the northbound bus, put your bags down, and get comfortable. As an old saying Arundhati Roy once recalled goes, you can wake someone who's sleeping; but you can't wake someone who's pretending to be asleep.[1]

Finding an animal-rights theory that works involves being comfortable with the theory in our daily lives—and automatically uncomfortable when we see the effects of humanity's systematic domination of others. The first matter for our agenda, though, is to sit down and describe a culture transformed. Start with the goal, and set the plan by working back from it. Start by asking: What does animal-rights advocacy want? Here's how my version looks: There is hardly an experience more joyful than lying down on a grassy hill in a park at dusk in summer, waiting for the bats to emerge and swoop and flutter overhead. There is hardly a more exhilarating feeling than camping quietly, watching a group of deer walk past—the feeling of letting other animals pass through our lives in peace. The more we think about it, the more exciting the plan to respect animals' freedom becomes. I think, yes! This is what animal rights looks like. What do you think animal rights would look like?

We don't achieve what we don't conceive, so let's think of what we want, and let's think in big, bold strokes. Acknowledge the magnitude of the change you seek, and then map your route. Social change is a big goal—so much so, many people wonder if they should even start. Don't get overwhelmed. Start by sitting down for an hour or two and mapping out the way. Once we've got our map, we can free ourselves from regretting the past or anticipating a fearsome future; we concentrate on the present moment. We'll continue along our route as a runner or hiker would, knowing where we're off to, but looking at the next step, and concentrating on the importance of each segment of the way.

Here are some possibilities to start yours. Read though this section first, then take time to write your own goals. It's important to write them down. Start with notes about what you wish to see occur on the planet in your lifetime. Imagine your ideal world. The following samples would fit with the experience on the North American continent, but the details can be adapted to fit any communities and regions. Note the use of present tense:

- Conscious living beings are now known as persons just as we are and their interests are taken seriously, just as human rights are—although we're aware that the point isn't to make other animals adjuncts to human culture, but rather to have a society that cultivates respect for animals on their terms.
- Today's circus performers are human artists.
- Wolves, horses, bison, deer, elk and moose freely roam their habitats. Bears flourish, bees flourish, and horses live freely on Chincoteague, Assateague, the western ranges of Nova Scotia and the Nemaiah Valley. No one is calling for roundups; after all, there are no cattle ranchers trying to take the land. Jaguars and nectar bats, humans as well, have the right to move as they wish over the face of the earth.
- The earth's CO_2 balance is restored, its wildlands are recovering, its air and its waters are clean and clear.
- Pesticides are things of the past and the only lethal mousetraps left in the world are in antique stores. The same for bird cages, spurs, guns, and fishing poles....

Ready? Start here:

Imagine a culture and a landscape where animal-rights theory is valued. Describe the traits that make it unique and appealing. Commit at least five ideas to writing. (This might be best done in the pages of a fresh journal book.)

Next, we see our personal role in bringing it to fruition. Of course, the transformation we seek will need to continue beyond our lives. So what would we like to personally accomplish over a lifetime in order to begin the cultivation of a fair and thoughtful culture? Imagine how you've cultivated this society. Plan your major lifetime efforts; imagine them accomplished!

For example:

- I live in an environmentally respectful space. [Include a description.]
- My respect for other animals, for my health, and in response to social and environmental concerns keeps growing.
- I am in the midst of thoughtful and talented people. [Describe what this would be like.]

Ready to commit to, say, five wonderful ideals connected to your personal role?

_____

_____

_____

_____

_____

_____

_____

_____

Next, we take these accomplishments and commit to writing the things we shall have done in ten years' time (this means some of the writing will be the same) to integrate our being with the society we are cultivating. Imagine, in ten years, what we have done and how we are living to make the transformation real.

For example:

- I have put together a vegan cookbook with contributions from people who have made exceptional dishes at my vegetarian club's potluck events.
- I cultivate a community vegetable garden. [Include a description.]
- I have developed an annual festival or conference to further a major animal-advocacy objective. [Include a description.]
- I live in an environmentally respectful space. [The description will match the one above, in the lifetime scenario.]

Go ahead and imagine your ten-year life ideals:

_____

_____

_____

_____

_____

_____

_____

Then five years. In this sample, planning a vegan festival starts off the goals. Vegan meals and festivals are wonderful conduits of information, combining pleasure and advocacy of the holistic approach to cultivating animal rights. Watch them attract nutritionists, churchgoers, woodworkers, employees at law offices, and astronomers—and their children. Start with these, or come up with your own resolutions, and a few more.

- On the local level, our popular vegan festival is now an annual event and it's inspired others in several communities.
- I nourish an organizational base for social change with national and worldwide impact, by supporting groups that work at that level of policy. [Describe how. Later in your worksheet, you can note how you'd get started volunteering or otherwise supporting in the coming year, the coming months, and weeks.]

_____

_____

_____

_____

_____

_____

_____

_____

_____

_____

Then one year....

- I have organized and presented a successful vegan festival (or conference, or vegan pledge).
- In my community, waste is now an alternate resource. Our local greens group has supplied training for former landfill workers to tend a composting project.
- I've written a booklet for campuses that raises consciousness

about the pet trade and discourages students from abandoning animals while they are in or leaving school.

Now, six months! Make these mini-goals that lead up to your one-year plans. Examples:

- Several activists and I have outlined plans to create the

first [describe conference, festival, or pledge project] in our community.

- I have joined or started a committee to promote hospitable, resource-efficient, and affordable public transport in order to lighten our dependence on roads and fuels.
- I am working for food justice. Fair trade shouldn't mean injustice to human workers—or the use of non-human beings. [Describe activity you are undertaking to expand the definition of fair trade.]

Now, one month.

- I've joined the board of my local vegetarian society in order to increase the vegan membership, educate, and to ensure the by-laws will never condone animal exploitation. I support, with the resources I am able to give, one or two vegetarian societies that promote vegan events and have a vegan definition of "vegetarian" in their by-laws.

_____

_____

_____

_____

_____

_____

_____

Now for the immediate gratification. What are you going to see yourself accomplishing this week?

_____

_____

_____

_____

_____

_____

_____

_____

_____

Now, in two hours, six hours, eight hours, ten hours—whatever you deem the right amount to complete today, what work will you do? Do this each morning.

_____

_____

_____

_____

_____

The work of radical change becomes less daunting once we see that it goes step by step, day by day. Consider noting the conversations you have with others as well; these conversations bring out new ideas and methods and are likely to help sharpen, arrange, and enrich your thinking and your work, and from time to time they might cause you to readjust your compass. If you've started your journal according to the steps shown above, you're ready to plan your journey in advocacy—on your own terms.

Some have asked for even more specific guidelines: How do we write our vegan guides? Together with my co-workers, I've planned and helped design a Vegan Starter Guide and listened to a lot of feedback. On the basis of that experience, here is what I could suggest…

Creating Ace Pamphlets
and Vegan Guides

Putting together a pamphlet or guidebook for your outreach? Make it ace! Select the simplest, most straightforward language.

As you're writing for everyone who's curious about vegan living, you'll likely want to be mindful of words and at the same time avoid language that's highly stilted or jargon-laden and could make you sound as though you are in an inner circle. *Converse* about equality issues rather than using extremely strict lingo to identify yourself as subscribing to an equality-minded perspective. There is no need to speak to the public from the standpoint of a subculture within veganism, or to modify the word "vegan" with a particular adjective to describe your group. There is no reason to say you're a *really strict vegan* who strives to avoid all animal products; all vegans do. You need not identify your group as the "abolitionist vegans" or as "ethical vegans"—as though there are pro-exploitation or unethical types of veganism. You shouldn't have to put the word "ethical" or "abolitionist" in front of vegan. Better to explain that veganism simply encompasses those concepts. No special subcategories. No levels of accomplishment. No passwords or secret handshakes. We need not make or adhere to special brands or subcategories of veganism; we just need to learn what vegan means, and that's not complicated at all.

Linking veganism to a specific kind of music or fashion can also inhibit the reach of your material. Of course, expressing vegan values through certain designs or music can reach various audiences; but the core identity is just vegan. Rather than connecting each of your utterances to a certain brand of veganism, it makes sense to remember we're surrounded by people with many ideas and backgrounds. Most are not born receivers of our message, so let's be as welcoming as we can. Although reading up on the history and theory of animal advocacy is valuable, special jargon and strict social groupings don't advance our cause as much as they advance our clubs. Some will disagree. But at least consider this point. Veganism rules out certain ingredients and habits, but should it ever rule out the potential of any person? Veganism is friendly and straightforward, and although it takes dedication, it takes no special skills or resources, and is no more complicated than any other set of customs. It's our responsibility to strive for the attitude that everyone in the world is a member of our inner circle.

Good principles are all connected at the root, and taking a broad view of what veganism stands for means questioning all forms of personal or systematic injustice, bullying or coercion. To put it in terms Donald Watson used, let your readers know they are on to something really big! They will find, perhaps to their surprise, that vegan living isn't a diet (although the vegan principle is applied to diet). And although it might be beautifully and compellingly expressed through art and music genres, it's certainly not a fashion trend.

A general vegan booklet (as distinct from a booklet that focuses mainly on a specific aspect—such as the climate impacts of agriculture—which is also good to have) will explore some of the many reasons people decide to be vegan, with an emphasis on agriculture as an unjust treatment of other conscious beings.

And the word "decide" is a good one. People resolve to go vegan, make a decision. A commitment. One makes a change more profound than selecting from choices or options when subscribing to the principle of rejecting dominion and cultivating respect. When talking about vegan dishes on a menu, rather than talking of vegan *options*, try the phrase vegan *offerings* instead. Not only is it less tentative; it also has a ring of generosity.

You could start with basics: the definitions.

Vegetarianism is commonly defined as a diet based on direct nutrition from plants: grains, vegetables and fruits. After many debates about whether vegetarianism could include some animal products, the term *vegan* was coined in 1944. Its originators were a small group of people including Donald Watson, Dorothy (Morgan) Watson, and Elsie Shrigley, who derived the new word from the first three and last two letters of "vegetarian"— explaining that veganism starts with vegetarianism and carries it through to its logical conclusion. Dairy products, fish, fish eggs, birds and birds' eggs are not plant-based foods, and therefore vegans avoid them as well as other animal-derived substances, such as leather, down, fur, honey, wool and silk. Vegans strive to live as harmoniously with the planet and all its inhabitants as possible. Sharing a bit of early vegan history not only helps explain the words; it also helps advocates and everyone else learn how a promising ethical movement took hold.

A discussion of animal dignity will, in most cases, be your first main conversational section.
Given the current human population, most of animal agribusiness will be made up of factory farms; in some cases, industrial farms are stacking animals vertically. Although all animal farms are the issue, it's appropriate to note that most non-human animals are processed in an assembly-line fashion, after being conceived through a variety of artificial or forced insemination techniques, routinely mutilated for easy handling, and forced away from their mothers. Slaughter methods and the exploitation of human workers are also appropriate to note.

Animals used for flesh, egg and dairy production are now subjected to genetic manipulation, growth hormones, and repeated pregnancies. The eating of cheese results in the production of veal—so no one can claim to consume cheese but renounce veal. If every time we gaze into the dairy case we reminded ourselves to imagine a calf fated to be cut into pieces of veal, we would gain a sense of the reality of cheese, cream, and milk. Picturing the veal calf has strengthened the resolve of many a new vegan to walk away without buying that cream or cheese.

There is no need to find shocking photos; simply explain the reality, and avoid using worst-case scenarios to make the point. People are used to thinking your message is "Animals suffer in factory farms" and their view is usually "Yes, factory farming is bad but it's important to remember that it's not the only way to raise animals for food." Anticipate that argument. Explain the ethical problem with all animal farming, including that which is advertised as organic, local or humane. If you've read this book, you know how to do this.

Take the utmost care to keep the readers' attention focused on the ethical bottom line: Even where businesses purport to offer humane or free-range animal products, the overall circumstances and fates of the animals still depend on the whims and the wallets of human shoppers, to whom the animals are, in the end, nothing more than a product. This is why farm animals, from big factories and pastures alike, eventually wind up facing the shock and trauma of slaughter—normally after they're loaded onto trucks and taken to the same miserable abattoirs.

A vegan booklet will also highlight fish, and this is especially important after years of "seafood boycotts" have gone on to protest Canada's seal-killing. Those campaigns inevitably suggested to the public that sea animals are our food, and that their sales value can and should be leveraged on a temporary basis to meet a certain goal. Why not instead encourage respect for the natural lives and experiences of the beings who inhabit seas, lakes and rivers? And when they are captive-raised, still more animals are used as feed. Mangrove swamps and other marine life are often casualties of the fish-farming industry, with all its antibiotics, artificial structures, and waste. And angling not only kills the fish it targets, but also leaves its treacherous hooks, nets and lines for seals, pelicans, and others to get caught in or swallow.

Then there is clothing. Leather involves the use of an animal's body, perpetuates animal agribusiness, and harms the ecology with harsh tanning chemicals. Wool too is an important topic; selective breeding for wool and taking the wool makes sheep into objects until they're killed. Vegans avoid silk, and honey, beeswax, and other consumer goods derived from bees. Bees have intricate neurological systems and use a complex form of communication, and now your readers will learn about this. Other topics will arise regularly; veganism means a lifetime of learning and striving.

You'll want to cover the social benefits veganism offers.

While the Ethiopian government hopes for food aid for millions of its people, animal agribusiness in the United States feeds grain to billions of cows and chickens who are bred to be eaten. Those who continue to consume fish, cheese and other dairy products, flesh or eggs all take a massive toll on the environment and climate—on which everyone in the world depends. Being vegan is the right ethical response to urgent human safety and social justice questions.

You'll note that avoiding animal products does not compromise human health.

According to the position statement on vegan diets from the American Dietetic Association, well-planned vegan diets are healthful for everyone (and in 2003, the Dietitians of Canada joined with the ADA to release a position paper stating the same view); you can quote the statement:

> Appropriately planned vegetarian diets, including total vegetarian or vegan diets, are healthful, nutritionally adequate, and may provide health benefits in the prevention and treatment of certain diseases. Well-planned vegetarian diets are appropriate for individuals during all stages of the life cycle, including pregnancy, lactation, infancy, childhood, and adolescence, and for athletes.

Many people think protein and iron must come from meat or eggs, and calcium must come from milk, so, in a general way, address this and other common nutritional myths.

Explain that vegan living can be handled affordably.

While there are many expensive packaged vegetarian foods, there are also plenty of staples from which delicious meals can be made, such as potatoes, rice, beans, and pasta. And good health saves money. Also, the price we pay for what we buy needs to be a discussion topic. Small, ethical businesses, while sometimes expensive, are important to support. Cheap chocolate and popular coffee, for example, are usually produced by people who have no choice but to work in terribly degrading conditions. Let people know how to find vegan chocolate and baking companies, and good clothes and shoes made from canvas, hemp and organic cotton, and encourage them to learn about human rights issues at the same time.

Explain that vegans can gracefully accept and offer meal invitations.

Parties are no obstacle. Many people know how to make traditional hummus—simply a mix of crushed chickpeas, sesame tahini, lemon juice, and garlic—which can be served with bagel crisps or any flat bread.

Do offer cooking and food preparation tips.

I have found, at numerous outreach events, that people have concerns about taking a brochure or booklet from me or someone in my group if they think it will horrify them. When offered a vegan starter guide, people will sometimes ask directly: "Are there gory pictures in this?" We tell them there are not, and they agree to take and read the booklet. This has happened enough times that I think it's worth stating as a practical matter: There are people going about their daily lives who will stop and listen if they feel it's about learning rather than becoming overwhelmed with pictures of harm and hurt.

Our outreach materials need not be sensational in a negative sense. We can, on the other hand, present food and our future in a sensuous way. We're excitable, joy-loving primates and we love attractive food. That's great; let's run with that. And let's make vegan growers worthy of hurrahs! Don't miss a chance to point people to the great vegan-organic resources in Britain and throughout Europe <veganorganic.net> and in the Americas and New Zealand <goveganic.net>.

Want to picture animals? Support and celebrate freedom; it still exists!

In general, farm animals are not our business—whether they're in or out of the factory farm cages. Refreshingly, vegan-organic sites focus on what is being cultivated, and the freedom of other animals to move, without experiencing violence or subjugation, over, around, and under that cultivation. The real influence we have entails insisting on regarding other animals' own power, not dominated, not eternally victimized, not domesticated. Our idea of the world we want to bring about (or work to restore) must be highlighted, must be clear. It's not enough to talk about what we don't want; we must have an idea of the dignity of fellow conscious beings.

Showing happy and abused domesticated animals side by side misses the point.

Even abolitionist pamphlets do it. One pamphlet implies that we should not kill animals because they can nuzzle us as puppies do. Popular advocacy brochures frequently admonish: "If we locked dogs in a cage so we could kill and skin them for their fur, the idea would seem revolting to most people." Or, "If it's wrong to harm a cat or a dog, then it's wrong to harm other animals for similar reasons."

People seem to think that if we could make sure animals get treated as pets, that's real progress—or even the ideal. Is this so? Perhaps it comes as no surprise that various human cultures divide animals into those who will make good pets, and those who will make a good meal. But that mental structure shouldn't be echoed in your vegan guide. Put yourself in the reader's position. Ask, "If I were to pick this up for the first time, might I think it suggests I treat certain domesticated animals (farm animals) as I treat other domesticated animals (dogs and cats)?"

Want to picture animals? Show them on their terms.

Imagery of miserable, victimized farm animals in grotesque scenes are problematic also if juxtaposed with farm animals who seem to be living on the pasture with the red barn. Truly valuable discussion in your pamphlet doesn't ask us to treat animals as we treat pets, or to make farm animals happy. It asks what animal rights really means: freedom from our dominion, domestication, and control. More than once I've heard that vegans *threaten* non-human animals because omnivores actually have a use for animals and therefore keep them on the planet. This indicates that most humans don't even consider the existence of any animals who aren't potentially useful to us! Does your pamphlet consider them?

If it does, instead of suggesting that animals bred as pets have the best life, the gold standard, your pamphlet is showing autonomy as the goal. What a powerful statement.

You'll mainly be covering the basics; applying vegan principles to food is simple.

People considering the case for vegan living will be grateful to know this can be as easy as the way they were eating before. Popular dishes to start are baked potatoes filled with chili or topped off with a refreshing picnic-style salad, bean burritos with vegetarian refried beans, three-bean salads, pasta salads, and selections from the health-food aisles popping up in various grocers, such as lemony Lebanese tabouli, a parsley and bulgur wheat salad that needs no cooking at all to make a wonderfully healthy and filling meal. Raw food is the topic of some controversy, but it certainly has environmental advantages: less use of packaging, less oil, less electricity needed to prepare it. It also inspires curiosity, creativity, and inventiveness. To some extent, humans may have evolved to rely on cooking. Therefore The Vegan Society recommends a varied diet including both cooked and raw foods as the proven basis for vegan health, particularly for infants and children who need a relatively high calorie density. Now, I am not a scientist or dietician. If you aren't, avoid making detailed nutrition claims; instead, you can point readers to sources such as research scientist Stephen Walsh, who published a concise yet detailed sample raw diet plan, with concerns about specific nutrients flagged. It is freely available from info@vegansociety.com. For more general information, you could start with *The New Becoming Vegetarian: The Essential Guide to a Healthy Vegetarian Diet* (by two registered dieticians, Brenda Davis and Vesanto Melina).

Here's a dish that just about everyone loves—that happens to be raw. You're welcome to include it, citing Friends of Animals' first cookbook, *Dining With Friends: The Art of North American Vegan Cuisine:*[1]

Guacamole

Ingredients:

2 avocados, peeled and seeded
1 scallion, sliced
½ red onion, diced
2 cloves minced garlic
1 jalapeño pepper, seeded and
   minced
1 fresh lime, juiced
½ tomato, diced
2 Tbsp. chopped fresh cilantro
Salt to taste

Preparation:

Choose an avocado that has give to it. Peel and seed the avocado and mash it with a fork. Transfer the mashed avocado to a bowl and combine with remaining ingredients. Cover and refrigerate for up to 2 hours. Stir lightly before serving. Note that leaving the avocado pit in the guacamole until you're ready to serve it, or adding a sprinkle of lemon or lime juice, helps to preserve the guacamole's hue of vibrant green.

It's a good idea to address young readers.

Young people can immediately grasp the concept of respect for all animals. But will their family accept the diet that puts this principle into action? Some parents don't, but many do. If a young person learns to prepare foods, and puts an emphasis on nutrition, that will benefit the whole family and friends too.

Yes, human population is a vegan issue. Address it.

The early vegans noted the presence of two billion humans on Earth when they began their movement. They noted that two billion is a lot, on a small planet with finite resources that must sustain all its animal life—the humans and everyone else. Today's population is several times that. The human population rate is an issue for all of us. Those of us in the world's affluent regions (even vegans) use an especially large share of the globe's natural resources. Let's be open to the idea that care is meaningful not because it's a gift to our biological offspring, but because it is a gift to anyone who receives our love.

Finish off with enthusiasm, because we can do it!

Level with people. They'll take some flak. And we know: It is virtually impossible to be 100% vegan. Books, sealants, building and art supplies—so many things might contain animal derivatives we can't see. But living as vegan as possible is essential if we hope to effect positive change in our society, and to ensure that our planet has a future. These difficult things will change as human minds change and make creative decisions.

Study references that provide tips on some of the finer points of veganism, including ingredients in cosmetics, testing policies, recipes for non-toxic, animal-friendly home-made cleaning solutions, and advice to young people. Vegan essays, pamphlets and booklets to review are offered in free form over the computer and by regular mail from Friends of Animals (www.friendsofanimals.org; 203.656.1522) and Vegan Means (www.veganmeans.com). Significantly, these are carefully based on the principles as originally set out by and also available through The Vegan Society (www.vegansociety.com) and similarly designed, as far as possible, to be applicable to an international readership. There are also local vegan societies to offer more area-focused information for you, and, as we've seen, there are groups on campuses and local communities that start vegan groups and projects. We can all empower ourselves to do it!

Beginning with the individual, a world of peace is possible. If we think it probably can't be done, or it will be too difficult, we might fail to try, when it could happen if a critical number of us *do* try. If no one tries, failure is guaranteed. But stay diligent, and you will win, because success is staying true to the fairest principles. You will, and you are, succeeding.

Key Definitions

Abolition

As generally used in animal-rights theory, abolition means the end of our commodification of other animals. Abolition accomplishes the critical task of ensuring animals are *not* property. Because animal rights is also a positive concept, abolition is necessary yet insufficient to ensure the respect for animals' dignity that is the point of animal rights.

Animal Rights

A social and legal movement to cultivate human respect for the dignity of non-human animals. It entails interceding on behalf of non-human individuals' and communities' ability to live autonomously. The essence of animal rights will mean that non-human animals are able to live on their own terms. The rights position, seen in its strongest form, understands animal use as domination; and that central affront—the domination—is not measured in degrees. It is actively going on *or* it is rejected.

Animal Welfare

Animal welfare is the well-being of non-human animals. The term is used in this book to refer to a caring ethic for domesticated animals or captive animals unable to fend on their own and thus dependent on human care. Not to be confused with *animal husbandry*, it does not refer to the breeding or handling of other beings to suit our desires or goals. The term "animal welfare" *does* apply to a person or non-profit caring for animals already born and in dependent circumstances, either because the animals were raised in captivity and would be unlikely to cope well apart from human control, or because they were selectively bred (as in the case of farm animals or animals born as pets). This attention to well-being can honestly merit the term "welfare" or "care" and is distinct from concepts of proper maintenance of the commercially owned animal.

Animal Husbandry

Refers to methods of housing, transporting, handling and maintaining animals who are captive, domesticated, or both—when they are inside the institutions of use. Professionals in the fields of animal agribusiness, pet shops, dog trainers, lab technicians and biomedical research specialists all apply certain methods of handling animals deemed suitable for the relevant kind of use.

Animal-handling methods serve to maintain the living raw materials owned by businesses and human society as a whole. Adjustments to these methods also comprise a safety valve which animal agribusiness uses to prevent rebellion against human control and commodification of living animals. If we can think, for example, that the milk, eggs and flesh of other animals can be consumed in some relatively harmless manner, we are likely to stop short of conscientious objection to the business.

Veganism

Veganism is a principle that *humanity has no right* to exert dominion and thereby exploit other creatures. It seeks to end the use of other animals for human food, commodities, work, hunting, vivisection and all other deliberately exploitive purposes. Veganism takes the war-resister's principle of conscientious objection and expands it to encompass respect for all conscious life. It operates as direct action to spare other animals from being dominated by humanity. Thus, while it is applied to diet, it is more—a principle in itself, and a movement to end the commodification of other animals, and, more profoundly yet, to respect all conscious beings on their terms.

Endnotes

Notes to Preface ∾ **Pages 9–16**

Note to the reader: Some references in this book, particularly when citing hard-to-find documents, will include the addresses of websites where copies have appeared. Addresses to websites can change without notice; those supplied here were current at the time of publication.

1 Richard Black, "Biodiversity Loss Is 'Wake-Up Call,' Warns UN" – *BBC News* (11 Jan. 2010).

2 See Julia Whitty, "Gone: Mass Extinction and the Hazards of Earth's Vanishing Biodiversity" – *Mother Jones* (25 Apr. 2007), citing figures available from the World Conservation Union.

3 Barnaby J. Feder, "Henry Spira, 71, Animal Rights Crusader" (obituary), *New York Times* (15 Sep. 1998). Spira campaigned successfully in the 1970s to end research on cats by the American Museum of Natural History. During the 1980s, Spira focused on the treatment of farm animals. A vegetarian for health-oriented and ecological reasons, Spira worked within the system of agribusiness, ending face-branding of cattle and negotiating with McDonald's and other fast-food companies to get them to supervise the practices of their suppliers more closely. Ibid. Spira's group Animal Rights International is now run by philosophy and bioethics professor Peter Singer.

4 The Albert Einstein Institution in Cambridge, Massachusetts, in "A Journalist's Brief Glossary of Nonviolent Struggle" (undated), defines a boycott as "[s]ocial, economic, or political noncooperation."

Notes to Chapter 1 ∾ **Pages 23–52**

1 See Henry S. Salt, *Animals' Rights Considered in Relation to Social Progress* (Macmillan & Co., published 1894, two years after manuscript date), at 51.

2 Ibid. at 48.

3 See U.S. Environmental Protection Agency press release: "Pesticide News Story: Petitioners Ask EPA to Revoke Import Tolerances for 13 Pesticides to Protect Migratory Birds; EPA Requests Public Comment" (1 Sep. 2009), regarding a petition from the American Bird Conservancy to end tolerances in imported food for 13 pesticides—cadusafos, cyproconazole, diazinon, dithianon, diquat, dimethoate, fenamiphos, mevinphos, methomyl, naled, phorate, terbufos, and dichlorvos—and asserting that the action is required by the Migratory Bird Treaty Act and the Endangered Species Act.

4 Friends of Animals (2009; Civil Action 04-01660); see also John Platt, "Endangered African Antelope Win Protection from American Hunters" at the *Scientific American* weblog's 60-Second Extinction Countdown (29 Jun. 2009).

5 The commentary appears in Salt's book in Chapter 1: "The Principle of Animals'

Rights." For the sake of simplicity and in furtherance of a plain-speaking movement, this book discusses animals as property in *legal* terms. The vague and occasionally perilous idea of moral rights has led some advocates to say domesticated animals, such as animals bred as pets, "are not our property; we are not their owners." That leads to problematic views: for example, notions that domesticated animals have acquired or will be gaining rights through laws or simply through enough love and caring on the part of those responsible for their welfare. Even deer, coyotes, and free-flying birds are subject to the regime that treats them as property of the State. Whether animals nonetheless have moral rights, or if moral rights exist, is not the focus of this book. We can keep things simple through language on which most all of us would agree: Conscious animals have interests; this book speaks of *rights* as socially created and enforceable protections for those interests.

6 See Carol Gilligan, *In a Different Voice: Psychological Theory and Women's Development* (Harvard University Press, 1993); see also Nel Noddings, *Caring: A Feminine Approach to Ethics and Moral Education* (University of California Press, 2nd edition, 2003).

7 As one writer put it, "the patriarchal conceptual framework that has maintained, perpetuated, and justified the oppression of women in Western culture has also, and in similar ways, maintained, perpetuated, and justified the oppression of nonhuman animals and the environment." See Deane Curtin's "Toward an Ecological Ethic of Care" in *Beyond Animal Rights: A Feminist Caring Ethic for the Treatment of Animals*, at 60 (Continuum, Josephine Donovan & Carol S. Adams eds., 1996).

The care ethic has been central to ecofeminism, in which, as described by the *Routledge International Encyclopedia of Women* (Cheris Kramarae and Dale Spender, eds., 2000, at 435) the "devaluation of both women and nature is understood in terms of a particularly deleterious construction of masculine consciousness that denigrates and manipulates everything defined as 'other,' whether nature, women, colonized cultures, or marginalized races." The French writer Françoise d'Eaubonne's coining of the term "ecofeminism" was noted in Mary Daly's *Gyn-Ecology*, published in the United States in 1978. In a text entitled *Le féminisme ou la mort* (1974; "Feminism or death"), D'Eaubonne argued that patriarchal control had wrought crises of environmental destruction through resource depletion connected with surplus human births; thus feminism's potential for bringing about an ecological revolution. The term "ecofeminism" has been applied to the activism of Vandana Shiva and other people whose perspectives often differ from those discussed in the text of this book; moreover, ecofeminist opinions vary widely on the matter of consuming animals and animal products. A care ethic that could be adopted temporarily by animal-rights advocacy, however, would be geared to ensuring the well-being of dependent animals—never the consumption of their animal products or the perpetuation of institutions of human dominion and control.

8 Introduction to *Beyond Animal Rights*, at 15.

9 Likewise, Rita C. Manning, throughout the chapter "Caring for Animals" in *Beyond Animal Rights*, writes approvingly of instances of domestication as opportunities for caring, and (at 121) takes the position (arguably at odds with that approval) that the care ethic does not require interference in the lives of "wild" animals.

10 For an excellent treatment of this point, one that finds overlapping concerns for the animal-rights and feminist movements, see Catharine A. MacKinnon, "Of Mice

and Men: A Feminist Fragment on Animal Rights" in Cass R. Sunstein and Martha C. Nussbaum, eds., *Animal Rights: Current Debates and New Directions* (Oxford University Press USA, 2005), at 263-76.

11 "In reality," Donovan and Adams add, in the introduction to *Beyond Animal Rights*, at 14-15, "animals are only with considerable strain appropriable to Cartesian man."

12 Several writers have made the point that talking of animal rights, as though all nonhumans occupied one amorphous group rather than various species, unjustifiably makes "human rights" into a special case. I acknowledge the point of the argument, but it is largely irrelevant to this book's view of animal rights. First, this is because humanity, as the only group that assigns and currently exercises legal rights, does comprise a special case; second, the right to live on their terms is essentially about controlling *our* group in relation to all others. This book is here to assert that we do have a responsibility to intervene and defend particular groups of animals identified as under assault by human communities, but at the same time acting holistically, so that complete and interwoven communities of nonhuman beings in the area at issue are respected.

13 Neutering animals bred as pets, such as rabbits, cats and dogs, should not be considered a violation of animal-rights principles. These animals have already had their reproductive systems manipulated, for reproduction in order to generate profit has been part of the goal in intensive pet breeding; these animals' free-living ancestors are able, in contrast, to experience meaningful reproductive autonomy.

14 "Is the fact that, from the human side, the animal-human relation is necessarily (epistemically and ontologically) a relation *within* human society more problematic than it has been seen to be?" MacKinnon, "Of Mice and Men" (note 10 above) at 263.

15 Jack L. Albright (professor of animal sciences and veterinary medicine, Purdue University), "A Critical Analysis" (internal citations omitted; the paper appears on the website of South Dakota State University's Department of Animal and Range Sciences; see http://ars.sdstate.edu/animaliss/critanal.html); published via Richard D. Reynnells and Basil R. Eastwood (facilitators), "Animal Welfare Issues Compendium: A Collection of 14 Discussion Papers (Sep. 1997)" – U.S. Department of Agriculture Cooperative State Research, Education & Extension Service; Plant and Animal Production, Protection and Processing; see http://www.nal.usda.gov/awic/pubs/97issues.htm. For related material see Tom Regan and Gary L. Francione, "The Animal Rights Movement Must Reject Animal Welfarism" in Andrew Harnack (ed.), *Animal Rights: Opposing Viewpoints* (Greenhaven Press) at 194-201 (publication dated 1996, edited and reprinted from a 1989 publication).

16 *Husbandry* is defined as agriculture or the application of scientific principles to agriculture, especially to animal breeding; or stewardship. It came into English from the Old Norse *husbondi*, meaning "master of a house," or a man who has land and stock. Such a person was usually married, and the word *husband* apparently arose from this overlap. The managerial connotations embedded in the word's history are troubling—and make the term apt for the systematic handling of animals in a way the term "animal welfare" is not.

17 Bruce Friedrich of PETA distributed a notice titled "KFC Investigation Unearths Shocking Abuse" over the Internet on 1 Sep. 2003; it reads, in part: "PETA is calling

on KFC to immediately adopt PETA's recommended animal welfare guidelines internationally. PETA's guidelines have been approved by members of KFC's own animal welfare advisory panel and represent the most up-to-date studies and research into animal welfare."

18 Yi-Fu Tuan, *Dominance and Affection: The Making of Pets* (Yale University Press, 1984), at 135.

19 National Park Service, "Chesapeake and Ohio Canal National Historical Park: Meet the Mules" (undated); posted at http://www.nps.gov/CHOH/planyourvisit/meetthemules.htm.

20 "Animals Being Fitted for Contact Lenses" – *ABC News* (WENN, Phoenix, Arizona; 20 Jul. 2009).

21 The e-mail message from Darcey Rakestraw, communications director for Worldwatch Institute, dated 6 Jan. 2009 (on file with author), states:

> *Our agriculture team thought carefully about partnering with Stonyfield on this initiative. While they have written about the many benefits associated with reduced meat and dairy consumption and livestock farming, their work has reinforced that not all meat and dairy production is created equal.*
>
> *Stonyfield does its best to ensure stringent animal welfare standards from its suppliers. Their business model also fits well into Worldwatch's goal of building sustainable industries that incorporate the needs of small farmers, the environment, and animals alike.*
>
> *Ultimately, we are interested in encouraging those forms of production that get animals out of feedlots and onto pasture, that improve their health and living conditions, and that reduce dependence on energy-intensive inputs. As far as we have determined, Stonyfield is head and shoulders above standard dairy operations, and a leader in the organic industry, including in its use of renewable energy. Stonyfield buys dairy from conscientious farmers and is constantly pushing those farmers to improve.*

22 The World Society for the Protection of Animals, "Eat Humane"—posted at http://www.wspa-usa.org/pages/2481_eat_humane.cfm.

23 Farm Sanctuary joined the Humane Society in urging advocates to thank Wolfgang Puck. See "Animal Welfare Has a Place at Wolfgang Puck's Table" (22 Mar. 2007); posted at: http://www.hsus.org/farm/news/ournews/wolfgang_puck_animal_welfare.html.

Notes to Chapter 2 ❧ Pages 53–70

1 Singer's opinion was part of an exchange with Tipu Aziz, an Oxford neurosurgeon who declared that 40,000 people had been helped by experimental work that involved giving Parkinson's disease to "only 100 monkeys." See "Monkeys, Rats and Me: Animal Testing" - *BBC2* (Nov. 2006). Even before the segment aired, the *Sunday Times* announced, "The father of the modern animal rights movement has endorsed the use of monkeys in research by an Oxford professor at the centre of anti-vivisection protests." Gareth Walsh, "Father of Animal Activism Backs Monkey Testing" (26 Nov. 2006). In a subsequent statement Singer wrote, "Whether or not the occasional experiment on animals is defensible, I remain opposed to the institutional practice of

using animals in research, because, despite some improvements over the past thirty years, that practice still fails to give equal consideration to the interests of animals." See Peter Singer's letter to the editor in response to the article "Animal Guru Gives Tests His Blessing" - *Guardian Observer* (26 Nov. 2006).

2 Tom Regan, "Tom Regan Replies to Peter Singer: Animal Rights and Animal Testing" (e-mailed statement dated 28 Nov. 2006).

3 *See generally* Tom Regan, *The Case for Animal Rights* (University of California Press; 1983).

4 See Michael Specter, "The Dangerous Philosopher" - *The New Yorker* (6 Sep. 1999); and Oliver Broudy, "The Practical Ethicist" - *Salon.com* (8 May 2006). Notably, Singer's *Animal Liberation* states that rights claims are "irrelevant"; Singer rejects rights theory, opting for the view that only the consequences of a given act, vis-à-vis the preferences of those affected, matter.

5 Rod Preece, "Animal Rights Advocacy: Right Ethics, Wrong Target" (*Logos*; Spring 2005).

Amongst a variety of works mentioned by Preece are the eighteenth-century writings of Joseph Butler, the Bishop of Durham, who takes it "as common knowledge that other animals as well as humans 'share apprehension, memory, reason...affection... enjoyments and sufferings'"; and "the veterinarian William Yoautt, writing in 1839... that animals possess senses, emotions, consciousness, attention, memory, sagacity, docility, association of ideas, imagination, reason, instinct, the moral qualities, friendship and loyalty — each of which is acknowledged to exist in other species and to differ from human attributes only by degree." Preece adds, "Nor did Youatt seem to think he was advancing a new and especially controversial doctrine."

To update Preece's list we might also add Henry Salt's 1892 book *Animals' Rights: Considered in Relation to Social Progress* (printed by MacMillan Co. in 1894), which asked, "Why should the law refuse its protection to any sensitive being? The time will come when humanity will extend its mantle over everything which breathes..." Salt, in turn, observed many cultural threads connecting the idea of respect outward to oppressed categories, threads connecting the Buddhist and Pythagorean principles to people such as Jeremy Bentham, Mahatma Gandhi, and Mary Wollstonecraft. The organizers of groups begun in the mid-1900s, including Eleanor Seiling, who started United Action for Animals, and Alice Herrington, founder of Friends of Animals, would provide a context for writers who emerged in the twentieth century to discuss the application of animal-rights ideology.

6 See Ewen Callaway, "Pain-Free Animals Could Take Suffering out of Farming" – *New Scientist* (2 Sep. 2009; issue 2724), citing an article in *Nature*.

7 Transcript of a keynote speech at Taking Action for Animals (event sponsored by the Humane Society of the United States, 2006). In the same talk, Singer says "there's nothing in *Animal Liberation* that says killing of animals themselves is necessarily always wrong. It's more about, as I say, on their capacity to suffer, is the key thing."

8 Bob Meyer, "Veal Growers Making the Transition to Group Housing" - *Brownfield Ag News* (8 Jun. 2009) (reporting that the American Veal Association voted to have all veal calf operations converted to group housing by the end of 2017, and that this presents "management challenges for veal operators as they deal with 'bully' calves").

The recommendation to owners is tethering at feeding time through 30 minutes post-feeding for six to eight weeks. See Ohio State University Animal Sciences Fact Sheet, "Raising Dairy Veal" by John M. Smith (with information adapted from the Guide for the Care and Production of Veal Calves, 4th Edition, 1993, American Veal Association).

9 UC (University of California) Davis News Service, "To Cage or Not to Cage: Research Coalition Seeks Answers" (13 Feb. 2008), reporting that the research team received $400,000 from the American Egg Board, an egg-marketing group, to fund the planning stage of research into the issue of whether it is better for egg-laying hens to be housed in cages or in barns.

10 Quoted by Sian Powell, in "The Beasts and the Bees" - *Weekend Australian* (21 Apr. 2001).

11 See "Eggs: Battery or Free Range?" in *The Independent* (31 Oct. 2005).

12 Jim Downing, "Modesto Egg Producer's 'Enriched Colony' Cages Draw Criticism" - *Sacramento Bee* (16 Sep. 2009).

13 See Peter Singer and Jenny Palmer, "A Step in the Right Direction" (opinion column) in *The Daily Princetonian* (28 Sep. 2007).

14 Bob Condor, "College Prof Hopes the Cafeteria Will Serve a Lesson in Ethics" - *Seattle Post-Intelligencer* (20 Nov. 2006). Condor also refers to Singer's 1975 book *Animal Liberation* as "credited with galvanizing a whole movement regarding more humane treatment of livestock."

15 Ibid.

16 All quotes are derived from an interview of Donald Watson by George D. Rodger (15 Dec. 2002). The full transcript appears at www.veganmeans.com courtesy of The Vegan Society and George D. Rodger.

17 "The meat, dairy and egg industries would gradually decline and disappear. This will enable farmers to breed fewer animals" during the transition, according to the question-and-answer material produced by The Vegan Society.

18 Henry S. Salt, *Animals' Rights Considered in Relation to Social Progress* (dated 1892 and published two years later), at page 49.

19 Oliver Broudy, "The Practical Ethicist" - *Salon.com* (8 May 2006).

20 Ibid.

21 Ibid. Singer is using the word "vegetarian" loosely — referring, evidently, to ovo-lacto vegetarians.

22 Peter Singer and Jim Mason, *The Way We Eat: Why Our Food Choices Matter* (Rodale, 2006), at 282-83.

23 Ibid., at 283 (allowing a law student's fine-restaurant "exemption" in an ethical principal).

24 See ibid., at 258.

25 Keynote speech, Taking Action for Animals (event sponsored by the Humane Society of the United States, 2006).

26 Ibid. Later in the speech, Singer says reform should be the priority rather than

abolition, but claims that the two are compatible. Notably, a panel dedicated to "approved" cattle ranchers was hosted at Taking Action for Animals 2007. For related discussion, see Lee Hall, "Hogwash! How Animal Advocates Enable Corporate Spin" - *Dissident Voice.org* (Sep. 2007).

27 Quoted in Rosamund Raha's "Animal Liberation: An Interview with Professor Peter Singer" in *The Vegan* (quarterly magazine of the Vegan Society; Autumn 2006), at 19.

28 Ibid.

29 Donald Watson, editorial in *The Vegan News: Quarterly Magazine of the Non-Dairy Vegetarians* (Issue No. 1, Nov. 1944). The modern animal-advocacy movement is often said to have started in the late 1970s and early 1980s, but a more realistic look shows that time as the point when the reduction of suffering became its all-encompassing theme. Arguably, that impeded a serious movement for autonomy. We might debate whether 1944 gave rise to the modern animal-rights movement; yet the date signals the presentation of a new and vital nexus of questions, a time when a paradigm shift was proposed. Watson, who pointed to the Essenes as one example of a group that had conscientiously avoided animal exploitation, also drew from the vegetarian movement that took hold in Britain and the United States in the 1850s; and Watson's uncompromising opposition to vivisection was doubtless influenced by Frances Power Cobbe, founder of the British Union for the Abolition of Vivisection. Also present at the time of The Vegan Society's formation were opponents of "cruel sport"; but the advent of The Vegan Society pulled a cohesive anti-exploitation movement together into comprehensive animal-rights advocacy with personal commitment as its basis, and an emphasis on continuous public outreach to raise awareness of, and challenge, humanity's ordinary uses of animals.

30 Leslie Cross published "Veganism Defined" through the Spring 1951 issue of *The Vegetarian World Forum*, a magazine that then served as the journal of the International Vegetarian Union. Available: http://www.veganmeans.com/vegan_who/VEGANISM_DEFINED.htm.

31 Ibid.

32 See Lee Hall, "Movement Watch: Vegetarian CEO Asked to Stop Selling Ducks" - Friends of Animals *ActionLine* (Spring 2004).

33 On 25 Jan. 2005, Whole Foods promoted a global five-percent day, designed to contribute a percentage of the day's profits into the foundation. On the same day, Friends of Animals picketed the company at five of its retail locations.

34 Ewen Callaway, "Pain-free Animals Could Take Suffering out of Farming" - *New Scientist* (Issue 2724; 2 Sep. 2009).

35 Oliver Broudy, "The Practical Ethicist" - *Salon.com* (8 May 2006).

36 "Because breeding the best possible stock improves the over-all health and disease resistance of animal populations, cloning should reduce animal suffering over time." This claim appears on the website *CloneSafety.org*, "FAQs" [Frequently Asked Questions] at http://www.clonesafety.org/cloning/facts/faq/. The website's listed sponsors are "Cyagra, stART Licensing, and ViaGen, Inc., the world's premier animal cloning and livestock genetics companies, in cooperation with the Biotechnology Industry Organization and leading scientists."

37 Oliver Broudy's interview "The Practical Ethicist" appears at *Salon.com* (8 May 2006).

38 Rosemary Kennedy, born into the Kennedy family a year after John F. Kennedy, began to engage in physical fights and to sneak out at night from the convent where she was being educated; so in 1941, Rosemary's father, who worried that Rosemary would gravitate to situations that could damage the family reputation, agreed with Walter Freeman's recommendation for a lobotomy that would calm the "mood swings that the family found difficult to handle at home." See Lolita C. Baldor (Associated Press), "Rose Kennedy, Champion of Special Olympics, Dies" - *Deseret [Salt Lake City] News* (8 Jan. 2005). The operation reduced Rosemary to an infantile state that left her incontinent and staring blankly at walls for hours; for years afterward the family kept Rosemary out of the public eye and in an institution in Wisconsin. For information on earlier examples of social control under the guise of medical science see Jeffrey Moussaieff Masson's *A Dark Science: Women, Sexuality and Psychiatry in the Nineteenth Century* (Farrar Straus & Giroux; 1986).

39 As quoted in Brian Doherty, "Ill-Treated: The Continuing History of Psychiatric Abuses" - *Reason Magazine* (May 2002), a book review of Robert Whitaker's *Mad in America: Bad Science, Bad Medicine, and the Enduring Mistreatment of the Mentally Ill* (Basic Books Perseus Books Group, 2001).

40 "Heavy Petting" is Singer's review of a book by Midas Dekkers, *Dearest Pet: On Bestiality* (Verso, 1994). Appearing in the March 2001 issue of *Nerve.com*, Singer's essay suggests that the social aversion to bestiality is outdated and conservative.

41 Singer only decries the sexual use of other animals in the case of a hen because birds have small genital openings and thus such activity would be "cruel to the hen." Singer's essay includes an incident between an orang-utan and a human volunteer at a rehabilitation site. Despite the orang-utan's strength, the story Singer mentions involved an individual who, like many of the great apes today, was ripped from the natural world early in life — a victim of deforestation.

42 This includes simply killing animals when they are of no further use to us. Hens past their laying prime have no industrial value, and Singer suggests the debt of conscience for their exploitation can somehow be paid off by making sure they aren't shredded up or suffocated at the end. "Those hens have been producing eggs for you for a year or 18 months. You have a responsibility to make sure they are killed humanely." Oliver Broudy, "The Practical Ethicist" - *Salon.com* (8 May 2006). Singer believes the argument against species bias is harder to maintain "when you get beyond mammals" and it's possible that this could explain this dismissive attitude about birds. But as we have seen earlier in this chapter, Singer also declines to rule out hamburgers.

43 Michael Specter, "The Dangerous Philosopher" - *The New Yorker* (6 Sep. 1999). The essay includes an insightful quote from Rosemary Crossley about the difficulty of judging the quality of other's preferences and the fullness of their lives:
> Most of us live through our own experiences, so Peter assumes that people would be happy if they had the experiences that he had. For most of us, it is hard to live without reading, if you are a reader, or having sex, or jogging, or eating Chinese food. Whatever makes you happy, if you see people who cannot experience those things, you assume they cannot be happy. But that is not necessarily the case, and I don't think Peter has ever fully come to grips with that.

44 Quoted in Rosamund Raha's "Animal Liberation: An Interview with Professor Peter Singer" in *The Vegan* (quarterly magazine of The Vegan Society; Autumn 2006), at 19.

45 Singer & Mason, *The Way We Eat*, at 255. The phrase "both human and animals" is copied as published in the original.

46 Ibid., at 252. Singer and Mason do (on pages 254-56) suggest including destruction of habitat and also the difficulty of ensuring that the pig was indeed "humanely" raised in the cost-benefit analysis, although this fails to contemplate the loss domestication visits on the communities of free-living animals who are, throughout the process, gradually erased.

Notes to Chapter 3 ∿ Pages 71–94

1 Tom Regan, *The Case for Animal Rights* (2nd edition, 2004), at xxvii.

2 See Tom Regan, *The Case for Animal Rights* (1st edition, 1985, at 235; 2nd edition, 2004, at xxxiv).

3 Tom Regan, *The Case for Animal Rights* (both editions), at page 268.

4 Tom Regan, *The Case for Animal Rights* (both editions), at page 328. Regan uses the easier-to-handle term "psychological beings" in more recent essays; see, e.g., "The Philosophy of Animal Rights by Dr. Tom Regan" (undated; published online by the Culture and Animals Foundation).

5 This statement on "independent value" and the excerpted quotes below it can be seen in Tom Regan, "The Case for Animal Rights" - *In Defense of Animals* (Peter Singer, ed., Basil Blackwell, 1985), 13-26.

6 Ibid.

7 Tom Laskawy, "Will Whole Foods' New Mobile Slaughterhouses Squeeze Small Farmers?" – *Grist* (20 Nov. 2009) (interviewing a Massachusetts farmer).

8 Perhaps, however, the nudity is intended simply to draw media attention. Soon after Igualdad Animal and Equanimal, both based in Spain, carried out the naked protests for seals in early 2009, Equanimal held a protest against bullfights in which all activists wore only briefs and offered no explanation of a connection between the near-nudity of the activists and the plight of bulls.

9 Tom Regan's letter "Defending Animal Rights From A 'Defender'" appeared 3 Apr. 2001 in *The News & Observer* of Raleigh, North Carolina, at A11.

10 See ibid.

11 Following Regan, abolitionism has made allowances to save the human over the dog in every situation. This tendency has been critically examined, however, in Paola Cavalieri, *The Animal Question* (Oxford University Press; 2001) at pages 95-96; in Joan Dunayer, *Speciesism* (Ryce Publishing; 2004) at pages 95-98; and in Lee Hall, *Capers in the Churchyard* (Friends of Animals: Nectar Bat Press; 2006) at pages 31-32. In the essay "Animal Rights and Feminist Theory" in *Beyond Animal Rights* (at page 53, note 10), in a brief footnote, ecofeminist writer Josephine Donovan rejects Regan's argument, believing it lacks logical consistency and preserves a hierarchy with humans at the top.

12 See Tom Regan, *The Case for Animal Rights* (University of California Press, 1983; reprinted 2004), at 314, 351.

13 See Tom Regan, *The Case for Animal Rights* (1983 and 2004) at 324-25.

14 See ibid. at 325, and the preface to the 2004 edition.

15 See the preface to the 2004 edition, at xxxv.

16 "Dolphin Rescues Stranded Whales: Conservation Official" - *The Age* (as reported by Conservation officer Malcolm Smith to Agence France-Presse; 12 Mar. 2008).

17 See "How Can a Dog Sniff Through Concrete?" in *BBC News Magazine* (26 Feb. 2008).

18 Robert C. Solomon, *A Passion for Justice: Emotions and the Origins of the Social Contract* (Rowman & Littlefield, 1995), at 143.

19 Joseph K. Bump, et al., "Wolves Modulate Soil Nutrient Heterogeneity and Foliar Nitrogen by Configuring the Distribution of Ungulate Carcasses" - *Ecology* (2009), led by Joseph Bump, an assistant professor at Michigan Technological University's School of Forest Resources and Environmental Science.

20 The Project Gutenberg electronic text of *Wild Animals I Have Known* by Ernest Thompson Seton is filed at http://www.gutenberg.org/dirs/etext02/wldam10.txt.

21 "The Wolf that Changed America"- *PBSNature* (2008).

22 Regan, *The Case for Animal Rights* (2004), at xxxv-xxxvi.

23 Hugo and Jane van Lawick-Goodall, *In the Shadow of Man* (Houghton Mifflin; 1971), at 236-37.

24 Ibid., at page 237. In fact, when tested in (alas!) captivity, birds in the crow family have been found to rival chimpanzees in dexterity and ingenuity related to tool-making and -using tasks. "Rooks Show Intelligence to Rival Chimpanzees in Tests With Tools" - *The Times Online* (26 May 2009).

25 Regan, *The Case for Animal Rights* (1983 and 2004), at 314; see also page xxxiii.

26 Regan, *The Case for Animal Rights* (2004), at xxxiv.

27 Gary L. Francione, "Animals – Property or Persons?", in *Animals as Persons* (Columbia University Press, 2008) at 25; and in Cass R. Sunstein and Martha C. Nussbaum, eds., *Animal Rights: Current Debates and New Directions* (Oxford University Press USA), at 108.

28 Gary L. Francione, *Introduction to Animal Rights*, at 151-52.

29 I appreciate thoughts shared with me by Scott Geiger and Allison Memmo Geiger, highlighting this point.

30 Tom Regan, *The Case for Animal Rights* (2004), at xxx-xxxi (discussing an objection made by L. W. Sumner that the Regan's lifeboat exception is inconsistent with Regan's general anti-vivisection position).

31 Ibid., at page xxxi (discussing an objection made by Rem B. Edwards).

32 Amy Hamilton, "Horse Problem: Abandonment Up in Rough Times" - *The Grand Junction Daily Sentinel* (15 Jan. 2010) quotes inspector Mike Walck, who oversees brand inspections from De Beque and Aspen, Colorado, reporting 14 or 15 abandoned horse cases in 2008, and calling this "a trend that is mirrored nationwide." A brand inspector checks animals during transfers to view the brands and compare them to the branding records.

33 "Pet Dogs Abandoned as Recession Bites" - *CNN.com* (dated 21 Dec. 2008; posted online 22 Dec. 2008).

34 Chris Richard, "Number of Malpractice Cases Spikes… For Pets" - *Christian Science Monitor* (28 Jul. 2003).

35 On page 153 of *Introduction to Animal Rights*, Francione does observe that we unnecessarily bring animals into a domesticated existence—"for uses that we would never consider appropriate for any humans—by having a 'meat' industry or an 'entertainment' industry or a 'game animal' industry"; and that's an important statement. It would also be important, as animal-rights theory evolves, to state with unequivocal clarity that we relinquish the custom of regarding other beings as our domestic companions, and at the same time to insist that the autonomy of wolves and other free-living animals be respected as a central point of the animal-rights platform.

36 Notably, a precedent for the lifeboat metaphor did take environmental catastrophe into account. Garret Hardin, seeing the burgeoning human population as outstripping the planet's food supply, likened financially wealthy countries to a lifeboat which less affluent people would like to enter, or from which they'd at least like to receive a share of the wealth. Hardin applied a consequentialist analysis, claiming the net result of helping people would be catastrophic. Originally published as Garret Hardin, "Lifeboat Ethics: The Case Against Helping the Poor" - *Psychology Today* (Sep. 1974).

37 Tom Regan, *The Case for Animal Rights* (updated edition, 2004), at page xxx.

38 Dogs were domesticated from wolves; Peter Savolainen et al. at the Royal Institute of Technology in Sweden offer strong evidence that this involved wolves in Eastern Asia, possibly China, about 15,000 years ago, published in the journal *Science* (22 Nov. 2002, Vol. 298, No. 5598, at 1610-13). See also Melissa M. Gray et al., "The IGF1 Small Dog Haplotype Is Derived From Middle Eastern Grey Wolves" — *BMC Biology* (24 Feb. 2010). The journal is part of a series of BMC journals published by BioMed Central.

39 Claudette Vaughan's interview: "The Abolitionist Theory of Gary Francione" - *Abolitionist Online* (2005). Francione states, "If the human interest in not suffering has any moral significance, then we cannot treat humans merely as resources." Francione applies the same principle to nonhuman beings. See Gary L. Francione, *Introduction to Animal Rights: Your Child or the Dog?* (Temple University Press, 2000), at 92-93, 100.

40 Tom Regan, *The Case for Animal Rights* (either the 1983 or 2004 edition) at 30. Emphasis in original text.

41 Francione, *Introduction to Animal Rights*, at 175-76.

42 Francione's introduction to *Animals as Persons* (at 11) states:
    Although whether a being is sentient may not be clear in all cases, such as those involving insects or mollusks, the overwhelming number of nonhuman animals we exploit are unquestionably subjectively aware and have an interest in continuing to exist, even if they do not have the same reflective self-awareness that we associate with normal humans.

43 See Phil Davison's Obituary for Donald Watson in *The Independent* (24 Nov. 2005). Francione, like Peter Singer in *Animal Liberation*, claims plants can't feel pain because it would be evolutionarily useless to sense a pain signal from which one cannot move. I can think of no explanation for their being less sure that the smallest animals— including earthworms and other insects, who can move away from intense heat, cold,

spades, and so forth—do experience physical sensations. This is not to suggest that vegans are able to live without causing harm to insects. The vegan position involves commitment to mindfulness and striving to act out of respect in as many aspects as we are able to learn and apply.

44 See Lee Hall's interview with Gary L. Francione on "The State of the U.S. Animal Rights Movement" in Friends of Animals' *ActionLine* (Summer 2002).

45 Francione's *Introduction to Animal Rights* (at page 5) cites Bentham's humane-treatment principle as the basis of anticruelty laws; the book posits that humans, as long as they are owners, cannot be expected to extend equal consideration to the animals they own, and will arrange these laws so as to put property interests first; thus, the status of nonhuman animals as property is what Francione seeks to change. Francione asserts that this would be a matter of taking seriously the humane-treatment principle, which almost everyone agrees upon: that it is wrong to inflict "unnecessary suffering" on non-human animals. Cass R. Sunstein, in a review in *New Republic* (29 Jan. 2001), has seen this as a merging of disparate philosophical traditions: "Francione is taking a complicated and unusual step here: he is merging the idea of animal welfare with the idea of animal rights…through the claim that animals have rights because they can suffer. It is not clear that the merger of the disparate traditions can be made to work. The importance of suffering, under the utilitarian framework, is inextricably intertwined with the insistence on the overriding importance of consequences." Sunstein's point is noteworthy. Bentham's appeal arguably carries its greatest appeal to the campaigner for husbandry improvements rather than to the proponent of animal rights. Consider Bentham's full explanatory note in Chapter 17 of *An Introduction to the Principals of Morals and Legislation* (first published 1789):

> Under the Gentoo and Mahometan religions, the interests of the rest of the animal creation seem to have met with some attention. Why have they not universally, with as much as those of human creatures, allowance made for the difference in point of sensibility? Because the laws that are have been the work of mutual fear; a sentiment which the less rational animals have not had the same means as man has of turning to account. Why *ought* they not? No reason can be given. If the being eaten were all, there is very good reason why we should be suffered to eat such of them as we like to eat: we are the better for it, and they are never the worse. They have none of those long-protracted anticipations of future misery which we have. The death they suffer in our hands commonly is, and always may be, a speedier, and by that means a less painful one, than that which would await them in the inevitable course of nature. If the being killed were all, there is very good reason why we should be suffered to kill such as molest us: we should be the worse for their living, and they are never the worse for being dead. But is there any reason why we should be suffered to torment them? Not any that I can see. Are there any why we should *not* be suffered to torment them? Yes, several. See B. I. tit. [Cruelty to animals]. The day has been, I grieve to say in many places it is not yet past, in which the greater part of the species, under the denomination of slaves, have been treated by the law exactly upon the same footing as, in England for example, the inferior races of animals are still. The day *may* come, when the rest of the animal creation may acquire those rights which never could have been withholden from them but by the hand of tyranny. The

French have already discovered that the blackness of the skin is no reason why a human being should be abandoned without redress to the caprice of a tormentor. [See Lewis XIV's Code Noir.] It may come one day to be recognized, that the number of the legs, the villosity of the skin, or the termination of the *os sacrum*, are reasons equally insufficient for abandoning a sensitive being to the same fate. What else is it that should trace the insuperable line? Is it the faculty of reason, or, perhaps, the faculty of discourse? But a full-grown horse or dog is beyond comparison a more rational, as well as a more conversable animal, than an infant of a day, or a week, or even a month, old. But suppose the case were otherwise, what would it avail? the question is not, Can they *reason?* nor, Can they *talk?* but, Can they *suffer?*

The full text of Bentham's *An Introduction to the Principles of Morals and Legislation* is available at the Library of Economics and Liberty: http://www.econlib.org/library/Bentham/bnthPML.html

46 *Rain without Thunder,* at 16. In *Introduction to Animal Rights* (at 137), Francione describes Singer's position "that killing a sentient being does not inflict harm on that being" and responds that "it would seem that the opposite is true: that death is the greatest harm for any sentient being and that merely being sentient logically implies an interest in continued existence and some awareness of that interest." Francione adds: "Animals may not have thoughts about the number of years they will live, but by virtue of having an interest in not suffering and in experiencing pleasure, they have an interest in remaining alive."

47 See Lee Hall's interview with Gary L. Francione on "The State of the U.S. Animal Rights Movement" (cited in note 44 above).

48 Transcript of the 11th IVU World Vegetarian Congress (1947; Stonehouse, England); available at http://www.ivu.org/congress/wvc47/veganism.html.

49 Henry Fountain, "Call of the Wild, or, Rather, the Grim Reaper?" - *New York Times* (28 Aug. 2005).

50 See Gary Rivlin, "In California Enclave, Cougars Keep the People at Bay" – *New York Times* (28 Aug. 2005).

Notes to Chapter 4 ∾ Pages 95–140

1 The 2008 study in the *Journal of Consumer Research* was done by Michael W. Allen at the University of Sydney, Richa Gupta from the University of Nashville, and Arnaud Monnier of the National Engineer School for Food Industries and Management, France.

2 See generally Gary L. Francione, *Rain without Thunder* (Temple University Press, 1996).

3 Ibid., at 211.

4 Francione, *Rain without Thunder,* at 210 (emphasis in the original).

5 *Ibid.,* at 210-11 (emphasis in the original).

6 See Joan Dunayer, *Speciesism* (Ryce Publishing, 2004), at 69, explaining that a caging ban isn't a ban at all, but rather a requirement that hens have more space.

7 *Rain without Thunder,* at 210, does not accept as a legitimate "incremental" step to

rights an agreement by the industrialist to change from four hens per cage to two hens per cage: "The problem with the proposal is that it endorses the status of animals as property without inherent value and trades away the basic right of the hens not to be property in favor of a recognition of moral status that falls short of recognition of the basic right, or the complete protection of some interest that the animal has, for example, in bodily movement."

8 "Some proposals that easily conform to the criteria are absolute bans on leghold traps to catch fur-bearing animals. The rule consists of a prohibition of an activity that is a constitutive part of the overall exploitation of animals for clothing or fur purposes. The interest recognized is extra-institutional and nontradable, and proposal does not substitute another form of exploitation, such as the padded trap." Francione, *Rain without Thunder, at* 212. See the next note for a general description of the "criteria" mentioned here.

9 The five criteria for "an incremental approach," taken together, are designed to identify a regulation that counts as a prohibition of a certain violation of animals' interests, and to guide activists who'd like to urge "incremental change on a sociolegal level (changes in law, regulations, policy)" without thwarting the eventual end to institutionalized exploitation. As the criteria rely on complex wording and interconnections, the reader is advised to see the text of *Rain without Thunder at* pages 190-219.

10 *Rain without Thunder,* at 202-3. Francione posits: "That is, assume that a prohibition abolishes the battery cage *entirely* and replaces it with a rearing system that accommodates *all* of the hen's interests in freedom of movement and thereby fully recognizes the interest of the hen in bodily integrity." Francione declares that "this sort of substitution differs considerably from that in which two hens are merely removed from the cage: although we have not yet abolished the institutionalized exploitation, the substitution eliminates the exploitation involved in the confinement system through a *full* recognition of the interest of the hens in their freedom of movement." Ibid. at 210 (emphasis in the original).

11 Ibid., at 2. Francione says, "Animal rights theory rejects the regulation of atrocities and calls unambiguously and unequivocally for their abolition." Yet there is, it might be noted, ambiguity in Francione's perspective, connected with the word "exclusively" as the comment continues: "Rights theory precludes the treatment of animals exclusively as means to human ends, which means that animals should not be regarded as the property of people." Ibid.

12 At page 215, Francione writes: "If animal exploiters accommodate animal interests and eliminate the battery cage in favor of some other form of hen enclosure that continues their status as property and does not fully respect their interest in, for example, body integrity, that does not necessarily undermine the incremental eradication of property status. This effect on property status has been accomplished by forcing the property owner to recognize, albeit in a limited way, that the animals have inherent value that must be respected whether or not the property owner thinks that such respect is cost-justified in light of the status of the animal as property."

13 Ibid. at 215.

14 Ibid. (emphasis in the original).

15 Gary L. Francione, "Reflections on *Animals, Property, and the Law* and *Rain without Thunder*" - *Law and Contemporary Problems* (Vol. 70:9, Winter 2007), at 46. At that point, Francione continues: "Moreover, the incremental change must protect interests beyond those necessary in order to exploit the animal in an efficient way (the limiting principle of most animal welfare) and should be explicitly promoted as recognizing that nonhumans have interests that are not tradable or able to be ignored merely because humans will benefit from doing so." Ibid. (internal citations omitted). This indicates that if specific interests of farm animals are legally protected at the farmers' cost, a step has been taken in the direction of animal rights. It fails to state that there simply cannot be incremental steps to the rights of calves.

16 Campaigns against the transport of injured cattle, veal crates, castration and dehorning are discussed on pages 214-17 of *Rain without Thunder* as "prohibitions" that "recognize interests that would be recognized were the animals not property at all" and therefore treat the farm animals "as more than a means to human ends."

17 Ibid. at page 216, stating: "Similarly, a complete prohibition on the selling of nonambulatory, or 'downed,' animals, a prohibition that would completely eradicate the market for these animals, may satisfy the five criteria as long as the supposed 'prohibition' does not substitute another form of exploitation."

But the absence of crippled animals in the food supply doesn't stop any form of exploitation in the first place; it means the animals are marked "condemned" and killed rather than being dragged to the slaughter plant.

18 U.S. Department of Agriculture news release No. 0218.08: "USDA Announces Proposed Rule for Requirements of the Disposition of Downer Cattle" (27 Aug. 2008).

19 Francione, *Rain without Thunder*, at 217.

20 *Rain without Thunder*, at 215. Francione has based this on their capacity to feel pain: "If a nonhuman can feel pain, then we have a moral obligation not to treat that nonhuman exclusively as a means to our ends." See Lee Hall's interview with Gary L. Francione on "The State of the U.S. Animal Rights Movement" in Friends of Animals' *Act·ionLine* (Summer 2002).

21 Cass R. Sunstein, "Slaughterhouse Jive" – *New Republic* (29 Jan. 2001) at 45.

22 Francione, "Reflections on *Animals, Property, and the Law* and *Rain without Thunder*" - *Law and Contemporary Problems*, at note 125, citing Gary L. Francione, *Introduction to Animal Rights: Your Child or the Dog?* (Temple University Press, 2000) at 90-91.

23 *Rain without Thunder*, at 216.

24 *Animals as Persons*, Introduction, at 21, reaffirming "a version of the abolitionist theory of animal rights" developed in *Introduction to Animal Rights* (2000), which states, "I conclude that our acceptance of the right of nonhumans not to be treated as property requires that we abolish institutionalized animal exploitation and stop producing domestic nonhumans for human use."

25 See Dennis Pollock, "Henhouse Options to Be Weighed by Experts" - *The Fresno Bee* (15 Feb. 2008), referring to facts provided by UC Davis researcher Joy Mench. See also UC Davis News Service, "To Cage or Not to Cage: Research Coalition Seeks

Answers" (27 Feb. 2008), stating that "most laying hens suffer from osteoporosis, and cage-free hens are more likely than caged hens to break bones while moving through the barn or on the range."

26 Organic, free-range chicken and cage-free eggs produce some 14 to 20% more greenhouse gases than conventionally raised birds due to factors such as the longer time they need to be raised and fed, and space considerations. See Mike Tidwell, "The Low-Carbon Diet" – *Audubon Magazine* (Jan.-Feb. 2009); for a case in point see, e.g., "Environmental Burdens of Agricultural and Horticultural Commodity Production" (Project ISO205; final report published 2006), funded by Britain's Department for Environment Food and Rural Affairs and conducted from 2003 to 2005 from Cranfield University, Bedfordshire, by a research team led by Adrian Williams. I do not cite these references to endorse battery egg production. In a vegan paradigm one need never select any eggs at all.

27 Eggs, flesh and dairy emit four times higher greenhouse gas emissions than other agricultural services combined. See Food & Agriculture Organization of the United Nations, "Livestock's Long Shadow: Environmental Issues and Options" (2006; prepared by Henning Steinfeld et al.), at 112.

28 Duncan Clark, *Guardian:* Green Living Blog: "Top 10 Green Living Myths" (26 Nov. 2009).

29 Frank Pope, "Climate Change Feared to Blame as Dead Zones Suffocate Pacific Ocean Life" – *Times Online* (10 Oct. 2009).

30 "A Whole New Alternative? 'Compassionate' Meat at Whole Foods" - *Satya* (quoting Lauren Ornelas as executive director of Vegetarian International Voice for Animals-USA (VIVA-USA).

31 It has been claimed, for example, that *Rain without Thunder* did not mean to advocate regulatory measures by setting out five criteria for pursuing them. Yet the book states that the criteria, applied conjunctively, are consistent with rights theory, even if Francione has a preference for grassroots education over regulatory measures, and thinks that groups that pursue these measures should do so with caution because they encourage a problematic "insider status" and are arguably an inefficient use of time and resources, and because may be met with fierce resistance. If Francione never meant to approve of using them, they needn't have been set forth at all — all the more so in a book that is expressly cautious with regard to regulatory measures.

32 Nick Paumgarten, "Food Fighter: Does Whole Foods' CEO Know What's Best for You?" (4 Jan. 2010).

33 The standards can be found at www.vegansociety.com (as of this writing, specifically located in the "View Trademark Products" section).

34 Product samples and coupons arrived from more than a dozen vegan companies, cookbooks were provided to each participant from Friends of Animals, and The Vegan Society in Britain donated enamel sunflower badges and copies of early vegan publications.

35 "World's Largest Salmon BBQ July 5" - Living Light Culinary Arts Institute (May-Jun. 2008 newsletter).

36 "Ghent Goes Vegetarian" – Life and Style Blog, *The Guardian* (14 May 2009;

reporting that Ghent, Belgium will be vegetarian every Thursday from that date on, but also that the city is "renowned for its fish and shellfish"; presumably such products will continue to be sold daily).

37 Marie Woolf, "Citizenship Lessons to Teach Children Respect for Worms" - *Times Online* (15 Nov. 2009).

38 As recounted in Lee Hall, "Synopsis and Commentary: The *Satya* Humane Meat Discussion of [12 Oct.] 2006" at Jivamukti Yoga Studio Café, New York City: Farmer-activist Harold Brown explained that "husbandry is already in the agricultural schools' curricula, so it doesn't need any promotion. The more we talk about the serious subject of animal rights, the more industry will respond with husbandry adjustments in an effort to pacify activists and the public. But it's not our job to compromise our views and meekly ask for those reforms. We can't 'dismantle' animal use by compromising with it." Full commentary available at *VeganMeans.com*.

39 Nigel Binns, as chief biologist for the Rentokil company, received a "Person of the Year" award from People for the Ethical Treatment of Animals for developing a new way to kill mice. In the trap's plastic enclosure, a pressure pad senses the animal's paw, and closes the door if the footfall matches the weight of a rat or mouse. Gas released from a carbon dioxide capsule then kills the mouse. Media coverage of the lobster-killing promotion was issued by Andy McSmith, "I'll Have My Lobster Electrocuted, Please" - *The Independent* (21 Nov. 2009).

40 *Git Along, Little Dogies,* a traditional ballad of the western United States, is also performed under the title *Whoopie Ti Yi Yo.* The song describes seasonal roundups in which cattle drivers "mark 'em and brand 'em and bob off their tails…then throw the little dogies out on the long trail."

41 See Samuel Warren and Louis Brandeis, "The Right to Privacy" - *Harvard Law Review* (Dec. 1890) and *Olmstead v. United States*, 277 U.S. 438, 478 (1928) (Brandeis, J. dissenting; with reference to the Fourth Amendment).

42 Francione, *Rain without Thunder*, at 2 (emphasis in the original).

43 Francione, *Introduction to Animal Rights*, at 50-51. Reindeer are thought to have been domesticated as early as 14000 BC; dogs, as previously noted, were domesticated from wolves about 13000 BC. Ancient Egyptian law, dating as far back as 3000 BC, had a civil code, although the Torah, which dates back no further than 1200 to 1500 BC, might be the oldest body of law relevant to modern legal regimes; the Torah refers to domesticated animals, and reflects the idea that animals generally were available to be used by humans who had dominion over them. And while Francione correctly points out that the Latin word for money, *pecunia*, is derived from *pecus*, meaning cattle, this highlights the domination already in place, upon which a system of exchanging animals was established. The modern concept that free-living animals may be made into the personal property of the person who first exercises complete control over their bodies can be traced in the 1805 case in the Supreme Court of New York, *Pierson vs. Post* (involving two parties' conflicting claims over a body of a fox). Among the early authorities cited by the court in its opinion were the works of William Blackstone (1723-1780), Fleta (a treatise written in the second century AD), Jean Barbeyrac (1674-1744), Baron Samuel von Pufendorf (1632-1694), Hugo Grotius (1583-1645), and Justinian I (AD 483-565).

44 Gary L. Francione, *Animals as Persons* (Columbia University Press; 2008), at
25 (reprinting writing originally published in 2004; internal citations omitted).
Elsewhere in the book, Francione reaffirms: "A central thesis in *Rain without Thunder,*
as well as my later work, is that, if animal interests are to be morally significant, we
must accord to nonhumans the basic right not to be treated as property, and this
requires that we seek to abolish, and not merely regulate, institutionalized animal
exploitation." *Animals as Persons,* at page 70 (reprinting writing originally published in
2007; internal citations omitted).

45 In *Animals as Persons* (page 125, Chapter 2, "Reflections on *Animals, Property and the
Law* and *Rain without Thunder*"; reprinted from an article originally published in
2007 in the journal *Law & Contemporary Problems*), Francione discusses the topic of
ascertaining which beings should be included in the "moral community" and points to
characteristics "relevant to whether we make a being suffer or kill that being." What
this does not observe (and an explicit observation is critical) is the importance of free
animals' need for habitat, and the need for affirmative advocacy on behalf of this need.

46 For related commentary see Julia Whitty, "Gone: Mass Extinction and the Hazards of
Earth's Vanishing Biodiversity" – *Mother Jones* (25 Apr. 2007).

47 "Mammals May Be Nearly Half Way Toward Mass Extinction" - *ScienceDaily* (18
Dec. 2009), describing research by Russell W. Graham, professor of geosciences
at Penn State University, Anthony Barnosky, UC Berkeley professor of integrative
biology, and UC Berkeley research associate Marc A. Carrasco. The analysis by
Barnosky, Carrasco and Graham appeared online the week of 13 Dec. 2009 in the
open-access journal *PLoS One.*

48 The Vegetarian Resource Group's most recent survey (with data collected in May
2009 by the Harris Interactive Service Bureau) shows .8% of the U.S. population as
vegan. By the time Donald Watson passed on in 2005, *Time* reported the existence of
about 250,000 self-identifying vegans in Britain and two million in the United States.
See Claire Suddath, "A Brief History of Veganism" - *Time* (30 Oct. 2008). Donald
Watson's November 2005 obituary in *The Independent* put the number of British
vegans at 300,000. Although these are particularly accessible estimates, vegans live in
many other places on every continent.

49 *The Vegan News: Quarterly Magazine of the Non-Dairy Vegetarians* (No. 1, 24 Nov. 1944).

50 Perhaps Francione now recognizes this. In a 2007 essay reprinted in *Animals as
Persons,* Francione writes, "Critics who claim that I propose no incremental legal
change have apparently overlooked this part of my work...I accept, however, that this
portion of *Rain without Thunder,* which I presented explicitly as a preliminary analysis,
was not as clear as it could have been and I plan to clarify my views on incremental
regulatory change in future writing." Francione, *Animals as Persons,* at 113 (note 148).

51 Monty Moran, Chipotle's president and chief operating officer, dispatched a letter
in March 2008 to an animal-advocacy group in order to say the company will add a
relevant statement to its supplier protocols: "We will give purchasing preference to
suppliers that utilize the most humane method of slaughter available, including new
and emerging technologies such as controlled-atmosphere killing (CAK), where the
suppliers also meet our naturally-raised meat protocols, offer a stable of supply of food
meeting our high quality standards, and in a way that is economically feasible." See

"How PETA Influences Restaurant Shareholders to Push Policies" - *QSR Magazine* (8 Mar. 2008).

52 See Paul Walsh, "PETA to Confront Hormel Tonight on Turkey Slaughter Methods" - [Minneapolis-St. Paul, Minnesota] *Star Tribune* (29 Jan. 2008).

53 See Geoffrey P. Lantos, "The Boundaries of Strategic Corporate Responsibility" - *Journal of Consumer Marketing* (2001) (concurring with Milton Friedman that for a publicly held business altruistic "corporate social responsibility" — doing good at the expense of profit maximization and the interests of shareholders — is not legitimate, and therefore that "companies should limit their philanthropy to *strategic CSR*"– doing "good works that are also good for the business").

54 *Dodge v. Ford Motor Co.*, 170 N.W. 668 (Mich. 1919) set the tone for this principle after shareholders sued Ford because the company had stopped paying special dividends in order to invest the money in building more plants to make the cars more affordable. The court found that the corporation's directors had to pay the special dividends to the shareholders because the corporation's primary purpose is to generate profits for the shareholders; it exists only secondarily for community benefit. Where substantial human interests are perceived (the most salient modern factors could include threats posed to endangered species or risks posed by climate change), a government could, however, move to impose ethical duties on companies. In Britain, Friends of the Earth pressed for the Company Law Reform Bill, through which Parliament could impose environmental responsibilities on companies. See Friends of the Earth press release, "Asda Joins Roundtable on Palm Oil" (16 Dec. 2005).

55 *JobCircle.com*, advertisement for "Philanthropy Sr. Manager" vacancy (job code 945793, posted 22 Jan. 2010).

56 David Schepp, "People at Work: Corporate Giving Boosts Image, Employee Involvement" - AOL Money & Finance via *DailyFinance.com* (Jan. 2010; citations omitted).

57 Paul Tharp, "Whole Foods Kills Them Softly" - *New York Post* (19 Jan. 2005). Whole Foods shares rose 2.7 percent to $97.50 as the foundation's first director, Anne Malleau, said, "The creation of the Animal Compassion Foundation offers a brighter future for farm animals."

58 Humane Society of the United States, Corporate Social Responsibility (CSRwire) press release: "Trader Joe's Gives Birds Something to Sing About" (8 Nov. 2005).

59 John Vyvyan, *In Pity and in Anger: A Study of the Use of Animals in Science* (1988, Micah Publications), at 14.

60 James LaVeck, "Compassion for Sale? Doublethink Meets Doublefeel as Happy Meat Comes of Age"- *Satya* (Sep. 2006), quoting John Mackey at the "Power of One" (20th annual International Compassionate Living Festival in Raleigh, North Carolina, 7-9 Oct. 2005), co-sponsored by the Culture and Animals Foundation and the Institute for Animals and Society).

61 Phuong Ly, "The Other Red Protein: Meat Is Rare No More in Takoma Park" - *Washington Post* (20 Mar. 2005).

62 Lierre Keith, *The Vegetarian Myth: Food, Justice, and Sustainability* (PM Press, 2009), at 145.

63 Ibid., at 153.

64 Ibid., at 154.

65 See http://www.balnafettach.com/; Alex Renton's blog column appears at http://www.guardian.co.uk/lifeandstyle/wordofmouth/2007/oct/19/happymeat

66 Whole Foods Market, "Products: Meat & Poultry" (as visited 13 Dec. 2009).

67 Tony Banks, a former member of the British Parliament, also received a keynote speaking invitation from the convenors, but was reportedly unable to appear.

Notes to Chapter 5 ∾ Pages 141–160

1 "Let's Respect Our Mother Earth: Letter from President Evo Morales Ayma to the member representatives of the United Nations on the issue of the environment" (24 Sep. 2007).

2 The piece, by Jeffrey Davis, is dated 18 Jan. 2010 and includes the added headline: "When it comes to sustainable farming and humanely raising animals, Niman Ranch is at the top of their field." The photo includes a caption indicating prior publication in *Men's Journal*.

3 "We have to go beyond the amelioration of prison practice," prison abolitionist Angela Davis has said, stating that prison reforms are also necessary. Beth Potier, "Abolish Prisons, Says Angela Davis"—*Harvard Gazette*; posted at http://www.hno.harvard.edu/gazette/2003/03.13/09-davis.html (dated 13 Mar. 2003).

4 University of Chicago News Office: "Study: Vegan Diets Healthier for Planet, People Than Meat Diets" (13 Apr. 2006), citing research by Gidon Eshel and Pamela Martin showing that the average U.S. diet requires the production of an extra ton and a half of carbon dioxide-equivalent, in the form of actual carbon dioxide as well as methane and other greenhouse gases, compared to a pure vegetarian diet.

5 See Kim Severson, "Bringing Moos and Oinks Into the Food Debate"—*New York Times* (25 Jul. 2007), reporting that animal-advocacy non-profits have been rewarded with support for having "learned to harness the power of celebrity in a tabloid culture" and that in order to gain access to mainstream media and politics they "don't demonize meat— with the exception of foie gras and veal— or the people who produce it. Instead, they use softer rhetoric, focusing on a campaign even committed carnivores can get behind: better conditions for farm animals."

6 As recorded (likely paraphrased) through a transcript of the 11th IVU World Vegetarian Congress (1947; Stonehouse, England); available at http://www.ivu.org/congress/wvc47/veganism.html.

7 Ibid.

8 Cormac Cullinan, *Wild Law: A Manifesto for Earth Justice* (Green Books, 2nd edition, 2003), at 62-63.

Notes to Chapter 6 ∾ Pages 163–174

1 Catharine A. MacKinnon, *Feminism Unmodified* (1987, Harvard University Press), at 51.

2 Catharine A. MacKinnon, "Of Mice and Men: A Feminist Fragment on Animal Rights" in Cass R. Sunstein and Martha C. Nussbaum, eds., *Animal Rights: Current Debates and New Directions* (Oxford University Press USA), at 264.

3 Alice Walker, "Coming Apart: By Way of Introduction to Lorde, Teish and Gardner" - *You Can't Keep a Good Woman Down* (The Women's Press, 1981), at 41-53 (combining a story originally done for an anthology on pornography with historical commentary).

4 Brannon Costello, *Plantation Airs: Racial Paternalism and the Transformations of Class in Southern Fiction, 1945-1971* (2007), at 19, quoting Zora Neale Hurston's 1948 novel *Seraph on the Suwanee*.

5 Colin Woodard, "Why Your Dog Is Smarter Than a Wolf" - *Christian Science Monitor* (26 Oct. 2005).

6 Yi-Fu Tuan, *Dominance and Affection: The Making of Pets* (Yale University Press, 1984), at 85-86.

7 Martha C. Nussbaum, "The Moral Status of Animals" - *Chronicle of Higher Education* (3 Feb. 2006). As noted previously, we should keep in mind that the Judeo-Christian concepts of dominion reflected a long pattern of practices. While the Torah dates back no further than 1200 to 1500 BC, domestication of animals dates back to around 14000 BC.

8 "Orangutans Monkey Around With Video Games" - *CNN.com* (Associated Press, 13 Apr. 2007).

9 Henry Fountain, "Call of the Wild, or, Rather, the Grim Reaper?" - *New York Times* (28 Aug. 2005).

10 Stefanie Olsen, "Animals in Utero: An Inside View" - *CNET News* (8 Dec. 2006; announcing and describing a December 2006 *National Geographic* television special called "In the Womb: Animals").

11 Defenders of Wildlife press release, "Defenders of Wildlife Calls on Lawmakers to Protect Sensitive Border Lands and Wildlife as They SECURE our Borders" (20 Sep. 2006), at http://tinyurl.com/4ajlzs (capitalization in original).

12 Biologist and lawyer Geordie Duckler proposed to classify zoo animals as National Historic Landmarks listed under the National Historic Preservation Act's provision to maintain "objects significant in American culture" given that they exist "as easily identifiable landmarks in every major metropolitan city" and described as "cultural artifacts" the "exotic animals which humans have captured, studied, enjoyed and bred." See Geordie Duckler, "Toward a More Appropriate Jurisprudence Regarding the Legal Status of Zoos and Zoo Animals" - *Animal Law* (Vol. 3, 1997), at 196.

13 For related commentary see Yew-Kwang Ng, "Towards Welfare Biology: Evolutionary Economics of Animal Consciousness and Suffering" - *Biology and Philosophy* (Vol. 10, No. 4; 1995), at 255-85. Steve F. Sapontzis argues that we are morally obliged to prevent predation in the wild, at least when doing so would not produce more suffering than it would prevent; see "Predation," *Ethics and Animals* (Vol. 5, No. 2; 1984) at 36. For discussion of cases in which the obligation to protect prey animals is not morally absurd, see Arne Naess, "Should We Try To Relieve Clear Cases of Extreme Suffering in Nature?" (*Pan Ecology*, Vol. 6, No. 1, Winter

1991), considering, for example, an insect known as *cephenomyia trompe,* whose larvae feed and grow in the nostrils of reindeer, slowly suffocating the animals to death, and discussing whether it could be acceptable to intervene if possible to do without disturbing the balance of nature.

14 David Pearce, "Reprogramming Predators: Blueprint for a Cruelty-Free World" (2009), published on the BLTC ["Better Living Through Chemistry"] Research website, whose mission statement asserts that "Post-Darwinian superminds" can and should abolish pain. Dr. Pearce has assured me that the website is not meant to be satire.

15 E-mail communication dated 17 Dec. 2009.

16 *The Case for Animal Rights* (1983), at 357.

Notes to Chapter 7 ∽ Pages 175–196

1 Yi-Fu Tuan, *Dominance and Affection: The Making of Pets* (Yale University Press, 1984), at 95.

2 Mary Rogan, "A Little Bird Told Me" - *Seed Magazine* (12 Sep. 2007).

3 The site's question-and-answer page elaborates: "Every week our employees and volunteers travel to destination farms to pick up deceased livestock."

4 Darren Freeman and Seth Seymour, "Two on PETA Staff Charged With Cruelty to Animals" - *The Virginian-Pilot* (17 Jun. 2005).

5 Statement of Ingrid Newkirk, PETA president, in "PETA Statement at News Conference Regarding Euthanasia" (17 Jun. 2005).

6 The group, People for the Ethical Treatment of Animals, routinely kills more than 90% of the animals they take in. Several writers have commented on this fact (which is available from open Virginia records), including, most notably, animal advocate and author Nathan Winograd.

7 PETA vice-president Bruce Friedrich, in a book tour talk at Singapore Vegetarian Restaurant in Philadelphia (6 Jun. 2009), used the term "clean up" in reference to what PETA's president has accomplished in the case of a Washington, D.C. shelter.

8 Sarah Ovaska, "New Class of Hairy Lawsuits Asserts Pets' Rights" - *The [Raleigh, North Carolina] News & Observer* (16 Mar. 2008).

9 Ibid. Joyce Tischler, as executive director of the Animal Legal Defense Fund, has stated, "Protecting companion animals is not just something a crazy little old lady in tennis shoes would do. It has touched a nerve with legislators, with judges, and with all sorts of others who consider animals as part of the family." Chris Richard, "Number of Malpractice Cases Spikes…For Pets" - *Christian Science Monitor* (28 Jul. 2003 edition).

10 Matthew Scully, *Dominion: The Power of Man, the Suffering of Animals, and the Call to Mercy* (St. Martin's Press, 2002), at 9.

11 Ibid., at 5.

12 Of those species recorded as becoming extinct between 1500 and 2004, more lived in the United States than anywhere else, followed by the United Republic of Tanzania, Uganda and Mauritius. *New Scientist* published a map of this 27 Oct. 2008, visible

at http://bit.ly/7TJD27. The maps were derived from *The Atlas of the Real World*, published by Thames and Hudson and produced by the researchers behind the Worldmapper website.

13 Scully, *Dominion*, at 115.

14 See, for example, Steven M. Wise, *Drawing the Line: Science and the Case for Animal Rights* (Perseus, 2003). New York City's *Newsday* reported on a former corporate lawyer who became an animal law specialist after swimming with dolphins used in cancer therapies. See Alfonso A. Castillo, "Animal Lawyers Share Passion to Protect Helpless" - *Newsday* (30 Sep. 2007).

15 Castillo, "Animal Lawyers Share Passion to Protect Helpless" (ibid).

16 Jennifer Dillard, "Concepts of Freedom: Companion Animals" – *Animal Blawg* (28 Apr. 2007). Another blog states: "If you believe your dog has a right to a life free of torture and slaughter for no reason, then you really ought to think about extending that right to mice, rats, chickens and fish."

17 See David Brown, "Why Do Cats Hang Around Us? (Hint: They Can't Open Cans)" - *Washington Post* (29 Jun. 2007), discussing conclusions of a genetic study, published the same day in the journal *Science*, of the origins of domestic cats.

18 References addressing domestication include Tuan, *Dominance and Affection*, at 101-2; and Danielle LaBruna, "Columbia University Introduced Species Summary Project: Domestic Cat (Felis catus)" (2001; stating that cats were likely domesticated in Egypt from local populations of *F. lybica*, in a domestication process that began around 6,000 BC).

19 "Pedigree Dogs Plagued by Disease" - *BBC News* (19 Aug. 2008), noting that a segment called "Pedigree Dogs Exposed" would be aired on *BBC One* on the same date.

20 Karlin Lillington, "Dog's Life for Pedigree Breeds Due to Inbreeding" - *Irish Times* (20 Aug. 2008).

21 Tuan, *Dominance and Affection*, at 96-98.

22 Amy Harmon, "As Breeders Test DNA, Dogs Become Guinea Pigs" – *New York Times* (12 Jun. 2007).

23 Tuan, *Dominance and Affection*, at 154.

24 Scully, *Dominion*, at 5.

25 *Animals as Persons*, page 146, Chapter 3, "Taking Sentience Seriously"; reprinted from an article originally published in 2006 in the *Journal of Animal Law and Ethics*. For similar statements see Gary L. Francione, *Introduction to Animal Rights: Your Child or the Dog?"* (Temple University Press, 2000), at 153-54.

26 "Taking Sentience Seriously" (ibid.) at 137. See also Francione, *Introduction to Animal Rights, 115-18, 138-42*.

27 Yi-Fu Tuan, "Humanistic Geography: A Personal View" – talk delivered at Beijing Normal University (posted electronically by Huang Qingxu, 2005).

28 Cass R. Sunstein, "Introduction: What Are Animal Rights?" - *Animal Rights: Current Debates and New Directions* (Cass R. Sunstein & Martha C. Nussbaum eds., 2004), at 7, under the header *Enforcing Existing Rights*.

29 Tom Regan uses the phrase "mere receptacles"; see Tom Regan, *The Case for Animal Rights* (both editions), at 328. Gary L. Francione asserts, "Although there is certainly a great deal of disagreement about precisely what rights human beings have, it is clear that we now regard every human being as holding the right not to be treated exclusively as a means to the ends of another. This is a basic right, and it is different from all other rights; it is a pre-legal right in that it is a necessary prerequisite to the enjoyment of any other right." *Introduction to Animal Rights*, at 93.

Notes to Chapter 8 ∾ Pages 197–216

1 See Henry Fountain, "Call of the Wild, or, Rather, the Grim Reaper?" - *New York Times* (28 Aug. 2005). A study in Alaska, the article states, showed bear attacks at the rate of about five a year, with one fatality every two years. (There are more human deaths involving domestic dogs.) In the years spanning 1990 to 2005 in Tanzania, however, there were more than 560 fatalities from lion attacks.

2 Melnick is quoted in Lily Huang, "It's Survival of the Weak and Scrawny" - *Newsweek* (issue dated 12 Jan. 2009). For related information see Anne Minard, "Hunters Speeding Up Evolution of Trophy Prey?" - *National Geographic News* (12 Jan. 2009), citing the same week's issue of the *Proceedings of the National Academy of Sciences.*

3 The Humane Society of the United States holds a permit to test contraceptive vaccines on animals. For more information on these methods, see Priscilla N. Cohn, Edward D. Plotka, and Ulysses S. Seal, eds., *Contraception in Wildlife, Book I* (Edwin Mellen Press, 1996).

4 Peter Singer, "Food for Thought" (reply to a letter by David Rosinger) - *New York Review of Books* (Vol. 20, No. 10; 14 Jun. 1973); available: http://www.nybooks.com/ articles/9822.

5 Peter Singer, *Animal Liberation: A New Ethics for Our Treatment of Animals* (New York, 1975), at 261.

6 See Gary L. Francione, *Introduction to Animal Rights: Your Child or the Dog"* (Temple University Press, 2000), at 155.

7 Ibid., at 19. See also page 196 (note 35), wherein Francione asserts (internal citation omitted): "Contraception has already proved to be an effective method of population control. It has been adopted by the U.S. government as a wildlife management tool and is being used in pilot studies in many other countries." To call for the neutering of cats or to prevent dogs from mating, given that we've already manipulated the reproductive processes of these animals by selective breeding to the point where they lack the genuine ability to reproduce and raise their young on their terms, doesn't offend animal rights; indeed, as argued elsewhere in this book, any rules that help to phase out the breeding of animals as pets could also be considered aligned with abolishing the treatment of animals as commodities, because these would spare *wildcats and wolves* from being selectively changed to suit our whims. But Francione's apparent acceptance of birth control for free-living animals is another matter. Once again it points to the importance of starting out by distinguishing selectively bred animals from communities of animals who could actually experience autonomy, and

shouldn't be denied that opportunity.

8   Mark Hume, "B.C.'s Quiet War on Wolves" - *Globe and Mail* (15 Dec. 2008).

9   Tom Regan, *The Case for Animal Rights* (1983), at 361 (emphasis in the original). This exclamation, written in both a positive and emphatic form, is, in my view, a much stronger prescription than asking that we simply "leave them alone." That phrase can be understood as meaning we need not be concerned about, or need not intervene on behalf of or take any affirmative actions for, free-roaming animals. To let autonomous animals be autonomous indicates a responsibility to control ourselves as a way of affirmatively yielding to the basic needs of others, and to acknowledge their stake in existing in their own ways.

10 See Jared Diamond, *Collapse* (Viking Press, 2005), at 55.

11 "Nurtured Chimps Rake It In" - *ScienceDaily* (18 Jun. 2007); source: Reuters, from material provided by Springer and citing a study by E.E. Furlong, K.J. Boose, and S.T. Boysen titled "Raking It In: The Impact of Enculturation on Chimpanzee Tool Use."

12 Lori Gruen, "False Friends" - *The Hartford [Connecticut] Courant* (5 Aug. 2007).

13 Paola Cavalieri and Peter Singer, eds., *The Great Ape Project* (first printing 1993 by Fourth Estate, London). The book articulated a goal of obtaining a United Nations declaration to welcome orang-utans, gorillas and chimpanzees into a "community of equals" with humans.

14 "Activists Pursue Basic Legal Rights for Great Apes" - *USA Today* (15 Jul. 2008).

15 Adam Cohen, Editorial Observer: "What's Next in the Law? The Unalienable Rights of Chimps" - *New York Times* (14 Jul. 2008).

16 Catharine A. MacKinnon, "A Feminist Fragment on Animal Rights" - in *Animal Rights: Current Debates and New Directions*, at 270 (Cass R. Sunstein & Martha C. Nussbaum eds., 2004).

17 Public Law 106-551 (HR 3514) was signed into effect in 2000 and applies to apes used in labs run for U.S. agencies. A site was started up in Louisiana known as Chimp Haven. This new entity (and any private entity which might, in the future, be awarded a contract under the Act) must provide at least $1 for each $3 of federal funds needed to run the housing system. (Maintaining a great ape in a research laboratory over a 5-year period can cost between $300,000 and $500,000, compared to an approximate cost of $275,000 for care outside that setting, according to the text of the subsequently proposed Great Ape Protection Act).

18 Singer's Great Ape Project never opposed this. The group openly supported the bill and only expressed reservations when it was amended, as GAP wrote, "to allow chimpanzees to be removed from the retirement facility"—but at all times the law permitted some types of research, saved money for federal research projects using apes, and accepted the idea that only "surplus" apes were to be moved to the euphemistically termed "retirement" sites. See Lee Hall, "A Primer on the CHIMP Act" - Friends of Animals' *ActionLine* (Spring 2002), at 28-33.

19 Although the statement is ambiguous, and could be read as endorsing operations for the health of chimpanzees, Goodall's remark was made in answer to this question from hearing chair Michael Bilirakis: "Dr. Strandberg, from the NIH, is going

to testify that the NIH can't support this legislation because it would make the animals permanently unavailable for study or monitoring. Expand upon that. What is your feeling there? How strongly do you feel about their not being available for invasive research procedures?" Goodall's immediate response began: "Well, I think the most important thing here is can they be left in the sanctuary and there are certain procedures, even over and above taking blood which could be carried out..." Statement of Jane Goodall, Ph.D. CBE, Director of Science and Research for the Jane Goodall Institute, before the House of Representatives' Committee on Commerce, Subcommittee on Health and Environment, hearing on H.R. 3514, Chimpanzee Health Improvement, Maintenance and Protection Act (18 May 2000).

20 For a detailed analysis see Lee Hall, "A Primer on the CHIMP Act" (note 18 above).

21 See Sue Savage-Rumbaugh, et al., *Apes, Language, and the Human Mind* (1998), at 7, 33.

22 This involves educational collaborations with the Jane Goodall Institute in Congo-Brazzaville, according to a March 2007 Spanish-language press release generated by the Great Ape Project in Spain.

Notes to Chapter 9 ⌖ Pages 217–244

1 Your Daily Vegan, "PETA Wastes Time and Money (Again)" – *YourDailyVegan.com* (Jun. 15, 2009). See also "Odd News: PETA's Pigs Allowed at Ohio Protest" – *UPI.com* (25 Jun. 2009). That message does appear self-contradictory, until one understands that most animal-advocacy groups are not against the use of animals *per se*. Rather, they trumpet the message that pain should be reduced. This very exhibit projected the opinion that the use of animals is a problem because severe pain occurs in high-volume farms. The advocacy group described its display as "an exhibit aimed at showing how factory farms are breeding grounds for diseases such as swine flu." See People for the Ethical Treatment of Animals' press release, "PETA Appeals After Ohio Statehouse Nixes Pig Manure From Factory-Farm Exhibit: Stench and Filth Are Vital to Understanding That Swine Flu and Other Deadly Diseases Are Directly Linked to Animal Agriculture, Argues Group" (6 Jul. 2009).

2 Catharine A. MacKinnon, "Of Mice and Men: A Feminist Fragment on Animal Rights" in Cass R. Sunstein and Martha C. Nussbaum, eds., *Animal Rights: Current Debates and New Directions* (Oxford University Press USA), at 265.

3 Leslie Cross, "Veganism Defined" - published through the Spring 1951 issue of *The Vegetarian World Forum*, a magazine that then served as the journal of the International Vegetarian Union. Available at www.veganmeans.com in the "Vegan: Who" section.

4 See A Leon Higginbotham, Jr., *In the Matter of Color- Race and the American Legal Process: The Colonial Period* (Oxford University Press, 1978), at 188-99. Argumentation derived in part from Higginbotham's writings as well as those of Alan Watson, applying those to the custom of animal commodification, appears in Gary L. Francione, *Animals, Property, and the Law* (Temple University, 1995) particularly at 110-111.

5 Higginbotham, *In the Matter of Color*, at 190.

6 This material was posted on a public Web log named "A Restless Mind" under the category "food" (as visited by the author on 27 Mar. 2008).

7   Richard Koenigsberg, "Nations Kill a Lot of People: Denial of the Destructiveness of Civilization" (published electronically on 25 Mar. 2008). For the record, Hitler did not adhere to a vegetarian diet either, although that myth is bizarrely persistent.

8   Presentation by Richard Koenigsberg, "Death to the Non-Believer: As I Have been Terrorized, so Shall You Be Terrorized." The Human Condition Series: "Terror 2008" (2-3 May 2008, Laurentian University at Georgian College campus, Barrie, Ontario).

9   David Bauder, "Group: TV Torture Influencing Real Life" (Associated Press, 11 Feb. 2007). One eerie possibility is that popular advocacy's use of exploitive advertising not only intensifies the mean-spiritedness of our times, but might even encourage people, particularly young people, to be stimulated by exhibitions of humiliation and violence. Of particular interest to those who pursue the possibility further is the 2006 murder of Pamela Vitale and cutting of the body. Henry K. Lee, "Two Views of Dyleski: Gentle Kid or Vicious Killer" - *San Francisco Chronicle* (28 Jul. 2006), quoting California deputy public defender Ellen Leonida, who identified Scott Dyleski, who was convicted, as "somebody who cared deeply about human rights and animal rights." See also Lisa Sweetingham (*Court TV*), "Teen to Serve Life Without Parole for Killing Lawyer's Wife" - *CNN.com* (27 Sep. 2006), stating: "According to witnesses at his trial, Dyleski was a gentle vegan kid who also had a fascination with Goth music and serial killers." Pictures of vivisection were found on Dyleski's computer. Just sixteen at the time of the murder, Dyleski was imprisoned for life.

10 See Finlo Rohrer, "China Drinks Its Milk" - *BBC News* (7 Aug. 2007).

11 Nathan Fiala, "Meeting the Demand: An Estimation of Potential Future Greenhouse Gas Emissions from Meat Production" - *Ecological Economics* (Vol. 67, 2008), at 413.

12 Asked by George D. Rodger in 2002 "What do you find most difficult about being vegan?", Donald Watson responded: "Well, I suppose it is the social aspect. Excommunicating myself from that part of life where people meet to eat, and the only way this problem can be eased is by having veganism more and more acceptable in guest houses, hotels, wherever one goes, until one hopes one day it will become the norm." The full interview appears at www.veganmeans.com.

13 See Liz Jones, "Why Is Gratuitous Nudity Being Used to Sell Everything From Handbags to Fruit Juice?" – *Daily Mail* (9 Oct. 2008).

14 Carol Lloyd, "Exploiting Women to Protect Animals?" - *Salon.com* (28 Mar. 2008).

15 Juliette Jowit, "Melting Glaciers Start Countdown to Climate Chaos" - *Guardian Observer* (16 Mar. 2008).

16 "Customers Find All Skin, No Meat at Vegan Strip Club" - Fox 12, via *KPTV.com* (11 Feb. 2008).

17 Quoted by Michael Benton in a call for submissions to *Reconstruction: Studies in Contemporary Culture* (ISSN: 1547-4348) on H-Net: Humanities and Social Sciences Online (2009).

18 The original playhouse was in Highgate, North London, near Waterlow Park—a short walk from Upstairs at The Gatehouse, where this author watched the play. See http://www.upstairsatthegatehouse.com. *Playhouse Creatures* was commissioned and first performed by The Sphinx (Women's National Touring Theatre) on 5 Oct. 1993, at the

Haymarket Theatre in Leicester. The script is copyrighted by April De Angelis; ISBN 0 573 13007 8 (1994).

Notes to Chapter 10 ⌒ Pages 245–260

1 The proposal was outlined in a letter written by Lincoln to Illinois Senator James A. McDougall in March 1862. Associated Press, "University Shares Its Lincoln Letters Online" (posted electronically by *MSNBC.com* on 2 Mar. 2008).

2 Herrington founded Friends of Animals, and served as the group's president from 1957 through 1986.

3 Paul Brown, "Land Reverts to Birds" - *The Guardian* (4 Mar. 2004).

4 The Associated Press, "Trappers Can Bait Bears to Aid Moose Survival" – *Anchorage Daily News* (6 Jun. 2009) stated: "The animal rights group Defenders of Wildlife has concerns because private citizens will do the trapping and not state wildlife officials."

5 Humane Society of the United States (HSUS) press release: "New York First State to Ban Electrocution of Animals for Fur" (29 Aug. 2007), quoting Assembly Member Deborah Glick. A similar campaign was conducted by People for the Ethical Treatment of Animals, as outlined in a public letter to Elizabeth Goldentyer, DVM (of the U.S. Department of Agriculture) from Mary Beth Sweetland, director of Research & Investigations Department, People for the Ethical Treatment of Animals (10 Aug. 2004), requesting government oversight for fur farms, and specifically pressing a Michigan chinchilla farmer to refrain from employing either a cervical dislocation method without sedation or an ear-to-foot electrocution technique, but instead to use carbon-monoxide poisoning.

6 Similarly, Francione wrote (in *Animals as Persons* at page 114, Chapter 2, "Reflections on *Animals, Property and the Law* and *Rain without Thunder*"; reprinted from an article originally published in 2007 in the journal *Law & Contemporary Problems*): "Finally, animal advocates should never be in a position of promoting an alternative, more 'humane' or 'better' form of exploitation, or substituting once species for another." The critical difference between Francione's proposal and the proposal in the book you now hold is this one's emphasis, through the threshold of the first criterion above (*"Let them be!"*), on the complete rejection of domination as the linchpin of the animal-right platform. In contrast to purported bans of animal agribusiness methods, a vegan initiative means conscientious objection to animals being dominated, used, domesticated, or consumed. It does not pertain to conditions in which animals are, against their will and against their own interests, trapped, confined, handled, or killed — except by precluding such situations in the first place. Francione considers "incrementalist" steps to eroding the property status of animals as difficult to achieve because "equal consideration is not possible as long as animals are property" while "most welfarist measures do nothing but require that animal exploiters act in a more rational way and do a more efficient job at exploiting their animal property" (*Animals as Persons*, at 112); animals in habitat, however, need to have their current status respected, and we must make this clear. But for our concept of dominion over them, and, consequently, their status as legal property of the state (a status advocates ought to work to change), they live just as they would were animal rights secured. The importance of habitat as the locus of animal rights, and how to take steps to achieve

animal-rights goals specifically in this context, has not, to date, been articulated in Francione's books; yet this importance cannot be overstated as the discourse of animal-rights moves forward.

Notes to Appendix I ～ Pages 261–274

1 *Power Politics* (South End Press, 2001), at 68.

Notes to Appendix II ～ Pages 275–286

1 Priscilla Feral and Lee Hall, *Dining with Friends: The Art of North American Vegan Cuisine* (Friends of Animals: Nectar Bat Press, 2005).

Index

A